Additional praise for *Leadership Is Language*

"Although we use language to express ourselves, language also uses us, creating patterns of thought and action. Drawing on a wide variety of examples from all kinds of organizations, David Marquet has written an impressive and engaging book which is not just thought-provoking, but offers simple, actionable ways of escaping the traps that our words lay for us."

—Stephen Bungay, author of *The Art of Action*

"This is the definitive guide for those seeking to be real leaders in transformative times. David not only shows us how business and leadership has drastically changed and why the structures of yesterday are hindering our ability to business but also how to reinvent our leadership style to meet the evolving demands of the new marketplace."

—Tamara Ghandour, creator of the Innovation Quotient Edge, host of *Inside LaunchStreet*, and author of *Innovation is Everybody's Business*

"This book is brilliant. Seriously."

—John Konrad, author of *Fire on the Horizon* and founder and CEO of gCaptain

"Too many leaders think leadership focuses only on results. David Marquet dares us to see leadership as a relationship built on language and dialogue. These, he demonstrates, enhance collaboration and engagement. With brilliant writing, he explains what leaders need to know: leadership is about language. I have seen David in action using words to truly inspire and empower. This is a must-read for every leader!"

—George Kohlrieser, author of *Hostage at the Table* and *Care to Dare*, and director of IMD's acclaimed High Performance Leadership program

LEADERSHIP
——— IS ———
LANGUAGE

LEADERSHIP

—— IS ——

LANGUAGE

The Hidden Power of What You Say
—and What You Don't

L. DAVID MARQUET

PORTFOLIO / PENGUIN

PORTFOLIO / PENGUIN
An imprint of Penguin Random House LLC
penguinrandomhouse.com

Most Portfolio books are available at a discount when purchased in quantity for sales promotions or corporate use. Special editions, which include personalized covers, excerpts, and corporate imprints, can be created when purchased in large quantities. For more information, please call (212) 572-2232 or e-mail specialmarkets@penguinrandomhouse.com. Your local bookstore can also assist with discounted bulk purchases using the Penguin Random House corporate Business-to-Business program. For assistance in locating a participating retailer, e-mail B2B@penguinrandomhouse.com.

Library of Congress Cataloging-in-Publication Data

Names: Marquet, L. David, author.
Title: Leadership is language : the hidden power of what you say, and what you don't / L. David Marquet.
Description: [New York] : Portfolio/Penguin, [2020] |
Includes bibliographical references and index.
Identifiers: LCCN 2019043345 (print) | LCCN 2019043346 (ebook) |
ISBN 9780735217539 (hardcover) | ISBN 9780735217546 (epub)
Subjects: LCSH: Transformational leadership. |
Communication in management. | Teams in the workplace.
Classification: LCC HD57.7 .M392445 2020 (print) |
LCC HD57.7 (ebook) | DDC 658.4/092—dc23
LC record available at https://lccn.loc.gov/2019043345
LC ebook record available at https://lccn.loc.gov/2019043346

Printed in the United States of America
1   3   5   7   9   10   8   6   4   2

BOOK DESIGN BY ELLEN CIPRIANO

MAP ON PAGE 19 BY DANIEL LAGIN

Penguin is committed to publishing works of quality and integrity. In that spirit, we are proud to offer this book to our readers; however, the story, the experiences, and the words are the author's alone.

Dedicated to the crew of El Faro, *with the belief that their example will invite self-reflection upon our own language, and the hope that they help us become better leaders.*

CONTENTS

FOREWORD   xi

INTRODUCTION   1

CHAPTER 1
Losing *El Faro*   17

CHAPTER 2
The New Playbook   37

CHAPTER 3
Exiting Redwork: Control the Clock   75

CHAPTER 4
Into the Bluework: Collaborate   105

CHAPTER 5
Leaving Bluework Behind: Commit   137

CHAPTER 6
The End of Redwork: Complete   159

CHAPTER 7

Completing the Cycle: Improve   187

CHAPTER 8

The Enabling Play: Connect   213

CHAPTER 9

Applying the Redwork-Bluework Principles in
Workplace Situations   247

CHAPTER 10

The Red-Blue Operating System   279

CHAPTER 11

Saving *El Faro*   301

ACKNOWLEDGMENTS   313

FURTHER READING   315

GLOSSARY   317

NOTES   321

INDEX   327

FOREWORD

Let me save you some time and heartbreak: listen to what David says. I only wish I did sooner. It would have saved me a lot of grief and millions of dollars.

Like many people you know (or maybe even you!), I've spent my life trying to make it look like I had all the answers. I needed everyone to think I was smart. Whatever the cause, I was raised to believe being right and having the answers was a hallmark of leadership. It wasn't until my last company that I realized something was wrong.

After raising over $30 million, recruiting some of the best people I've ever worked with, and having the opportunity to lead and build product at one of the hottest start-ups in Silicon Valley, I couldn't escape a gnawing, enigmatic dread. We had enough capital, we had the right people, and yet everyone was miserable.

It took me a long time to see and admit it—but I was the problem. When I didn't know the answers, I felt insecure and I did not want people to see it. So I overcompensated by pushing. I cajoled people to get on board, go my way or get out. I had convinced myself that this was the right approach because of course I had the answers.

Everyone left. The company was recapitalized, and all the investors lost their money. No one else got a dollar. And I was depressed.

A few years before these events, I saw David Marquet speak. Everything he said was the opposite of the approach I later adopted at that failed business. In moments of clarity during those times, I would remember David's words and wish I could find a way to apply them to our work.

The chastening experience of that failure caused me to recommit to developing my leadership skills. At my next company, Assist, I rebuilt my approach from the ground up with David's guidance as my foundation. With my cofounder—Robert Stephens, the founder of Geek Squad—Assist became the leader in the AI space, powering brands on new platforms like Google Assistant, Alexa, and messaging apps. There is zero question that David's insight and guidance contributed in a giant way to our success.

From the first word I wrote to start the company, everything was through the lens of what this book is about. Curiosity was our core value. We celebrated what we didn't know, and know-it-alls weren't welcome. How we used our words became how we respected people and operated effectively. We practiced using language with one another that forced people to own making decisions. We would remind people it's OK to say, "I don't know." I hired people and asked them to teach me. We helped people go from saying "I think we should . . ." to "I've already done . . ." There was no need to ask for permission.

Today, my number one priority is partnering to create a workplace culture that expands the range of empowerment so more people have the skills and agency to act in the service of the greatest good. Inversely, the more permission that is needed, the less people will be empowered to think and lead, and the worse the place will be to work. It wasn't always easy; many people don't believe they can or should operate in this way.

Ultimately, I saw my job as CEO evolve to a place where my goal was to make as few decisions as possible. That's a long distance away from the guy who had to hide behind a mask of All Knowledge.

Everything in this book is exactly how I strived to lead Assist, and in 2019, Assist was acquired for millions. As I watched my colleagues move to great positions at prestigious companies, I felt incredibly lucky to have had the opportunity to learn and grow alongside some of the best leaders I've ever worked with.

David's not promising an easier, shorter path, but, in my experience, it's one that leaves everyone feeling whole, empowered, and eager to dive back in the next day. That works for me.

Shane Mac
Nashville, June 2019
Feel free to say "Hi" on Twitter: @shanemac

INTRODUCTION

I used to think I was special.

It started in high school, when I earned better grades than almost everyone around me. This trend continued into my time at the US Naval Academy. Truth was, I was just a prescient and skilled test-taker, but after graduating and rising to the rank of captain in the navy's submarine force, I mistakenly concluded that I'd risen so quickly because I was more observant, disciplined, committed, thoughtful, and caring than the people around me. It's hard to admit, but at the time I felt pretty sure I was better at getting stuff done—and just plain better—than the people I worked with.

Secure in my sense of superiority, I became the first one to spot problems and the first to see solutions to those problems, too. I told people what they should do and—through rank, influence, and sheer rhetorical force—coerced them into complying with my instructions. In my haste to get stuff done, I left no time for others to make their own contributions. My division or department was an assembly line, one that cranked out actions instead of cars or lawnmowers. I was the foreman of the action factory because I knew better than everyone else.

There were plenty of signs that my view was distorted—had I been willing to see them. People would hesitantly offer a good idea every now and then. Occasionally, they would take smart, decisive action without my direction. Once in a while, I would make a mistake, directing my team in a way that wasn't optimal or was just plain wrong. In these scenarios, my subordinates would comply with bad orders, despite all my lectures to speak up if they ever saw a problem. Afterward, when things went off the rails, they would shrug and say they were just doing what they'd been told. In response, I would double down on giving clear, concise, and correct orders.

I spent twenty-eight years being evaluated and ranked. The navy is highly competitive; top spots are scarce. In this environment of continuous judgment and evaluation, I experienced constant pressure to prove myself. Every exam, every monthly report, every inspection, every meeting, every *day* was another trial, another opportunity to prove and perform. A single bad outcome might affect a promotion, a pay raise, my social standing, even my sense of self-worth.

As I regarded my achievements with pride, I chafed at the sense that others didn't give me adequate recognition for my contributions. I adopted a closed, invulnerable persona, firmly rooted in a performance mindset. If life was going to be a rat race, you can bet your whiskers I was going to win it, however hard I had to drive my people to do so.

Operating this way—conforming to hierarchical roles, maintaining emotional distance from others, avoiding vulnerability at all costs—is lonely and unfulfilling. Although I was proud of my promotions and awards, something profoundly important was missing.

TURNING THE SHIP AROUND

My journey took an unexpected detour when the captain of the nuclear-powered submarine USS *Santa Fe* abruptly quit and I was suddenly put in command. *Santa Fe* was the laughingstock of the fleet. At the time, I joked that it had only two problems: the fleet's worst morale, and its worst performance to boot. Each month, the navy would publish the twelve-month reenlistment and retention rate for all fifty or so submarines and, inevitably, *Santa Fe* would be at the bottom of the list. Not near the bottom. All the way at the bottom, by a good margin, with 90 percent of *Santa Fe*'s crew getting out of the navy at the end of their time on board.

That was the morale problem I had to solve. The other problem was bad performance. *Santa Fe* was getting poor inspection scores across all its operations, from food service to firing torpedoes, from navigation to the nuclear power plant. It also had higher-than-average safety incidents.

Normally, my prove-and-perform leadership approach would have been just what the doctor ordered—if I had known the ship. But, as it turned out, I had spent twelve months preparing to take over a different submarine. I was driving blind.

When I came aboard my new submarine, I started asking questions. In the past, I'd always made a practice of asking questions, but they were more like test questions: I already knew the answers. Did they? Now, I was asking questions because I needed to know how the ship worked. This meant I had to admit to my crew that for many of the details, I did not know the answers. That was scary.

On our first day at sea, the crew and I were sizing each other up. I instinctively conformed to the role of captain as I'd been programmed: I would give the orders and they would follow them. Then, early on, I ordered something technically impossible for *Santa Fe*: second gear on a motor that had only one. The order was immediately parroted by an officer, though he knew it made no sense. The sailor ordered to carry it out just shrugged helplessly and my error was revealed to all.

This was a life-changing moment for me. I'd always known ninety-nine out of every one hundred parts of my job. When there was the occasional gap in my decision-making, I simply resolved to "give better orders" in the future. Here on *Santa Fe*, I felt like I knew only one out of one hundred parts of what I needed to do. If I couldn't count on my own officers to point out an obvious mistake like this one, we'd end up killing the wrong people. Maybe even ourselves. Something needed to change.

All my leadership training up to that point had been about making decisions and getting the team to implement them. I had never questioned this paradigm until that moment aboard *Santa Fe*. Improving my decisions simply couldn't happen fast enough to matter. I needed a different solution entirely. The problem, I realized, wasn't that I'd given a bad order, it was that I was giving orders in the first place. By making tactical and operational decisions for the team, I was absolving them of their responsibility for outcomes. Moreover, I was giving them a pass on thinking itself. It was a pass I had to revoke if we were going to survive.

Like many organizations, the USS *Santa Fe* prided itself on its can-do culture. But can-do is fragile. As long as whatever we're can-doing is right, things are fine, but in our take-no-prisoners enthusiasm, we can easily propagate errors throughout the organization. We needed to match our zest for can-do with a zeal for "can-think."

The officers of *Santa Fe* and I made a deal that day. I agreed to never give another order. Instead, I would provide intent, the goal of what it was we were trying to achieve. They agreed never to wait to be told what to do. Instead, they would provide their intentions to me, how they were going to achieve my intent. This shift was reflected in a simple change of language, replacing "request permission to" with "I intend to."

We shook hands on it. Then we went back to work.

Over the next twelve months, *Santa Fe* set a record when each and every one of the thirty-three sailors eligible for reenlistment that following year signed up to stay in the navy. The ship also performed brilliantly in every task the navy asked of it. *Santa Fe* received an all-time record inspection score for operating the submarine. All without firing anyone. For both performance and morale, *Santa Fe* had risen from worst to first.

This did not happen because I leaned harder on the officers and crew. It happened because I leaned back and invited them to lean in to me. As a result, we went from one leader and 134 followers to 135 leaders with a bias for action and thinking.

What happened over the next ten years was even more remarkable. The crew of *Santa Fe* continued to outperform their peers after I left. Ten of the officers from that time period were themselves selected to command submarines, five became squadron commanders or the equivalent, and two (so far) have been promoted to admiral. In the navy, this track record is, to put it mildly, extraordinary.

LEADERSHIP IS LANGUAGE

None of this happened because we became more skilled, knowledgeable, or dedicated to the job. We tinkered with some of the navy regulations, but we could only make minor modifications. This was a system over which we had little control. We couldn't change our schedule, major assignments, promotions, technical requirements, legal obligations, most procedures and policies, or even who was assigned to the ship.

What we could control was how we talked to each other, the words we used. Starting with me. After all, what is leadership but language? As I changed the way I communicated with the rest of the crew, it affected the way they communicated with me and with each other. Changing the way we communicated changed the culture. Changing the culture transformed our results.

Changing our words changed our world.

The language changed in three ways:

- We replaced a reactive language of convince, coerce, comply, and conform with a proactive language of intent and commitment to action.
- We replaced a language of "prove and perform" with a language of "improve and learn."
- We replaced a language of invulnerability and certainty with a language of vulnerability and curiosity.

We were still speaking English, of course, but in many ways, it really felt as though we had learned a new language entirely.

Language was the starting point for all the other positive changes that happened aboard *Santa Fe*. Words went both ways—our language revealed our thinking and changed our thinking. Language was the way we could measure empowerment and collaboration, as well as improve it.

As captain of the ship, the way I said things made all the difference. Language was my lever. Everything started with me. I'd always believed that I couldn't remain quiet because people wouldn't speak up. Finally, I realized that people weren't speaking up because I couldn't remain quiet.

Something else I learned was that waiting for people to prove themselves in order for me to trust them was backward. I needed to entrust people with authority and autonomy in order to give them the opportunity to prove themselves.

When I came aboard *Santa Fe*, I had it in my head that I would improve the crew's performance. Better performance would then lead to better morale. It didn't end up working that way. Instead, once people were given autonomy over their work, became connected to a purpose that mattered, and felt like part of a team, they became happier. Morale soared. *Then* the performance improved.

This started happening within a week.

SPREADING THE WORD ABOUT LANGUAGE

If you're curious about the full details of the transformation that occurred aboard *Santa Fe*, you can read my first book, *Turn the Ship Around!*. It was a humbling experience. It taught me that I wasn't special in the way I'd thought I was. Still, I am tremendously grateful to have faced that reckoning. I learned that if I can only keep my mouth shut for a few extra seconds, ask the kinds of questions that encourage people to share their thoughts, and actually pay attention to what others are saying, their ideas, points of view, and suggested actions are often as good as—often even better (!)—than what I'd had in mind.

In my rush to get people to do the things I wanted them to do, I'd been suppressing their engagement, openness, and creativity. While I felt a short-term psychological boost from making things happen, this behavior sapped the potential contributions of the people around me. Meanwhile, as the organizations I led grew in scale, my ability to know everything and manage everything myself diminished relative to the potential contributions of everyone around me. I'd been my own worst enemy all along.

Since leaving the service, I've worked to use my experience to help others become better leaders themselves. I show them how to create the ideal environment for their people and unleash all the passion, intellect, and initiative just waiting to be tapped within the organization. We do this through language, by addressing the way we communicate with others. It works.

In my new role as a coach and mentor for other leaders, I have become convinced that the lessons I learned on *Santa Fe* are effective across all organizations:

- The call center that reduced quarterly attrition from eight people to zero.
- The tech company that doubled revenue and size.
- The research center that started making award-winning products.
- The nuclear power plant that achieved top-level performance.
- The company selected "Best Place to Work."
- The mom who says her kids' bedtime is no longer a struggle.
- The police district that reduced crime by 3 percent.
- The operations manager who lost fifty pounds because she has so much less stress in her life.

All through language. All through changing the words we use to communicate and collaborate with others.*

For years, I have been working to change the way I talk to people, but I am still on my journey. It takes continuous self-awareness and reprogramming to avoid the imperative mode of communication that

---

* We call this approach Intent-Based Leadership® because leaders state their intent, not their instructions, to the team. Then the members of the team say how they intend to achieve that intent, instead of asking for permission.

is the default in our society. Today, I try to pause before responding or reacting in order to give myself ample opportunity to phrase things in a more effective way. I've seen how powerful the right words can be at achieving results.

A NEW LEADERSHIP PLAYBOOK

As I developed my thinking around the language of leadership, I formulated responses for leaders in various situations at work. I started thinking about these preplanned and preprogrammed responses that we have—patterns of action (and in our case, language) in response to, and triggered by, certain events or scenarios. Just like a sports play, you choose your play by reading the field and then making a deliberate decision about how to act. But I wasn't sure about that metaphor and was still struggling with the overall structure of the book.

While this was going on, I boarded United flight 1139, the redeye from San Francisco to Tampa. I was headed home. Just after I buckled in, a man sat down next to me with a large duffle bag that he pushed under the seat in front of him. He pulled out a three-inch, three-ring binder and I could see a couple others in the duffle. It was a playbook, a football playbook! I did not recognize him, but it was Jon Gruden, who had just signed a contract to be head coach of the Oakland Raiders (again). He had served as head coach from 1998 to 2001. These were the playbooks for the Oakland Raiders.

I asked him about the playbooks. He accommodated me and flipped open to the front of the binder. The first "plays" had nothing to do with football. They were about how the players, coaches, and staff would act off the field, in the locker room, at team events, and at practice. It was only in volumes two and three that the traditional pass plays and running plays were portrayed.

When we started discussing the organization of the binders, the first words out of his mouth were, "Well, it's all about language." I took that as a sign from the heavens and settled on the playbook metaphor.

Because of how I got there that when I say "play," I often picture football, because in that sport there is a break between each action. The field is reset and the offense has time to deliberately decide their next action: run, pass, or something else. So does the defense. And both sides are trying to read the other in determining their plan.

This pattern of executing plays or preplanned responses already exists in human behavior, business leadership, and language. The problem is that most of us are working with an outdated playbook: plays that we have been programmed to run from an older paradigm of leadership—the Industrial Revolution. In the early chapters of this book, I'll explain how we inherited our language of leadership from the industrial era and why it's so poorly suited to today's work environment.

Above all, the promise of this book is to reveal not only the new plays appropriate for today's challenges but also their underlying structure, the logic behind them, and how to use them with your team. Once you understand not only what to say but why and how, you will be able to find the right language for any situation. This will help establish a more effective working environment, leading to better outcomes across the board and a more satisfying and meaningful work experience for everyone in the organization.

Over the course of this book, I'll introduce you to six new leadership plays, contrasting each one with the old plays. I will also show how the new plays work together, revealing an underlying approach that oscillates between action and reflection, doing and deciding. They are, in order:

1. Control the clock instead of obeying the clock.
2. Collaborate instead of coercing.

3. Commitment rather than compliance.
4. Complete defined goals instead of continuing work indefinitely.
5. Improve outcomes rather than prove ability.
6. Connect with people instead of conforming to your role.

Each of these plays hinges on specific use of language, and I'll explain in detail how to execute them in the chapters to come.

BALANCING DELIBERATION AND ACTION

Fred is a hardworking executive at a manufacturing company. Every day, he faces a list of problems to solve, from making machines run better to hiring new workers, from improving overall output to dealing with trade tariffs. He feels the relentless pressure of the clock and, in his rush to get things done, he tends to run roughshod over other people. Fred spends the day coercing the team to do what he thinks best, then goes home feeling depleted, without any sense of having made much progress. He maintains a "professional," arm's-length distance from his employees, conforming to the role of boss.

Fred isn't happy. Fred's team members aren't happy, either. They feel like Fred doesn't trust them. He tells them what to do constantly and micromanages their work. They feel like they have to leave their humanity at the door: their creativity, empathy, and sense of purpose. There is little sense of progress for them, either. Every day feels much like the last. Everyone complies with what they're told to do, but there's little passion in it. They give just enough to get by and save as much of themselves as they can for after the end-of-day whistle.

. . .

SUE IS A hardworking executive at a technology company across the street. Prone to contemplation, rumination, even depression, she struggles to make decisions. Everything seems like a big commitment. It's overwhelming. Sue has a good sense of what she wants each project to look like at the end, but is often paralyzed in figuring out where to start. While the company founder urges her to "fail fast" and "break things," she isn't exactly sure what those things mean to her. When she does make decisions, she feels like she gets second-guessed a lot.

Sue is frustrated. Sue's team members are frustrated, too. They see projects that need to happen and ways of improving existing products, but they can't get Sue's sign-off on making meaningful changes. When they bring forward suggestions, she asks them question after question until there's one they can't answer—at which point they are sent back for more research. There is little sense of progress and every day seems like the last. The lack of progress and completion wears at morale. Turnover is high and people are disengaged.

It might seem like Fred and Sue have opposite problems. In reality, their problem is the same: an imbalance in the rhythm between doing and thinking.

Doing and thinking are the basic building blocks of all human activity. The correct balance of these two activities helps us achieve our goals. Unfortunately, many organizations struggle to maintain a healthy balance, tilting too far toward action, as at Fred's manufacturing company, or too far toward deliberation, as at Sue's technology company. Rather than being deliberately engineered, the think-do rhythm in most organizations arises accidentally, from the many small decisions we make every day.

The right balance of doing and thinking keeps an organization adaptive and agile, innovative and entrepreneurial. It gives the people in the organization a sense of purpose and progress, which helps drive continuous improvement. In short, the right balance of doing and thinking drives learning. It keeps the company relevant and solvent. It keeps employees happy. It leads to happy customers, too.

By *doing*, I mean physical interaction with the world, whether that means driving a forklift or making a presentation to investors. Doing something doesn't mean you aren't thinking, but the brain operates much more automatically. For familiar behaviors like deeply ingrained habits—getting dressed or driving home, for example—our brains can go into almost fully automatic mode, wandering freely even as we shave with a razor or drive seventy miles an hour down the highway. As a result, doing does not tax the mind the way thinking does. Doing is our default mode because it is faster and more efficient, and our brains are nothing if not efficient.

By *thinking*, I mean the deliberate, curious, and open exploration of information, beliefs, stories, and assumptions in order to interpret the world around us. In our model, thinking occurs before and after doing. Before an action, the outputs of thinking are decisions and hypotheses: What are we going to do and what are we going to learn? After an action, the output of thinking is reflection upon what we have learned. In stark contrast with doing, the process of thinking is cognitively taxing and leads to mental fatigue.

The difference between doing and thinking can be described in several ways:

Our interaction with the world is doing.
Improving our interaction with the world is thinking.

Proving and performing is doing.

Growing and improving is thinking.

A focused, exclusive, driving, proving mindset
is best for doing.

An open, curious, seeking, improving mindset
is best for thinking.

The doing self is fully present in the moment, acting upon
the world and reacting to stimuli dynamically.

The thinking self observes and reflects upon the doing self
from a detached and levelheaded perspective.

We will keep Fred and Sue with us because we have some of both of them in all of us. Sometimes we are like Fred, running around with too little reflection. Sometimes we are like Sue, overwhelmed by the magnitude of the task before us and finding it hard to move forward.

HOW DID WE GET HERE?

The key to understanding the playbook we inherited and what we need to do to change it comes from understanding Industrial Age organizations. They divided their people into leaders and followers, deciders and doers. You can see the legacy of this division in the titles and uniforms people wear at work.

Since the deciders and the doers were two different groups of people, leaders needed to convince followers to perform work they had not been part of conceiving, work they had not "bought into." Leadership was, by necessity, coercive. It was all about getting people to comply with external directions.

For the doers, variability was treated as the enemy. Factory work needs to be as consistent as possible to achieve consistent results. So the language patterns developed in ways that naturally reduced variability.

Finally, since we were always trying to squeeze in more pieces of work per unit of time, there was always a sense of "obeying the clock," resulting in a performance mindset.

Now, that is all changed. For organizations to survive, the doers must also be the deciders. We need the same people who used to view variability solely as the enemy to periodically view variability as an ally. We need the same people who used to have only a performance mindset to periodically have an improving mindset.

The book is laid out in the following format:

At the beginning, I describe the reasons behind the changes we are seeing at work. I explain how to think about learning and illuminate the proper interaction between thinking and doing.

The main part of the book is organized into the six leadership plays we have been programmed for, and the six new leadership plays we want to replace those with.

Then I provide some examples of how you might apply these new plays to your life and work. I also explain what an operating rhythm based on this approach looks like at the tactical, operational, and strategic levels.

To give credence to this argument, we will begin with the gripping story of a real team in a real-life situation trying and failing to achieve a mission against tough odds. Our objective is to fully understand how today's teams actually talk—and therefore make decisions—even in high-stakes, life-and-death scenarios. Not how we teach them to talk, not how we hope they will talk, not how we tell them to talk, but how they actually talk.

The case comes from a 2015 incident in which a container ship, equipped with modern radios and navigation equipment, sailed directly into a hurricane and sank. All thirty-three people on board were lost. To understand how this happened, we don't have to rely on anyone's shaky memory of a specific conversation. We are fortunate to be able to draw on the full transcript of twenty-five hours of conversation on the bridge of that ship.

The name of that ship was *El Faro*, and this book will conclude by presenting an imagined scenario in which the crew might have been saved by following a different leadership playbook. But first, we must understand what actually happened on board *El Faro* during what would be its final journey . . .

Losing *El Faro*

TUESDAY

1,000 MILES FROM STORM CENTER

Tuesday, September 29, 2015, was a busy day on board the container ship *El Faro*, as the crew of thirty-three mariners finished their final preparations for sea. As with most ships, the time in port would have been quite busy, with the ship having arrived from its previous trip just the day before. The cargo needed to be unloaded, and the new containers and cargo loaded and lashed down. They would have been rushing to meet their normal underway time of 7:00 p.m. Like the crew of *Santa Fe*, the crew of *El Faro* was a "can-do" bunch.

It was the height of hurricane season, but the seas were calm in Jacksonville, Florida. Presently, the ship, over two football fields in length, would traverse the familiar 1,300-mile stretch directly from the northeast corner of Florida to San Juan on the island of Puerto Rico. In fact, the forty-year-old *El Faro* had originally been called the *Puerto Rico* when it started its life making runs between America's east coast and the small US island territory.

At 8:06 p.m., *El Faro* set sail. Directly in its path on the Atlantic side of the Bahamas, Tropical Storm Joaquin was strengthening. The next morning, as *El Faro* made its way southeast, meteorologists upgraded Joaquin to a Category 1 hurricane and issued a hurricane warning for the Central Bahamas. By the end of the day, Joaquin would be classified a Category 3, capable of devastating damage, with winds of 129 miles per hour or more. Hurricane Joaquin would end up being the strongest hurricane to hit the Bahamas since 1866.

Prior to the ship setting for sea, an off-duty *El Faro* officer texted the captain, to make sure he was aware of the storm and to ask about his intended route. The captain replied that he planned to take the normal, direct route to Puerto Rico. Being the most direct, *El Faro*'s chosen course was the fastest, but also the most exposed to the hurricane. An alternate route, the Old Bahama Channel, was 160 miles longer and would take the ship an extra eight hours to traverse. But this route would put the Bahamas between the ship and the storm, buffering the vessel from the wind and waves.

You don't need experience in maritime navigation to understand the choice facing the captain and crew of *El Faro*. Once you've departed Jacksonville en route south to Puerto Rico, you have only two opportunities to cross over to the protected channel: at the north end of the Bahamas, where you turn right and follow the Florida coastline, or farther down the Atlantic side of the Bahamas, at the halfway point near an island called Rum Cay. At this point, there is a wide channel that cuts through the Bahamas. Once you pass that second turn at Rum Cay, you've committed yourself to the direct path, and to facing the full brunt of anything blowing in from the east. But the captain seems to have already made that decision, by himself, without discussion with his team, prior to getting under way.

At its current speed, *El Faro* would reach the first turning point at 7:00 Wednesday morning, the second decision point at 1:00 Thursday morning.

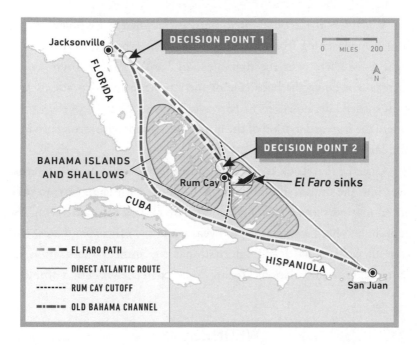

This chapter is about the power of our programmed language, rooted in the Industrial Age playbook. It uses the example of an oceangoing vessel facing a hurricane, but it could be about any team working on any big project. What makes *El Faro* worth discussing is that we have records of the actual words spoken and the actual actions taken by the captain and crew. This gives us an unparalleled glimpse into the language a team actually used when faced with life-and-death decisions.

This was a familiar route for the captain and crew of *El Faro*. They made the trip both ways on a regular basis and knew it inside and out. In other words, navigating from Jacksonville to San Juan was a classic, nose-to-the-grindstone task for everyone on board. In a situation like this, every member of the crew knew exactly what to do and when to do it.

Then the situation changed.

When *El Faro* left port, Joaquin was classified as a tropical storm. It was approaching from the central Atlantic, expected to turn to the right somewhere near the Bahamas. *El Faro*'s Atlantic route would then take it down the back side of the storm, the gentler side. If Joaquin turned late, however, *El Faro* would cross the front of the storm, where the forward motion of the hurricane would drive stronger winds and larger waves.

Once *El Faro* took the Atlantic route, it wouldn't be able to cross over into the protected Old Bahama Channel until Rum Cay. Experienced mariners know this, and these were experienced mariners. The captain had been a master for ten years, and the officers and crew had met all Coast Guard and International Maritime Organization requirements and regulations. Technical competence was not a problem.

WEDNESDAY

600 MILES FROM STORM CENTER

At 7:02 Wednesday morning, as the ship approached the northern Bahamas, the captain decided to take the Atlantic route, committing the ship to a route down the storm side of the Bahamas.

How was this decision made?

You could say that it was not deliberately made. There was a discussion on board *El Faro* between the captain and the chief mate. No one else was involved or even informed. It seems as though they did not even completely register it *as* a decision. On some level, the captain had already decided on the standard Atlantic route before leaving port. Early in the discussion, the captain said to the chief mate, "So we'll just have to tough this one out." Decision made. Done.

The only thing to be done was to continue with the plan. The rest of the conversation was about what they needed to do to make the ship as seaworthy as possible. The discussion was not *whether* they should take the Atlantic route, but *how* to take the Atlantic route. This is the Industrial Age play of *continue*. Continue is what has many of us chasing our tails in continuous action without reflection.

Looking at the transcript, it's clear there was no discussion of the assumptions that supported the decision, nor much of a plan for gathering evidence to support those assumptions. Later, as it became evident that the decision was a bad one, the captain fell into the trap of an escalation of commitment—sticking with a failing course of action simply because the decision had been made.

Why did they decide to take the exposed route? It was the faster one. Container ships do not make money steaming through the oceans—they make money once they have arrived at their destination and get their cargo off-loaded. For this reason, all commercial mariners tend toward obeying the clock. This is what we call the Industrial Age play of *obey the clock*. Under obey the clock, we feel the stress of time pressure and are motivated to get our work done within our allotted time.

In the best cases, obeying the clock creates focus. It puts us into a performance mindset. This helps us get things done, which is fine, as long as the things getting done are the things that *need to* get done. As a stressor, however, it creates all the effects any stressor will have on us: we retreat into self-preservation mode, with a resultant reduction of cognitive activity and a narrowing of perspective.

THE LANGUAGE OF INVULNERABILITY

Later that day, while the ship steamed toward the exposed side of the Bahamas, here are some of the things the captain said to various crew members:

"We're good."

"It should be fine. We are gunna be fine—not should be—we are gunna be fine."

He mocked novice mariners willing to deviate for "every single weather pattern."

"Oh. No no no. We're not gunna turn around—we're not gunna turn around."

His was the language of "getting it done" at all costs, the language of invulnerability and invincibility, the language that discourages any expression of concern. It sends the message that these decisions should not be questioned, our path is set, do not challenge me or make me explain this again.

What was the captain's motivation in saying these kinds of things? What is any leader's motivation? Inspire confidence? Focus people on task? Get them to comply? It's language we see over and over again and it is part of the Industrial Age play of *coercion*. We are too polite to use that word so we call it "inspiration" or "motivation," but the fundamental issue is that the captain needed to get people who were not part of making the decision to comply with the decision to take the exposed Atlantic route. He just needed them to go along.

It would be easy to blame the captain, but let's take a closer look at his operating conditions. The company was planning to replace *El Faro* and its sister ships with a pair of newer vessels. Three ships would shortly become two. One captain had already been selected, leaving only one open spot for the two remaining captains. The captain of *El Faro* needed to prove himself.

As the day developed, the captain of *El Faro* sent an email to his operational supervisors. Beginning to experience some concern about the weather, he asked about the *return* trip. He suggested the possibility of taking the Old Bahama Channel while returning. Only the possibility; he added that he would await approval from his supervisors.

The response authorized him to take the longer route if necessary. This exchange makes clear that the captain was operating in a permission-based environment. Technically, captains hold the authority to make operational decisions about their vessels while at sea, but the captain of *El Faro* apparently did not feel that way. Instead, he conformed to the role of an obedient bureaucrat. *Conform* is another, often counterproductive, Industrial Age play.

Since they had not yet reached the Rum Cay cutoff for the southward leg and the hurricane was still in front of them, why not propose taking the Rum Cay cutoff at this point? The reason is that the decision to take the Atlantic route was seen by the captain as a single, monolithic commitment, a one-time decision spanning the entire stretch of ocean to Puerto Rico. Since he had made fun of mariners who would deviate for "every single weather pattern," how could he now deviate for a weather pattern? His own words had trapped him into continuing the doomed course of action.

Only the return trip, which he saw as a separate decision requiring a separate commitment, left him free to propose an alternate course of action.

Through Wednesday evening and into Thursday morning, discussions on board indicate that several crew members were uncomfortable with taking the ship into the path of the storm. Judging from the transcript, there is no doubt they understood *El Faro* was heading directly toward the eye of a hurricane.

Meanwhile, Joaquin continued to track slowly to the southwest, seemingly refusing to turn right as expected. Remember that the farther it went before turning, the greater the chance *El Faro* would end up on the dangerous front side of the storm. The second mate complained shortly after midnight: ". . . can't win. Every time we come [turn] further south the storm keeps trying to follow us."

. . .

200 MILES FROM STORM CENTER

The third mate came on for the evening watch, from 8:00 p.m. to midnight. The captain departed the bridge at the immediate beginning of his watch and would not return for eight hours. His final words to the third mate just before 8:00 p.m. were, "I will definitely be up for the better part of your watch. So if you see anything you don't like don't (hesitate to change) course and give me a shout."

The situation steadily worsened, but *El Faro* had committed to the exposed Atlantic side of the Bahamas eighteen hours earlier. It would have only one more chance to seek shelter on the other side of the Bahamas, at 1:00 Thursday morning. This was fast approaching. About two hours prior to reaching this point, the third mate, on watch, called the captain with a report of the storm's location and a suggestion: turn south. Here are the words from the third mate to the captain over the internal phone at 11:05 p.m.:

> uhh, well it's—the—the—the current forecast has it uhh—max winds um a hundred miles—an hour. at the center.—umm and if I'm lookin' at this right—um—and it's moving at—at two-three-zero at uh five knots. so I assume it stays on that same—moves that same direction for say the next five hours. and uh so it's advancing toward our trackline—and uhh—puts us real close to it. umm you know like—I could be more specific—I could um—plot that out. but it's gunna be like real close (and). and uh—don't know. uh—uh I can give ya a better number and call ya back. we're lookin' a meet it at say like four o'clock in the morning. (you know).

Immediately after that, he said, "OK." The captain had told him to stay on course. When the captain gave the order to continue as planned, there was a short pause, and then compliance.

The language is hesitant, self-diminishing, deferential, and nervous. This makes it easy for the captain to reject the unwanted information. The captain's previous comments were having their intended effect: they suppressed discussion; but of course, they did nothing to suppress doubt or alter the strength of the winds and seas.

What happened to the advice the captain had given four hours earlier about not hesitating to change course or give the captain a shout? Understanding why that advice is ineffective is critical to understanding leadership. We tend to focus on what others should do—for example, encouraging them to speak up even when we have demonstrated a reluctance to listen. Rather than doing the hard work and spending the time to change our own behavior, it's easier and cognitively convenient to push the action onto others. Encouraging people to speak up, or even "empowering" them with statements like "don't hesitate to change course" in an environment of top-down decision-making, simply does not work.

Leaders say these things to assuage their conscience. When things go wrong, they can blame others for not speaking up despite the leader's encouragement to do so. But leadership is about making the lives of others easier, not blaming them. Leadership is about the hard work of taking responsibility for how our actions and words affect the lives of others.

THURSDAY

At midnight, the watch shifted from the third mate to the second mate. They discussed their situation openly. The third mate pointed out that their current plan would have them within twenty-five miles of the hurricane's eye in four hours. They laughed. They talked about taking the Rum Cay cutoff, cutting south to join the Old Bahama Channel on the protected side of the Bahamas. The second mate said, "He [the captain] is not gunna like this."

The seamen were turning over at the same time. They joked about having a personal distress beacon ready that would activate upon contact with seawater. They invoked gallows humor. "We're the only idiots out here," the off-going seaman said.

The transcript doesn't tell us where the third mate went after he left the bridge, but I'm guessing he went to bed. On board the USS *Santa Fe* the off-going officers made an in-person report to the captain. These reports allowed the officer to convey a more nuanced picture of the situation and communicate a sense of any impending danger. I suspect this did not happen on *El Faro* as there is no evidence of it.

By 1:00 a.m. Thursday, the storm was battering the 790-foot-long container ship. Winds were whipping along the deck and personnel needed to be secured before going outside. Waves were rocking the ship up and down and side to side. The crew knew the storm was out ahead, but not its precise shape. The eye of the storm was about a hundred miles east of the ship, moving slowly in a westerly direction as *El Faro* made maximum speed directly toward it.

On the bridge, the second mate talked through the option to turn south at Rum Cay with the helmsman: ". . . and we could be gettin' away from it. Going south getting away from it and then from there we connect with the um Old Bahama Channel. We have one more waypoint course one oh one and that—bloop—go right into the Old Bahama Channel. Right in to San Juan [Puerto Rico]."

She knew there was a way out. There was relief in her voice at the possibility of escape. But notice the language: "we *could* be . . ." Not we will, or we should, but we *could* be. It's like she was talking about a crew in a parallel universe that had options her crew did not.

Critically, *she did not order the turn to the south.* The second mate was held back by an organizational structure where she needed permission from the captain, a captain who did not want to deviate from the plan. She conformed to the culture.

The second mate and the helmsman knew their situation was dire. They joked about having their survival suits ready. They chatted nervously about the size of the coffee cups. They laughed about all the other ships being "outta here," with only *El Faro* in this part of the ocean. They discussed the storm's upgrade to a Category 3 hurricane, with winds as strong as 129 miles per hour.

The helmsman asked, ". . . sure we gunna change course at two o'clock?"

The second mate hesitated, then said, "I don't know. Gosh. I might call the captain here shortly if he doesn't come up [to the bridge]." She talked through the course change to safety again and again, building up her courage. Twenty minutes later, she called the captain. She knew she would have to overcome a high barrier to get the captain to change his mind.

The bridge transcript gives only her side of the report (the asterisks indicate where the recording was unintelligible):

(uh) I just wanted * * * (runs) south (of the) (island) * * * (old Bahama/weather) channel * * * we'll be meeting the storm. umm Fox News just said it's up to category * * *. yeah—yes (that's what I heard) * * *. it isn't lookin' good right now.—right now my uh—trackline I have zero-two hundred—alter course straight south and then (we'll) * go through all these * shallow areas. umm (and the next) course change (will/gunna) be (through the Bahamas) and then (just gunna) turn * * *.

Like the call from the third mate, the language is hesitant and deferential, with uhs and umms. It is weakened with evasions: "that's what I heard . . ." versus "that's how it is." Communicating this way allows a mental escape from the reality of the situation. It is vague—"isn't looking good right now"—rather than clear and direct: "We are sailing into danger."

The voice recorder does not capture the captain's words at the other end of the phone, but he must have told the second mate to continue. No invitation to discuss, no curiosity, no course correction, only an escalated commitment to continue on course. The second mate, in response, made no attempt to persuade the captain. Each person conformed to his or her role. Four seconds after she said her piece all we hear is "OK" and then she reports a minor adjustment in course to the captain and tells the helmsman the captain wants to continue.

I believe the watch team realized they were at a critical decision point that would have a momentous impact on their future, but they didn't have the words to express it. They were trapped in a set of old plays—CONTINUE and COMPLY. Follow the plan, don't question the plan.

When the National Transportation Safety Board report came out, finding number eighty-one of eighty-one was, "Had the deck officers more assertively stated their concerns, in accordance with effective bridge resource management principles, the captain's situational awareness might have been improved." While true, this statement addresses a symptom of the disease, not the disease itself. It is the responsibility of the captain and company leadership to create a structure that makes it easy for the deck officers to assertively state their concerns, not create a culture where questioning the plan is an uphill battle.

Within thirty minutes, the bridge team was talking about seeing flashes of light and hearing slams and clanks as the ship was tossed in the waves. The waves were knocking them off course. It takes a big wave to knock a 790-foot-long ship off course. Of course, by then it was too late. They had passed the second turning point and there was only shallow water to the south of them now. They could no longer escape the storm. Gallows humor ensued.

They talked about how hard it was to stand up. At one point, the second mate uttered some expletives, followed by: "That was a bad one." By 3:30 a.m., the bridge crew was discussing the shifting wind direction. It was now hitting *El Faro* across the front and right side. No one said it out loud, but they knew what this meant: they were on the wrong side of the storm. The movement of the storm was now adding to the wind speed. A few minutes later, the chief mate, second in command, came to the bridge to take the watch. The second mate had a chance to tell him about her rejected recommendation to the captain, but she did not. Why bother? It wouldn't change anything now. Might as well conserve the energy.

100 MILES FROM STORM CENTER

The captain finally returned to the bridge at 4:10 a.m.. He had been gone from the bridge for eight hours and ten minutes. Since the watches were four hours long, he had missed all but seventeen minutes of the third mate's watch and the entirety of the second mate's watch.

The captain made several comments upon returning to the bridge, including, "There's nothing bad about this ride," "Sleepin' like a baby," and "A typical winter day in Alaska."

Whether he was trying to reassure his crew or justify his decision with these remarks, it didn't change the outcome. The ship would sink in three and a half hours with the loss of all hands. By this point, *El Faro* was likely within thirty miles of the eye of the hurricane.

THE DANGER OF OLD THINKING
IN NEW SITUATIONS

Shortly before sinking, *El Faro* triggered an alarm. Search parties could find only wreckage where they expected to find the massive ship. As they combed the waters, people found it hard to fathom that such a large, modern vessel could sink, even considering the intensity of the storm. But it had, indeed, sunk. Modern technology had been no match for outdated thinking.

Fortunately, the National Transportation Safety Board found the place where the ship sank and retrieved the voice recorder, which is why we have the entire set of conversations that occurred on the bridge. It is a treasure left behind by this tragedy.

In the 511-page transcript, the captain makes 1,203 statements and asks 165 questions over a 25-hour window. Yet many of his questions are not really questions at all:

- "You know what I'm saying?" (binary affirmation)
- "What do you want to call this waypoint? How's Alpha?" (answering own question)
- "Alright, course 140 now?" (answering own question, affirmation)
- "It's going to be between these two, right?" (binary affirmation)
- "Does that make sense?" (binary affirmation)
- "Everything good as far as RPM [speed] goes?" (begs the right answer, binary affirmation)

The words are false comfort designed to keep people on task, conforming to their roles, and continuing on course.

The morning of the fateful decision to take the Atlantic route, the captain says the following things to various crew members:

- "So we'll just have to tough this one out."
- "We're going into the storm. I wouldn't have it any other way."
- "Should (all) work out OK."

This is the captain justifying the decision to himself and to others. After he leaves the bridge, the crew mocks the captain's words among themselves:

> he's tellin' everybody down there—"ohhh it's not a bad storm.
> it's not so bad. * * it's not even that windy out * * seen worse."

The captain's attitude has an effect on these officers. You can see it in the hesitant, ambiguous, and ineffective language they later use. What started as an escalated commitment in one person's mind has now spread through the organization.

It didn't have to be this way. As we'll see in the chapters that follow, it is possible to create a safe environment for every member of the team to express their views, to invite dissent, and to collaborate on a decision, which results in a commitment to execute and thinking in terms of smaller completion chunks; this process inoculates us from escalation of commitment. The crew has a lot of what ails Fred and his addiction to action—a can-do attitude above all. But they also have a bit of Sue, stuck in discussion and unable to turn the ship to the safe route.

On the bridge of *El Faro*, a relatively small shift in the captain's language could have saved the ship:

- "We could tough this one out, but man, I don't know about these conditions. The odds aren't great."

- "It should be fine, but let's stay alert to the conditions—we may need to change course."
- "How is everyone else feeling about this? Don't hold your tongues now."
- "How sure are we that we should stay the course?"

If the captain had displayed vulnerability, the other crew members would have felt safe enough to chime in. Emotions are necessary for decision-making. The idea that workplaces are emotion-free zones reflects the dominance of process work and our immersion in the performance mindset. It is a mode where decision-making is simply not part of the job. Only when we start to bring in thinking work, decision work, do we need to care about the emotional health of the workers. But with our programmed Industrial Age play of conform, we avoid the connection that allows our emotional engagement in decision-making.

SHARE OF VOICE

It's also worth noting the "share of voice" on the bridge. Share of voice is the proportion of words attributed to each person in a conversation and is an excellent indicator of the power gradient within an organization. If there are four people and each person says exactly 25 percent of the words spoken, you have a perfectly balanced share of voice. If the leader says 100 percent of the words and no one else says anything, that share of voice is completely skewed. When we work with an organization, we look closely at the share of voice, how balanced or skewed it is.

We use a methodology to convert the various shares of voices to a single number. This was inspired by the way income inequality is

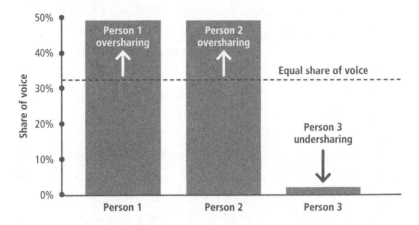

The Team Language Coefficient (TLC) is a number between 0 and 1 that represents the inequality in speaking among people in a conversation. For a three-person conversation where two people each say half the words and the third person is silent, the TLC is 0.5.

calculated for countries.* The number measures the deviation from a perfectly balanced share of voice. We call this the Team Language Coefficient (TLC). A perfectly balanced share of voice results in a TLC of 0.0 because there is no deviation from perfectly balanced. A situation where one person says all the words and everyone else is silent is perfectly unbalanced and results in a TLC of 1.0. To calibrate yourself, in a three-person team where two people say half the words each and the third person is silent, the TLC score is 0.5.

Based on what we've seen so far, you might suspect that a more balanced share of voice and a lower coefficient would lead to more team thinking and better decision outcomes. Not only is this true in practice, it is observable and measurable.

---

* The calculation for income inequality is called the "Gini coefficient," named after the Italian statistician who devised it.

In his book *Superminds*, MIT professor Thomas Malone probes what makes groups smarter than individuals. He found that one of the factors is the degree to which the words are evenly distributed among the participants.

The other two factors Professor Malone attributes the superior group intelligence to are the social intelligence of the members of the group and the proportion of women in the group.

Once you start to understand the factors that lead to poor decision-making, you can't help seeing those factors in play at the most dysfunctional organizations.

On board *El Faro*, share of voice is highly skewed toward the more senior people. When there are three people on the bridge, basically only the top two talk and the third person is nearly silent. When the most senior person leaves, the next two have a conversation.

For example, on Wednesday from 5:36 a.m. to 7:25 a.m., there are three people on the bridge. The captain, the deck officer, and a seaman. For an hour, the only words spoken are by the captain and the officer. Then, at 6:40 a.m. the seaman says, "One-four-two." He is responding to a question from the captain about what course they are on. That's it. Then he says nothing for the next fifty-two minutes. He does not speak again until after the captain leaves the bridge and there are just two of them left: the officer and the seaman.

This skew in share of voice is measurable. Here are the percentage of words and TLC for the times when the captain is on the bridge with the three different watch officers.

PERCENTAGE OF WORDS	CAPTAIN	OFFICER	SEAMAN	TEAM LANGUAGE COEFFICIENT
Team 1	57%	39%	3%	0.55
Team 2	50%	45%	5%	0.45
Team 3	54%	43%	2%	0.53

Think about this. Imagine you know only the number of words each person says: the captain, the officer, and the seaman during each of the periods that the captain is on the bridge. Knowing only that—nothing about what they said or who they said it to or how they said it—you would be able to perfectly predict who was where in the hierarchy with 100 percent accuracy.

AND HERE'S ANOTHER THING: the most junior person in all three situations is being treated as if they are not even there. Imagine how that feels. Then we tell these junior people things like "your voice matters" and "you are empowered to speak up."

This may seem tremendously obvious, but the more you talk, the less you are listening. If you want to hear more from your team, you need to talk less. The sequence is you talk less first, then they talk more—not, "When they talk more, I will talk less." It's as simple as that. The TLC is the hard data behind so-called soft skills.

Because we have the transcript from *El Faro*, it is possible for us to learn from the way the crew operated. It also gives us the ability to scrutinize and critique every utterance. This leads to the temptation to find fault—fault with the people.

As I read the transcript over and over again, I heard the voices of fellow mariners, professionals, trying their best to do their jobs, save their ship, and complete their mission. I could hear the voices of many of my previous captains: leaders running the same plays the captain of *El Faro* ran. I could hear myself.

It breaks my heart to see how they were doomed, not because they were bad mariners or bad people. They were doomed because they were playing from the wrong playbook. It is a pattern I've seen over and over: good people doing what they think is right and suffering bad outcomes. Obeying the clock, coercing compliance, conforming to role, a focus on doing, and a performance mindset. Sometimes the outcomes are bad products, lost sales, wasted time, or simply not feeling useful. Sometimes, running the wrong plays kills people, plain and simple.

We need to always remember that the organization is perfectly tuned to deliver the behavior we see, and people's behaviors are the perfect result of the organization's design.

As individuals, we should embrace our responsibility for being the best we can be within the design of the organization. But as leaders, our responsibility is to design the organization so that individuals can be the best versions of themselves.

We don't need to perform these old plays better. We need a new playbook. With a different playbook, the crew of *El Faro* might be alive today—and in the final chapter of this book, we'll imagine how that might have played out.

The New Playbook

Executives of a global corporation are sitting in a leadership seminar. Eleven tables of five. This company has a reputation for enlightened leadership, is consistently rated "one of the best places to work," and has generated significant profits over the past decade.

I've just told the attendees about a psychological phenomenon called "overclaiming," in which people participating in shared tasks tend to take more credit than warranted for an outcome. The classic studies on overclaiming go back to the 1970s. Husbands and wives were separately asked to estimate their share of the household chores, as a percentage. When combined, the sums consistently exceeded 100 percent.

Overclaiming happens because our own efforts are more visible to us. I know how much hard work I put in—the late hours, the weekends I gave up, and so on—but I'm only distantly aware of what everyone else was doing all that time. Overclaiming explains why I always felt like I was contributing more than my peers, while being appreciated less.

I ask the executives in the seminar to estimate the average overclaiming total found in the husband-and-wife experiments. One guess per table. Ninety seconds. Their competitive juices flow; they feel the pressure to obey the clock. But I have a hidden agenda: I want to see how each group of leaders makes decisions under pressure.

True to form, they run the Industrial Age playbook. At every table in the room—and at most tables nearly everywhere I run this exercise—the sequence of events is essentially the same. Almost immediately, someone, typically the senior participant, throws out the first guess. Then others chime in with estimates slightly above or below this original estimate. If there is a quiet person at the table, they may not speak up at all, especially if their personal estimate differs significantly from the rapidly forming consensus.

It is an Industrial Age play because the structure of the decision-making process (discuss, then vote) results in reducing variability before the decision is made.

You might call the results of this style of decision-making the *wisdom of the loud*. The first number, underpinned by authority, anchors the group, ensuring a final estimate within an arm's length away no matter how far off it was to begin with. (If you're curious, the correct answer is 130 percent.) Group members who think along different lines decline to contribute, depriving the group of possibly relevant information and analysis. The process of anchoring, public discussion, and a quick vote of agreement is convergent. It is intended to quickly reduce variability.

If you've been reading along so far, it should be obvious that this is not the best way for a group to make a decision. Yet this is exactly how most "group" decisions are made. It mimics how the decisions were made on *El Faro*—the captain decided and then let people know.

For better results, diverge first: allow each member to make his or her guess *before* being influenced by the group and, most importantly, the boss. We want an uncorrupted look at what each person believes to ensure the greatest possible diversity of thought. A simple way to do this is to ask each person to write down an estimate before any discussion occurs. Now converge: review the estimates as a group without identifying who made each one, and then narrow the possibilities down collectively.

The result this time is the *wisdom of the crowd*. Under the right conditions, the group is consistently smarter than any individual in the group. It's a term coined by James Surowiecki in his enlightening book *The Wisdom of Crowds*.

I have run this exercise with many hundreds of tables full of executives. In all that time, I have only once seen a table engage in divergent thinking. Seminar after seminar, the tables come within spitting distance of the senior person's first guess.

Why do groups answer questions this way? Thinking through complex variables is hard work. Zeroing in on a clear consensus unified around the voice of authority, on the other hand, is deeply satisfying. It takes a rigorous and systematic approach to resist the natural human tendency to reduce uncertainty as quickly as possible.

There's another reason, too. We make decisions this way because we have been programmed to do so, just like the captain and crew of *El Faro*.

ANCHORED TO AN OUTDATED PLAYBOOK

The captain and crew of *El Faro* were doomed because they'd also been programmed to run certain plays, behave in certain ways, and use certain language. They were trapped by an outdated playbook and unable to see a different way of doing things. Even if they could envision an alternative approach, it would have been extremely difficult to break out of patterns they'd been following their entire careers. We see the angst in the words of the officers as they *try*—and fail—to break these hardwired patterns.

Here are the six plays the crew of *El Faro* were programmed for, and the six plays that would have saved them:

- They obeyed the clock when they should have controlled the clock.
- The captain coerced the crew into compliance when he should have collaborated for a commitment.
- The coerced crew complied when they should have made their own commitment.
- They continued following a monolithic plan to take the Atlantic route when they should have completed one section at a time—to the first decision point at the top of the Bahamas and then to the second decision point at Rum Cay.
- They were in prove mode when they should have been in improve mode. This was a result of being in a can-do mode when they should have been in a can-think mode.
- Throughout it all, they conformed to their roles when they should have connected with each other.

Doing is important, but action must be balanced with thinking. Just like Fred and Sue in the introduction—too much activity without thought results in wasted or erroneous actions and bad decisions, and too much thinking without action results in inaction and frustration.

The key to learning and growing, as a company and as a person, is correctly balancing these two activities. Thinking about something, even making decisions, without committing to action to test your ideas will not result in learning. Nor will the mindless activity of complying with the instructions of others.

While balance is necessary, we have long been biased toward

doing, down to the language we use and the ways we design our organizations. We need to call the plays that will balance all that doing
with more thinking at every level of the hierarchy, not just at the top.
That is the message of this book.

EMBRACING VS. REDUCING VARIABILITY

Here is the key difference: Thinking benefits from embracing variability. Doing benefits from reducing variability.

When it comes to thinking and decision-making, variability is an
ally. Greater variability in possible actions means greater innovation,
greater creativity, more options. When it comes to ideas, we want to
cast a wide net, inviting many different opinions. In order to learn, we
will need to change our ideas, discarding old ones and adopting new
ones. In order to improve our ways of working, we will need to open
our perspectives, inviting other points of view. Variability is one of the
benefits of diversity.

Thinking benefits from embracing variability.

- In brainstorming, I would like as many different ideas as
  possible.
- In decision-making, I would like a wide range of options.
- In determining the truth, I would like to hear different perspectives.

The language of embracing variability is open, curious, probabilistic, and improvement focused. It sounds like "How do we know?"
or "How safe is it?" It is the language of curiosity and vulnerability.

When everyone thinks the same thing, that's low variability.
Sometimes we use the term "consensus." When people have different

ideas, especially opposing ideas, that's high variability. That's team debate. But it also means a lack of consensus.

The word "consensus" is normally used as a positive. Consensus means reduced variability, which is not what we want for thinking. Often, leaders driving toward consensus are reducing variability when they should be embracing variability and driving away from consensus. Then they wonder why they're not hearing new ideas from their team. The problem is they're calling the wrong play. They've brought a reduce-variability playbook to an embrace-variability game.

Why is our bias toward reducing variability? For one thing, all those options created by adding variability come with increased cognitive burden—they must be considered and weighed. That's hard work. And our brains, wired as they are to exert minimal effort, resist that hard work. Shoppers presented with too many choices simply do not buy at all.

But more important, variability is the enemy of what we've always designed organizations to handle: doing.

- In manufacturing, the parts should be as similar as possible. Variation is an error in manufacturing.
- In operating a submarine, the operators should adhere precisely to the procedure. Variation from the set sequence in a procedure is a process violation. Step 1: Shut hatch. Step 2: Submerge. Reverse the steps, that's an error.
- In a fast-food restaurant, every hamburger should be the same unless the customer requests a variation. Variation of quality and quantity confuses customers and makes it harder to plan purchases and to budget costs. Standardization wins.

The language of reducing variability is focused and goal driven. It means strict compliance with rules and adherence to process. It sounds like "Do it this way" or "It is safe." It is the language of control and compliance.

REDWORK AND BLUEWORK

Because the two different kinds of work—decision-making (thinking) and execution (doing)—take two opposite approaches to variability, they require two distinctly different mental processes and two different kinds of language. It's helpful to label these two different modes so you can clearly identify which one you're in. Let's call thinking, decision-making, embrace-variability work "bluework." Let's call doing, execution, reduce-variability work "redwork."

I label the action side of this rhythm as redwork because red is the color of energy and determination. Blue, on the other hand, is the color of calm and creativity.

Fred and Sue, in the introduction, were stuck on opposite sides of the redwork-bluework barrier. Fred was stuck in red, forever doing without reflection, whereas Sue was stuck in blue, perpetual reflection without committing to action. Either redwork or bluework by itself is inadequate; we need the right amount of each.

Finding that balance and doing both kinds of work effectively requires shifting deliberately, as a team, from one to the other.

On the submarine, we would hold a thinking, embrace-variability session called a "certification by the team." During the certification, variability was encouraged. What do people think? How ready are we? How do you see it differently? This was our period of bluework.

Once an officer or chief was satisfied that the team was ready, we would then switch from thinking mode to doing mode. After this commitment to action, variability was avoided, and precision was embraced. Follow the procedure. This was the period of redwork.

During this period, we wanted to adhere as closely as possible to the decided action, say, the torpedo-loading procedure. Each torpedo was loaded in exactly the same way as the one before it. Loading a torpedo is physically demanding, but it requires far less mental effort than the effort that goes into deciding which torpedo to load into which tube and when. Because executing a task like loading a torpedo increases our sense of certainty and completion, we lean into it. Humans are easily seduced by the good feelings triggered by "getting stuff done." It is only with time that the churn of getting stuff done starts to feel empty if not properly balanced with reflection.

There is nothing inherently wrong with either mode of operation. To be effective, we need to weave back and forth between thinking and doing. *The problem is that the language we use is only about doing, not thinking.* It reduces variability by default. As a result, we don't shift from redwork to bluework often enough, and when we do shift to thinking mode, our reduce variability language impairs our efforts.

To fix this pattern, to shift from redwork to bluework mode when you need to make decisions, requires going against what feels natural, because we're used to talking in a language that is deterministic, binary, and unchallenging. For example, it feels more natural to say "Are you sure?" rather than "How sure are you?" The first is cognitively effortless. It reduces the possible responses to two: yes or no. "How sure are you?" feels forced, unnatural. It feels cognitively taxing, inviting a wide range of responses. It can get messy—"Are you sure?" cannot.

Which one feels more natural to you: "Does that make sense?" or "What am I missing?" The first moves things from discussion to decision. It feeds our natural desire to keep things progressing, to obey the clock. I hear it all the time. "What am I missing?" causes delay. It feels like a waste of time. It requires us to be in control of the clock for once.

Redwork sounds like this:

- "Get it done!"
- "Make it happen."
- "Let's finish this."
- "Are we on track?"

Bluework benefits from a broadening of focus, quiet reflection, curiosity about what others see and think, and development of possible alternatives.

Bluework is the cognitive work of making decisions. It happens in our heads. It's invisible, making it hard to monitor. Bluework might not require lifting a finger, but it's mentally taxing. Engaging in bluework for long periods leaves us depleted.

Bluework sounds like this:

- "How do you see it?"
- "How ready are we for this?"
- "What can we do better?"
- "What did we learn?"

Now think about how this would be reflected in the share of voice in each of these cases. Because redwork statements require only a simple OK or a yes/no response, the share of voice is naturally skewed. One or more of the participants—the subordinates—say almost no words. They don't have to say much. The deviation from an even share of voice is high and the TLC is high—maybe 0.40 or 0.50 or higher. Since the TLC measures the deviation from a balanced share of voice, a higher number (approaching 1.0) indicates greater inequality in sharing the speaking. In theory, a team with perfectly balanced share of voice would have a TLC of 0.0, but achieving this perfect balance is neither realistic nor necessarily desirable. The coefficient is a tool to measure the degree of imbalance in the team's share of voice.

The bluework set of questions invite longer responses from the team. As a result, the share of voice will be more evenly distributed and there will be less deviation from a balanced conversation. The TLC is lower—maybe 0.20 or 0.10. This is the general pattern—the better the team is at bluework, the more even the share of voice and the closer the TLC (which shows deviation from perfectly even) approaches 0.0.

There are two common situations that result in skewed share of voice and high TLC. The first is when the leader monopolizes the conversation and we get the echo chamber effect. The second is when there is one person on the team who says little and his or her views, thoughts, and ideas are lost to the team. To what degree are these silent people the innovative (but divergent) thinkers, women or minorities, or other team members we have deliberately brought on board *because* of their different perspectives? You can imagine that in either case effective team decision-making is impaired.

THE END OF BLUEWORKERS AND REDWORKERS

Some readers might point out that by the definition of these labels, the productive, manual work of redwork is what is traditionally done by *blue-collar* workers—this mismatch is intentional. By referring to the work done by the "thinking" white-collar workers as bluework and the work done by the "nonthinking" blue-collar workers as redwork, I hope to accelerate the demise of these counterproductive labels.

After all, while bluework and redwork have been around forever, the rise of the factory led to a particularly pernicious management approach—one that separated the bluework and redwork by class. We did not have just bluework and redwork, we had blueworkers and redworkers. One group—the blueworkers—made the decisions, while another group—the redworkers—executed those decisions. One group did the thinking; the other did the doing. One group embraced variability; the other group worked to reduce variability. One group led; the other followed. Assigning the different modes of work to different groups of workers simplified the task of management and fit the times. It drove the organizational design of the Industrial Age. It also shaped the management practices and even the default language of the workplace.

This approach to management is exemplified by Frederick Winslow Taylor's 1911 book, *The Principles of Scientific Management*. Taylor started work as an apprentice machinist after the American Civil War, at a time when the country was industrializing rapidly. Most shops were still relatively small, run by individual craftsmen who would develop their own ways of doing things as needed. As industry grew in size and complexity, Taylor could see the inefficiencies in this approach and decided to do something about it.

Taylor studied the movement of workers in steel mills, determining the single most efficient way to perform each task. For example, Taylor determined that the typical worker was most efficient when shoveling twenty-one pounds of raw material at a time—not twenty, not twenty-two, but twenty-one. Reduction of variability was his trade. He even designed different sizes of shovels, accounting for the density of different materials, thus taking any skill out of shoveling the appropriate amount of material. Workers did the doing and were not to make decisions—even about how much to shovel—and management did the thinking. In this model, where no decisions are needed on the front line and workers are hired solely for physical work, initiative and thinking become unnecessary distractions.

Taylor rapidly became famous, his services in high demand. He was the first management guru, responsible for reducing variability, reducing waste, and improving quality and efficiency across many industries. His partnership with Henry Ford proved particularly influential.

Here's how Taylor described the role of management:

> It is only through enforced standardization of methods, enforced adoption of the best implements and working conditions, and enforced cooperation that this faster work can be assured. And the duty of enforcing the adoption of standards and enforcing this cooperation rests with management alone.

Notice, first, the focus on reducing variability—"standardization" is the word Taylor uses. Also notice the division of the world into two groups: management that sees the light and workers who must be forced to see the light. Because one group is making decisions and another is executing them, coercion is integral to this approach. Taylor does not shy away from management's need to enforce standards and methods of working.

Further, in a world that assigns thinking to the blueworker class, there is no need for redworkers to think. Taylor makes that clear:

> In our scheme, we do not ask the initiative of our men. We do not want any initiative. All we want of them is to obey the orders we give them, do what we say, and do it quick.

Taylor told workers that they were hired for their physical efforts alone, and that "we have other men for thinking." You've got to give him credit for the clarity of his language.

Taylor's methods were intended to prevent the workers from choosing their own way of working. Allowing them to choose meant different approaches and greater variability. Taylor sought to reduce variability by getting all the workers to do each task in the one best way. And that one best way was determined by someone else.

Factory owners benefited tremendously by implementing Taylor's ideas. They hired uneducated workers at lower wages and then taught them to do one specific, small part of a vast manufacturing process. It was unnecessary to explain how that task contributed to the whole, or even what they were actually making. In the closed system of a factory, with little variability in the process, there was an unending focus on production work.

While bluework and redwork exist in every organization today, blueworkers and redworkers do not have to. However, as a result of the legacy of an artificial construct invented during the Industrial Revolution, we have cultural labels and uniforms to identify which group you are in: leader or follower, salary worker or hourly worker, white hard hat or blue hard hat, lab coat or overalls. We still want to make it clear which team you are on.

While right for the time, there are problems with Taylor's approach for the modern organization. First, the system is fragile and nonadaptive. While efficient, the system is not adaptive because workers can operate only within a narrow range of situations. Conditions change, whether globally or on the production line, but we don't notice because we are too focused on getting our work done and too stressed to notice.

The fragility of this system is reflected in the inability of the crew of *El Faro* to adapt their plan to a changing weather situation.

Second, the system results in getting exactly as much effort out of people as is needed to meet the minimum requirements. The reward for going above and beyond is to increase your quota to the new higher number; since you've proved you could do it once, why not every day? Discretionary effort is reduced to zero.

Third, this system takes a toll on the people in it. The mind-numbing tedium of continuous redwork means minds may wander and attention stray. In the harsh environment of the factory, inattention can prove fatal. An early study of workplace accidents covered one county in Pennsylvania—Allegheny County, home to Pittsburgh, a major steel mill town. In that one county, in the first twelve-month period of the study ending in 1907, 526 workers died in industrial accidents.

Finally, life in such an environment is taxing and depleting. People working in highly industrialized environments tend to show lower levels of conscientiousness, self-control, and life satisfaction and have shorter life expectancy. These scars remain long after the heavy industry, like coal mining, might have moved on—and people in counties that previously housed those industries have the same psychological markers generations later.

A *Harvard Business Review* article by Martin Obschonka explains how the work environment affects workers' values, which then get passed from parent to child:

> For example, highly repetitive, exhausting, and low-autonomy work [i.e., redwork] can affect the values of workers, in that they put less value on intellectual virtues and critical thinking, and these values then often get transmitted to the children of these workers as well.

When we involve everyone in thinking, we get a win-win situation. The company wins because it becomes more adaptive, more agile, more resilient, and more profitable. The people in the company win because they have more fulfilling jobs, as well as richer, fuller, healthier, and longer lives—and their children do, too!

The challenge facing organizations in the twenty-first century is this: How do we create environments where we have both redwork and bluework, but not redworkers and blueworkers? How do we integrate the redworkers, previously labeled as the followers or doers, into the decision-making business of bluework?

CAN I GET SOME THINKING?

In Taylor's world, the blueworkers, clipboards in hand, observed the redworkers and decided what they should be doing, then passed down instructions. After World War II, a shift began to take place in this strict approach, first appearing in Japanese automotive manufacturing. Instigated by statistician W. Edwards Deming, leaders started to move from simply observing workers to asking them what they thought.

At the time, American automakers enjoyed an eager, relatively noncompetitive market for their products, while both Japan and Germany were rebuilding their manufacturing capacities. This sudden lack of international competition encouraged a complacent attitude toward quality, and American cars soon reflected that complacency.

After the war, Deming was stationed in Japan to assist in reconstruction. He spent the next three decades teaching Japanese firms how to build quality products. As a statistician, Deming recognized that if greater variability in the manufacturing process meant higher costs and products that felt cheaper, the reverse must also be true: reducing variability in the manufacturing process would *lower* costs while producing *higher-quality* products. In other words, Deming's first key insight was that quality did not cost money, it saved money. This approach came to be known as Total Quality Management or Total Quality Leadership.

Deming's second insight dealt with how to achieve quality. The traditional approach at that point was to ensure quality by inspecting parts after they were made and then eliminating any substandard ones. This process increased costs in two ways: first, the firm had to pay inspectors and, second, waste was produced when inferior products were scrapped or sold at a discount.

Instead, Deming advised integrating quality into the manufacturing process and eliminating the inspectors altogether. Take, for example, painting the body of a car. The car goes into a stall and several layers of paint are applied, from a base layer to a protective coating. The quality is determined by the coverage and evenness of application, or the consistency of the paint's thickness across the surface. This consistency depends upon many factors, including the paint formula, application nozzles, rate of movement, distance from the metal, baking temperatures, and pause before the next application.

In the traditional model, the car would be painted and the results inspected. In Deming's new model, management would continuously experiment with different paint formulas, nozzles, application techniques, and bake temperatures and times. This ongoing bluework was slow, difficult, and expensive, but it improved the consistency of the redwork, reducing mistakes and obviating the need for inspectors. The savings could then be passed along to customers. As a result of this kind of continuous refinement, today's average car is of a much higher quality than the average car of even twenty years ago.

Deming's third insight was that the previously classed redworkers, in this case the assembly line workers, should be involved in bluework. This approach obviously differed greatly from Taylor's, which advocated a less effective but more efficient division of labor: never delay production by asking workers what they think.

By involving the redworkers in bluework, Deming taught them how to transition between reducing variability and embracing variability. They knew the shop-floor processes better than anyone else, what their flaws were, and how they might be improved. In pulling them into bluework, Deming drove learning for both redworkers and blueworkers, while also reducing errors and improving job satisfaction.

As the Japanese honed this new approach to alternating between redwork and bluework, they developed ever-increasing degrees of precision. When the oil price shocks of the 1970s hit, American automobile makers struggled to build smaller, more fuel-efficient cars (we will visit the sad tale of Ford's Pinto later). High-quality, reliable, and efficient Japanese vehicles began to take the lead.

The notion of quality is in fact *defined* by a manufacturer's ability to repeat a process with as close to zero variability as possible: With cars, the more variability in paint and bolt alignment, the more thin spots that are prone to rusting. With furniture, the more variability in the hole and peg alignments, the wobblier the piece will be, and the more rapidly it will wear down and break.

So while the focus of the manufacturing process itself is the redwork of reducing variability, it is improved through the bluework of embracing variability, inviting thinking and dissent.

As the share of Japanese imports began to rise and American automakers turned out uninspired models like the Ford Pinto, Deming's philosophy was introduced to American businesses in a 1980 documentary, *If Japan Can, Why Can't We?* Manufacturing processes like the Toyota Production System were spawned, in part, by Deming's influence.

In 1981, for the first time ever, Japan produced more cars in one year than the United States. The integration of redwork and bluework had proven superior.

Despite Deming's crucial insights, he stopped short of eliminating the distinction between redworkers and blueworkers. The best he could do was get management (blueworkers) to involve the redworkers in the bluework. It was a step forward from Taylor, where blueworkers would observe the redworkers like lab rats, but the fundamental structure remained. Turning thinking, decision-making, and responsibility for improvement over to the redworkers was a step too far. But that is what we need now.

RED-BLUE APPROACHES

New red-blue approaches such as Total Quality Leadership (TQL), pioneered by Deming, significantly advanced manufacturing by applying statistical methods and involving the workers in developing solutions to manufacturing problems. TQL, and the Toyota Production System after it, resulted in higher-quality products with less variability.

Crew Resource Management (CRM) is another modern management practice grappling with the same fundamental problem of breaking down the redworker-blueworker class system and involving subordinates in the bluework of thinking and decision-making. CRM is a process applied to how teams operate; in particular, how teams fly airplanes. It deserves special mention.

CRM addresses the way the cockpit crew members communicate among themselves, stressing both the need for the copilot, or first officer, to speak up in an escalating manner to express concern, as well as the need for the pilot to create an environment conducive to such escalation. Pilots are trained to then listen to the concerns and ideas of subordinates when they are raised. The near universal practice of CRM by major airlines has saved thousands of lives. For example, when Captain Chesley "Sully" Sullenberger saved US Airways Flight 1549 by landing on the Hudson River in January 2009 after losing both engines to bird strikes, the language he and the copilot used was heavily influenced by CRM.

It is clear that many leaders want to create an environment where their people speak up when they see problems, bring their full creative minds to work, and contribute discretionary effort, like new ideas and solutions. In addition to CRM, there are a host of other modern management approaches with an overall objective centered around an idea like empowerment, engagement, ownership, having people think, allowing people to speak up, creating psychological safety, coaching instead of commanding, or asking the right questions. Intent-Based Leadership, the management style developed on board *Santa Fe* and refined through its application and analysis in other organizations, is an approach that strives to incorporate all of these attributes.

I think all these programs fundamentally address the same root problem: the legacy of the redworker-blueworker class structure from the Industrial Revolution.

Yet, we still have problems. We still have deeply divided workforces, workplaces that marginalize people, and people suffering stress and burnout at work. Why? The limitation of many of these programs is that they attempt to patch over problems in an inherently broken structure, or playbook. In essence, they encourage us to run the old plays better, more effectively, and in some cases replace them with new plays—but the overall playbook of leadership and language remains intact. The result is that leaders unwittingly sabotage their efforts to create better workplaces by using automatic and programmed language patterns that stem from the Industrial Revolution, stifling the emergence of any true red-blue approach. They don't know they are doing it and don't see the connection between the leadership plays they are used to relying on and the behaviors at work.

THE RHYTHM OF REDWORK-BLUEWORK

In our own lives, we regularly cycle between bluework and redwork without thinking too much about it. Here's an example:

Let's say you commute to work by car. At the end of the workday, you face a choice: go home, go to the gym, or go to the bar. You may make this decision effortlessly, but you consider the attractiveness of each of the three options before selecting one. You choose to go home. You've just completed the bluework portion of this daily task—making a decision.

Now that the decision is made and you head toward your car, you are no longer thinking about the task ahead. You have entered redwork. Unless you've just started this job and you're in an unfamiliar city, chances are you intimately know the way home. This knowledge frees your brain from the taxing work of planning. You may even daydream a bit as you drive. Once you arrive home, you probably can't recall the specifics of the drive that got you there. You have completed the redwork portion of the task.

Here's another example, from sport. In open-water swimming, the course is typically indicated by large orange buoys. Swimming is more efficient with your head down and your hips elevated, so swimmers spend most of their time in that position. They travel faster, but they can't see where they're going. Occasionally, they find it necessary to check their location by raising their heads, sighting the buoys, and adjusting course. This process creates a rhythm: (1) sight the buoys (bluework), (2) swim in that direction for a while (redwork), (3) raise your head to check your progress. Keeping their heads down for longer periods means faster swimming overall, but they may end up much farther off course, erasing any lead their pace had given them.

I like this example because it is exactly analogous to what I see in businesses that make decisions and then let things run. There's a natural tendency in businesses to avoid interrupting production work to pause and reflect. As with the swimmers, they're moving faster, but possibly in the wrong direction. Likewise, stopping production to engage in bluework too frequently results in unnecessary interference and reduced performance.

There is an optimal balance for any business, but finding it takes skill and experience. As swimmers gain proficiency in open-water swimming, they learn how to swim straighter for longer lengths, allowing them to safely extend the period between bluework looks. They use cues to the left and right and sometimes other swimmers, thereby reducing the drag and delay of a head raise. Over time, they find a balance between redwork and bluework that allows for maximum efficiency.

Decision-making (bluework) aboard *El Faro* included getting under way despite the storm, taking the exposed Atlantic route, and continuing along that route past the Rum Cay cutoff point. Execution work (redwork) aboard *El Faro* included operating the lube oil system for the power plant in rough seas, securing the cargo in the hold, and responding to the ship taking on water. We'll never know for certain, but the crew may have made mistakes on the execution side. That said, the ship's fate was ultimately sealed by the initial decisions that were made. The outcome hinged on whether *El Faro* traveled the exposed Atlantic route, not on how well it traveled that route.

On board *El Faro*, the captain and crew did not structurally view these as discrete decisions. The captain said he'd take the exposed Atlantic route (with the implication that he'd take that route all the way to Puerto Rico). Think of it like a swimmer who takes one look for the buoy then puts their head down and just keeps swimming, never looking to sight the buoy again.

A better balance between bluework and redwork here would have involved identifying those additional decision points at the outset. We will decide to get under way; we will decide whether to start the Atlantic route; and then at Rum Cay we will decide whether to take the Atlantic route or the Old Bahama Channel. Between those decision points, the team can commit to focusing on redwork.

Across organizations, especially those that are heavily process oriented like power plants, hospitals, and manufacturing, there is a tendency to focus on the errors in redwork and to underappreciate the errors in bluework and, critically, errors in structuring the redwork-bluework balance.

The reason for this is that errors in execution work are immediately visible: a pilot turns the autopilot to the wrong position; a patient is administered the wrong drug; a power plant operator opens the wrong breaker. Execution errors look like violations of policy and procedure or technical mistakes. Inspectors and evaluators love these types of errors because they are irrefutable and unambiguous: Did you wash your hands or not? Did you start the lube oil pump before the diesel engine or not? Did you check the airplane flaps or not? Easy.

This is how we become slaves to procedure. Say we want an outcome such as safer flight, so we gather ideas from operators on what makes flights safer. We notice a correlation between failure to check flaps on the ground and being surprised by a problem in the air. We then write a procedure that specifies testing flaps on the ground. The inspectors inspect against that procedure.

Errors in decision-making are more difficult to uncover and measure. It was not until shortly before sinking that the crew of *El Faro* was certain that taking the exposed Atlantic route—a decision made over forty-eight hours earlier—had been a bad one. In business, the same is true. Is buying a lottery ticket a good decision? What about going to college or getting married or taking a job at a start-up with stock options? We think through each one of these questions, but we can't know the outcome for some time.

At a trucking company, the decisions for pickup loads, times, and locations are determined by management (blueworkers). So are the maintenance plans for the trucks. Drivers (redworkers) are relegated to simply driving a predetermined load from a predetermined location along a predetermined route. It's a classic case of assigning bluework to the blueworker class and redwork to the redworker class.

What happens when a truck breaks down on the road? The driver gets blamed. It's an operational error, but the root cause most likely rests in the workload of the vehicle, along with the maintenance program.

The next time you have a problem at your company, think about this: Is this simply a problem in execution, or was there a decision in the past, perhaps the distant past, that set us down the path where this operational problem was more likely to happen? Is the problem rooted in faulty bluework in the past?

Even more difficult to identify are situations in which the problem results from simply not engaging in bluework. There's no decision to evaluate because it's not clear anyone made a decision to do, or not do, something. They just kept doing what they were doing. We call this the Industrial Age play of continue, and this can be one of the subtlest root causes to discern.

THE THINKING ANIMAL

With the development of large primate brains, Mother Nature was simply operating on her principle of adaptive variability: create species with a wide diversity of designs and see which are beneficial and which are harmful, defined in terms of the ability to reach reproductive age and continue the species.

Nature is nothing if not efficient, so the fact that the human brain uses an astonishing 20 to 25 percent of our daily calories speaks to the survival value of this decision-making power. While most animals possess approximately proportional brains for their size, the human brain is an outlier, three times larger than it should be.

Our enhanced decision-making capacity was useful as early humans needed to hunt their food. Lacking the large teeth and claws of other predators, humans relied on their ability to outthink their prey. Their brains allowed them to communicate and team up to bring down much larger animals. A big brain also made innovations like language possible, which was driven by, and in turn facilitated, teamwork and persistence hunting.

This big brain, with its ability for thought, imagination, and reflection, makes bluework a uniquely human endeavor, which is why removing bluework from human activities creates deeply dissatisfying conditions.

But for all its marvelous power and complexity, the brain, like everything else in nature, is efficient—that is, lazy; it wants to do the least amount of work possible.

When thinking, the brain seeks to get the process over with as soon as possible, and in order to do so, it searches endlessly for patterns. When it spots even the hint of a pattern, it creates a related heuristic—a rule of thumb—to minimize further thinking.* This cognitive shortcut helps avoid any future thinking about that issue. Get sick after eating a certain red berry, simply avoid those red berries in the future: problem solved.

While our brains are expert at developing these shortcuts, and we *believe* them, experience-derived rules can become unhelpful biases that distort our thinking and prevent us from seeing things as they truly are.

In *Thinking, Fast and Slow*, Nobel Prize–winning economist Daniel Kahneman playfully and credibly identifies many such biases. One of these is the anchoring bias, in which we over-rely on an initial

---

* Counterintuitively, thinking deeply does not consume that many more calories than following heuristics, but our brains are wired to avoid heavy lifting nonetheless.

piece of information when making decisions. For example, if you ask a group of people to estimate a number aloud, the guesses will cluster near the first guess offered, regardless of whether it's correct. We do this instinctively, *even if we're aware of the anchoring bias.* It takes deliberate effort to avoid falling into this trap, and this is only one of many such biases.

The example of teams answering the overclaiming question at the beginning of this chapter is an example of the anchoring bias. At one table, the first person to speak said, "One twenty-five," when guessing the sum of the percentage of the household chores claimed by both the husband and wife. Pretty soon, that table had agreed with 125, and then, remarkably, the neighboring table also agreed with 125.

It happened that the person to speak first was also the CEO and founder of the company, so the anchoring bias was particularly strong in this case, but even when the person speaking first has no formal authority, the anchoring bias does influence where the group ends up.

Think about how the anchoring effect serves to reduce variability, thus subtly undermining our desire to embrace variability during bluework. Once someone says a number, we reduce outliers and cluster thinking more tightly together, so anchoring is naturally an ally of redwork. But in almost every meeting where a decision is to be made, we observe the same pattern: discussion first, then voting. The discussion serves to anchor thought to a smaller range, suppressing outliers and leaving only one of two or three options that are not significantly different.

Such meetings rely on bluework, however, and should embrace variability. Therefore, we need to actively avoid the anchoring effect. *This requires running meetings much differently than most groups do: vote first, then discuss.* This order will result in greater variability of ideas and cognitive diversity, leading to better decisions.

Kahneman describes two modes of thinking in the brain, system 1 and system 2. System 1 is more primitive: emotional, instinctive, immediate, and sometimes impulsive. On the plus side, it's also efficient and fast, and it doesn't deplete our mental resources. System 2 is rational and thoughtful, less susceptible to biases, but slower. Its job is to monitor system 1. When things aren't working as our brain expects, it shifts to system 2 thinking, but its motivation will always be to limit that effort by getting the job done and returning to autopilot, system 1. As you might expect, redwork uses system 1 and bluework uses system 2.

When we engage in bluework, we broaden our perspective, challenge our assumptions, and work to identify and try to deliberately sidestep any biases. This requires a conscious decision to engage, even if that engagement is as simple as making a list of pros and cons or discussing possible outcomes with a colleague.

I suspect that when the captain of *El Faro* "made" the decision to take the exposed Atlantic route, it was a quick system 1 decision. There's no evidence in the record of deliberate engagement in system 2 thinking with regard to that decision.

Another system 1 cognitive shortcut manifests as the overconfidence bias.

In this bias, the brain tends to believe that we'll succeed at whatever we attempt to do, nudging us to take risks that may result in significant rewards. From the species perspective, I am grateful that humans have this bias because many advances in society, science, and technology have happened despite long odds against success. But for all its value, overconfidence can also fuel impulsive, wrongheaded decision-making.

To conduct a clear-eyed, unbiased examination of costs and benefits, you must *consciously invoke* system 2 thinking. This would be a period of bluework: broadening your perspective *before* committing. System 2 thinking asks questions like:

- "What are we missing?"
- "How might this go wrong?"
- "If we do this and it ends up going south, what would be the most likely culprit?"

Again, I suspect that this bias also affected the captain of *El Faro*. He wanted to think the Atlantic route would be successful, so his brain mustered arguments that made it feel like it was a safer option than it was. The captain's quick decision to take the Atlantic route wasn't a symptom of being a bad person, it was a symptom of being human and of being a leader in an environment that did not deliberately have a playbook to mitigate our natural human biases.

Engaging in bluework isn't easy. It involves a deliberate summoning of the reluctant system 2 brain to engage in reflective, unhurried, and open-ended thought. It will feel wrong, awkward, effortful. We know it will be cognitively taxing, but we do it anyway because it promises better decision-making and faster learning.

Both system 1 and system 2, redwork and bluework, can be applied to meetings. Certain approaches are better at reducing variability, while others are better at embracing it. If you want to reduce variability in a meeting, summon the anchoring bias and discuss first, then vote. Better yet, tell the group what you think and force them to push you off that position. If you want to embrace variability, avoid the anchoring bias by voting first—simultaneously and anonymously—then discussing second. This approach will result in the widest variability and lead to greater collaboration.

No matter what approach leaders take, however, they must be

willing to face the consequences, understanding the ways in which they are motivating, or suppressing, the separate modes of work.

THE BRAIN'S RESPONSE TO STRESS AND MOTIVATION

Since redwork doesn't tax us cognitively but bluework does, stress affects each type of work quite differently. Deadlines, incentives, and other forms of external pressure have a positive, or at least a neutral, effect on redwork, but the same factors can quickly diminish our effectiveness at bluework. Stress depletes the same cognitive resources that bluework demands, overwhelming the prefrontal cortex, where the brain conducts deliberative thought, and moving activity to the more primitive reptile brain.

In 1908, psychologists Robert Yerkes and John Dodson designed an experiment to explore the relationship between stress and learning. They set up model houses for lab mice and then had the rodents choose which house to enter. If the mice chose the wrong house, they would receive a "disagreeable shock" intended to teach the mice which house was "correct." Yerkes and Dodson then varied the size of that "lesson" to see how it affected the learning process. As they expected, more powerful shocks conveyed the lesson more quickly, but only up to a point. Once the shocks became intensely "disagreeable," the mice were too aroused by fear to properly learn the correct habit. Excess stress disrupted the learning process altogether.

This phenomenon showed that it is almost impossible for people engaged in simple, individual, physical, repeated tasks (picture the assembly line) to be overstressed to the point of interfering with the task. Additional stress might improve performance to a point, then it would plateau, but it would not get worse. Since the Industrial Age specialized in reducing human effort to simple, individual, physical, and repeated tasks, adding stress became the go-to motivational technique for managers. It's important to remember that chronic stress still takes a long-term toll on humans, but in the short run, for managers concerned only with task accomplishment, it's an effective tool.

Unfortunately, managers also add stress when it is not helpful, which is during bluework. For complex, collective, cognitive challenges, stress can and does have a strong negative impact on performance. Stress impairs the prefrontal cortex. It turns that big, gray, calorie-burning investment into a shoulder-weight. Our mental activity is reduced to primitive instincts controlled by the oldest part of our brain: our reptile brain.

The reptile brain uses flight, fight, or freeze to achieve self-preservation. Key point: *self*-preservation. In highly stressed environments, we often see individuals become much more self-serving than in relaxed environments. When teams have difficult problems to solve, and we, as leaders, put them under stress, team members turn into lizards. Then we don't understand why we see antisocial behavior, low empathy, and reduced creativity. It's because we led them to these behaviors and emotions!

When we're stressed out and overwhelmed, we may become resistant to asking for help, leading us to an unhelpful subset of the performance mindset: the protect mindset.

There are two sides to the performance mindset. We either try to *prove* competence (I can do the project) or *protect* ourselves against evidence of incompetence (I don't want to be discovered as incompetent). I will label these two subsets either a prove or protect mindset. The prove mindset is motivated to demonstrate something positive, the protect mindset is motivated to hide something negative.

Both feel similar to us. We become closed and defensive, feedback hurts, criticism stings.

A prove mindset sounds like this:

- "I did it!"
- "We need to show we can do this!"
- "Nailed it."

A protect mindset sounds like:

- "Wasn't me."
- "No, I'm fine."
- "We did the best we could with the time we had."

While performing short bursts of redwork, focusing on the end goal, filtering out other distractions, and dedicating cognitive resources to "getting it done" that comes with the prove mindset all benefit performance. For these short-term, one-off, or milestone tasks, the prove mindset correlates to the strongest performance. A protect mindset, motivated toward avoiding errors and hiding incompetence, does not do as well. This makes sense because the best way not to make an error is to do nothing, and organizations where people have been stressed into protect mindsets exhibit a bias toward inaction. In other words, when in "can-do" mode where task performance (rather than task improvement) matters most, the appropriate mindset is a prove (not a protect) mindset.

I will often label the prove mindset a "prove and perform" mindset so we remember that it is a subset of the performance mindset.

At the other end of the spectrum, bluework centers on learning and getting better. Higher performance in bluework correlates to an *improve* mindset. An improve mindset is open, seeking, and welcoming of criticism and feedback. It is the openness of the improve mindset that allows us to detach emotionally from our past work and improve it.

The improve mindset sounds like this:

- "How can we make it better?"
- "How could I do better?"
- "What have we learned?"

We must find a way to activate the appropriate mindset for the work we are doing: avoiding a protect mindset in all cases, and adopting a prove mindset for redwork and an improve mindset for bluework. This requires two different languages. Navigating the difference between prove and improve is so critical to our effectiveness that it is one of our six plays, IMPROVE, and forms the basis of chapter 7.

ADAPTING FOR THE FUTURE

Bluework and redwork exercise the brain in different ways, calling upon distinct leadership behaviors, mindsets, and, critically, language. When it comes to the words we use, and how we use them in the workplace, our current language is heavily weighted toward redwork:

- Knowledge companies hold "all hands" meetings.*
- Companies' employees are divided into two groups of people: "leaders and followers," "white collar and blue collar," "management and labor," "nonunion and union."

---

* "All hands" is an old nautical term referring to getting every crewman up to pull on a heavy line. It was, literally, about using your hands.

- Special "innovation brainstorming sessions" are scheduled, implying that innovation and creativity are not part of "normal" work.
- We aspire to be "can-do" teams.
- Bosses direct and subordinates report (we even call them "direct reports").

The language that sounds "natural" to you has probably been optimized for redwork—we're used to talking this way. But we need to learn to adjust the way we communicate to properly engage in bluework when needed. If we try to use redwork language while doing bluework, we'll be unable to enact bluework plays that embrace variability and foster an improve mindset.

Thinking back to the *El Faro* tragedy, every play and every conversation was rooted in redwork. When the weather changed for the worse, the operational mode needed to change from redwork to bluework, from "Sail the Atlantic route to San Juan" to "Which route should we sail to San Juan?" or even "Should we sail to San Juan?" When the officers called the captain to report the hurricane and recommend the detour at Rum Cay, their attempts at bluework language were clumsy, full of ums, ahs, and self-negating qualifiers. The results were awkward, tentative, and ineffective, which only makes sense: they had never practiced bluework plays. The reason? They had no playbook for bluework. All they had were redwork plays.

The captain was equally lost, trapped in redwork plays despite the obvious concern and skepticism of his crew. Again, he could only respond as he knew how, using the practiced language of redwork.

The problem was not with the captain or the officers; it was with an outdated leadership playbook, one that had not yet been adapted for a red-blue approach to problem solving or even day-to-day operations. Similar outdated playbooks can be found across industries, though newer industries tend to have adapted more readily.

In the world of computer software, for example, many companies are adopting "agile" development practices. The agile approach was launched in 2001 with the publication of *The Agile Manifesto*, which attempted to guide a more effective way for teams to develop software. At the time, most software programs were managed the way the Industrial Age projects were managed. That approach stressed significant upfront planning and then a long execution period that might extend for years. As the pace of change increased, this approach became more expensive, wasteful, and painful.

The goal of agile development was to start with the most basic product feasible, test it, then decide what to do next. This approach differed from the Industrial Age. First, working products were to be delivered frequently, as frequently as every two weeks. These short bursts of work were called "sprints." Early and frequent testing exposure to users allowed early and frequent adjustments.

Second, the team would work with the product owners to decide which features they would include during the next sprint. Rather than the Industrial Age approach of separating doers and deciders, the agile approach turned the doers into deciders.

Software companies large and small have adopted many of the tenets of *The Agile Manifesto* and reorganized teams and processes to align with agile software development practices. The structure of the red-blue operating rhythm and the plays here should allow a similar approach throughout all leadership levels.

One challenge is that the pressure to obey the clock keeps teams moving from redwork to redwork without thoughtful reflection. Take the navy, for example. In a typical submarine environment, the scene is one of unending doing—continuous action. Once one action is completed, the next task on the schedule is tackled, without pausing for deliberate consideration about whether the next task is appropriate. All are locked in redwork mode.

As a submarine captain, if I were to announce that we were going to conduct a certain tactical operation, it should be clear to everyone that a particular arrangement of engineering systems, sonar systems, missiles, and torpedoes would be appropriate. However, in a redwork culture, even if the crew in the torpedo room are aware of the mission, they do not typically think through the implications. Nor do they take initiative to get the right torpedoes loaded. Instead, they wait to be explicitly directed on whether to change the loadout.

If, with little time to spare, I happen to ask about the loadout, only to realize it's still suboptimal, I am faced with a tough decision: either go into the operation unprepared or rush around to fix the problem at the last minute. In the latter case, intense stress will be placed on the torpedo room operators, increasing the chances they will make a critical mistake. This stress will plunge them even further into a prove-and-perform, redwork mindset. If they make a mistake in the torpedo load, it's easy to notice and to blame the torpedo operators. But how much of the mistake occurred because we had a culture devoid of bluework?

This example illustrates how important the balance between redwork and bluework is in a system as a whole. The situation won't improve until the team learns to shift modes of work as seamlessly as the experienced open-water swimmer swims and navigates for maximum progress.

Let's go back to a question posed earlier in the chapter: Why do almost all executives in workshops jump straight to the cognitively satisfying task of reducing variability? When viewed in the context of the Industrial Revolution, it makes sense. The entire objective has long been to reduce variability. When stress is introduced into the workshops, by creating a time pressure, participants are driven to find an answer quickly, before they understand what everybody else knows and sees. They have been conditioned this way by the language and structures of the Industrial Revolution. To improve, a new form of conditioning must supplant this old one.

This is the new playbook, which comprises six main plays:

- CONTROL THE CLOCK, not obey the clock.
- COLLABORATE, not coerce.
- COMMIT, not comply.
- COMPLETE, not continue.
- IMPROVE, not prove.
- CONNECT, not conform.

But before we can even be in a position to call a play rather than just react to situations, we need to *control the clock, not obey the clock*—which gets us to our first play.

REDWORK AND BLUEWORK

Redwork is doing. Redwork is clockwork. Redwork consists of a constant battle for efficiency and for getting work done against the clock. This is why workers clock in and clock out and many people are paid "by the hour."

People performing redwork feel the effects of this pressure as stress and are "under the influence of redwork." They cannot help it.

Our mindset in redwork is a prove-and-perform mindset.

The protect mindset is an unhelpful subset of the performance mindset and is to be avoided.

Variability is an enemy to redwork.

Bluework is thinking. Bluework is cognitive work. Bluework is harder to measure based upon the time input. Bluework is about creative input and decision-making. Bluework lives in service to redwork.

Stress has a strong negative impact on people trying to perform bluework.

Our mindset in bluework is an improve and learn mindset.

Variability is an ally to bluework.

Redwork and bluework require two different languages.

The Industrial Age company separated who did the bluework and redwork by class, into blueworkers and redworkers. We use different cultural signals to indicate these classes: leaders and followers, salary and hourly, white collar and blue collar, lab coats and overalls.

The need to shorten periods of redwork and inject more bluework has increased as the world moves faster and the future horizon shortens.

Without our knowing or thinking about it, our language and organizational structure are biased toward performing redwork.

The differences between redwork and bluework can be summarized in the table below.

REDWORK	BLUEWORK
Avoid variability	Embrace variability
Prove	Improve
Do	Decide
Repetitious	Dissimilar
Blue collar	White collar
Physical	Cognitive
Individual	Team
Homogeneity	Heterogeneity
Production	Reflection
Performance	Planning
Process	Prediction
Compliant	Creative
Conformity	Diversity
Simple	Complex
Hourly work	Salary work
Narrow focus	Broad focus
Steep hierarchy	Flat hierarchy

Exiting Redwork: Control the Clock

On February 26, 2017, as the Oscars drew to a close, Faye Dunaway and Warren Beatty prepared to present the final and most prestigious award of the night. This was what viewers had been waiting for: the Academy Award for Best Picture. So far, everything was going according to plan.

Ahead of time, to ensure the integrity of the voting process, two PricewaterhouseCoopers (PwC) partners had tabulated the 6,687 Academy votes and stuffed twenty-four red envelopes with cards identifying the winners. Only they knew the results.

The PwC partners stood on either side of the stage, ready to hand the envelopes to the presenters. Each partner had a complete set of envelopes, so there was an envelope available whether a presenter emerged from stage left or stage right. As the evening went on, the envelopes were handed to the presenters, and the off-side envelopes were set aside, keeping everything in sync.

One small aesthetic change had been made this year. The envelopes were redesigned, now deep red with dark gold lettering on the front to identify the award category. The new design made it harder to

The

OSC∧RS.

EMMA STONE
"LA LA LAND"

_____

Actress in a Leading Role

The layout of the winner card caused confusion.

read the category than in the past. Inside, a card listed the award winner and, in small letters at the bottom, the award category.

Leonardo DiCaprio presented the penultimate award, for best actress in a leading role. While Dunaway and Beatty stood in the wings stage right, DiCaprio entered from stage left. He opened the envelope and announced, "Emma Stone, *La La Land*."

After she accepted the award, Emma Stone just happened to exit stage right, passing the PwC partner just as he was handing the envelope to Dunaway and Beatty, right before they walked onstage. The PwC partner also took the opportunity to take a photo of Stone and tweet it.

Unfortunately, the PwC partner had not set aside the spare envelope for best actress in a leading role. He gave Beatty the duplicate, instead of the envelope marked BEST PICTURE. It was an error that was likely caused, at least in part, by his inattention to the task. Dunaway and Beatty did not suspect anything was amiss when they walked onstage.

They had the wrong envelope, but there was still an opportunity to avoid announcing the wrong winner.

Dunaway and Beatty had been selected to present the award because it was the fiftieth anniversary of the movie *Bonnie and Clyde*, which they had starred in together.

However, their rehearsal for the presentation had not gone well. They'd disagreed about who would read the card. Finally, a compromise was struck: Beatty would open the envelope and Dunaway would read the award. Still, they did not part amicably. Beatty reportedly left rehearsal early and there was a lockdown on the video of their heated exchange. This set the stage for a lack of trust and cooperation between them and for misinterpretation of each other's actions onstage.

After Dunaway and Beatty walked onstage, they stood and listened to the list of nominees, which included *Moonlight* (the actual winner) and *La La Land*. While the trailers for the nominees ran, for a full five minutes, Beatty held the erroneous red envelope. Not once did he look at the front to verify it was the right one. But why would he?

The trailers ended and it was time to announce the winner. As planned, Beatty opened the envelope, pulled out the card, and looked down at it. The print read: EMMA STONE "LA LA LAND". It was the card for best actress. He paused, did a double take. His face contorted, he looked in the envelope for a second card. He was probably asking himself, "Why would the card for Best Picture have the name of an actress on it?"

In small letters at the bottom, the award category for that card was correctly identified: ACTRESS IN A LEADING ROLE. But reading that would have required another pause and the clock was ticking.

After another moment's hesitation, he started into his script, "And the winner of the best picture . . ."

Again, though, he paused, face tightened and brow furrowed. He looked in the envelope. Hesitancy, double-checking, stalling.

Dunaway was exasperated by the delay. She'd had enough. She pursed her lips, looked at him disapprovingly, and then placed her hand on his arm and said, "You're impossible!"

Beatty looked past Dunaway, offstage, for help, or a sign, or something. Nothing came. He was on his own. Dunaway prodded him again with, "C'mon."

He then showed her the card and she immediately called out, "*La La Land.*"

She had just announced the wrong movie.

WHO'S TO BLAME?

Why didn't Beatty stop the proceedings when he saw something unexpected on the card? What made it so hard to simply hold up his hand and say, "Something doesn't look right here"?

Perhaps the tension and lack of trust between the two actors resulted in Beatty relishing the opportunity to set up Dunaway.

Or maybe he felt that it was not his job, deciding instead to pass the buck to Dunaway, who could make her own choice about the card.

Another possibility: he didn't care.

I do not think any of these hypotheses is right. There is a simpler explanation that doesn't involve distrust or malicious intent. Beatty was trapped in redwork and could not get out. He (along with the rest of the Oscar producers) was running the Industrial Age play of obeying the clock. What they needed to do was a CONTROL THE CLOCK play, but this wasn't in their playbook.

Here's what I think happened:

Beatty and Dunaway have been primed to think of their jobs as redwork, following a sequence of steps: dress nicely, walk onstage, open the envelope, read the card. There is no expectation of thinking or decision-making. And they want to prove they can do this work. They do not expect bluework—deciding whether they should read the card—to be part of their job.

And why would they doubt the system? The card was delivered by the PwC partner, a trusted source, and in the fifty years since *Bonnie and Clyde* hit the silver screen, there has never been an incorrect card handed to a presenter.

But then Beatty opens the envelope and sees something unexpected: the name of an actress on the "Best Picture" card. How can that be? He questions whether it is the right card. A thoughtful decision is needed.

This is bluework and he needs his prefrontal cortex, the part of the brain best able to help him in problem solving. But his prefrontal cortex is impaired by stressors. He is in front of a live TV audience. Plus, there is that relentless feeling that he must obey the clock. Stress causes the activity in that big brain that Mother Nature invested so much in to shut down.

Stress pushes us all back to the oldest part of our brain, that original reptile brain at the top of our spines. That reptile brain is interested in one thing: self-preservation (not the preservation of the Oscars, not the preservation of the teams that worked on *La La Land* and *Moonlight*, and not the preservation of Dunaway). The reptile brain has to make a decision, and fast. Go on with the show or stop the Oscars. But Beatty hasn't been given a tool, a code word, to request a pause. That focus on *self*-preservation pushes us back behind our own eyeballs. It feels lonely. At this point, Beatty's brain functions really are all about himself.

His reptile brain is worried. It reasons, "If I stop the Oscars and it turns out that the card is right, I will be embarrassed for being wrong."

Why *wrong*? Almost every person who goes through this analysis with me uses that word—they will say, "He's afraid of being wrong."

This is one of the barriers to speaking up: labeling as "wrong" a pause which is simply asking for a check that turns out to be unnecessary. To call it resilience, verification, or a questioning attitude would be a better label.

Or, he could go on with the show. To the reptile brain, this seems like the safer option. The card has never been wrong and it came from an authoritative source. It's not your job, anyway, to question the card. After all, you are supposed to pass it to Dunaway, and she'll read it. This thought process happens in the blink of an eye. The reptile brain sides with self-preservation.

Decision made: go on with the show.

After that first glimpse at the card, once that decision is made, the stress leaves Beatty's face and his prefrontal cortex comes back to life. The human brain now evaluates the decision the reptile brain has already made. In essence, it says, "Hey, reptile brain, good job. Too scary to stop the Oscars. Besides, it's not your job to question the card."

But the deliberation is not quite closed yet. The possibility the card is wrong weighs heavily on Beatty. He pauses again, still trying to figure out how to stop the show, but he does not have the right play.

There are two final chances to trap the error. First, when he looks offstage. The organizational design has separated information from authority. The show managers offstage can't see the information on the card, only Beatty can. And Beatty, who can see the information, does not feel he has the authority to stop the Oscars. That decision rests with the show managers. He is trying to close that gap, hoping they will pick up on his distress signals. They do not.

Finally, there is the chance that Dunaway will notice the problem. Then, maybe they can collaborate on what to do. He shows her the card, but she has misread his delay. She immediately announces, "*La La Land.*"

What he needed was a pause, a moment to read the small writing at the bottom of the card, or an opportunity to have someone else, perhaps Dunaway, look at the card, too, in a deliberate way. That pause would have given him the opportunity to pivot from "We need to read this card correctly" to "Do we have the correct card?" Instead of being locked into the redwork of task completion, he would have shifted to the bluework of deciding whether they should read the card or not.

But like our executive Fred, he is stuck in red.

Remember the division of labor in the Industrial Age: a few do the bluework and most do the redwork. It isn't the redwork that gets us in trouble. Instead, it is the division of labor, which creates redworkers who are expected to perform only redwork. This labor strategy is fragile because performing the task sequence of passing the card and reading the card with more expertise would not have prevented the mistake. Only a pause to reevaluate whether they *should* read the card would have prevented the error from propagating. Redwork is brittle. The bluework allows us to adapt. But unless we control the clock, we have no chance to do our bluework.

So, the question is not "Who's to blame?" but "What's to blame?"

And the answer is programming to follow the Industrial Age play of obeying the clock.

This is what sank *El Faro*.

HOW TO CONTROL THE CLOCK

The traditional organizational response is to encourage people to speak up. We invest in lectures, posters, and assertiveness classes. None of these addresses the root causes that make it hard for people to speak up. All they accomplish is encouraging us to drive harder at the barriers. Instead, we need to remove the barriers. As leaders, we do this by controlling the clock instead of obeying the clock and by giving our team the tools to control the clock as well.

There are four ways to run the CONTROL THE CLOCK play.

TO MOVE TOWARD CONTROLLING THE CLOCK

1. Instead of preempting a pause, make a pause possible.
2. Instead of hoping the team knows what to say, give the pause a name.
3. Instead of pressing on with redwork, call a pause.
4. Instead of relying on someone to signal a pause, preplan the next pause.

Let's look at these one at a time.

1. Make a Pause Possible

Part of Industrial Age leadership is to condition people to keep working and to avoid pauses. This starts with good intentions from management but creates bad results. A "pause" is a delay when no products are being made. Therefore, it shows up on the spreadsheet as "waste" and should be eliminated.

In most organizations, people get promoted for being go-getters, by making quick decisions and executing them in short order. Being such a go-getter myself, I experienced this in the navy. My ability to urge, cajole, and motivate people to get stuff done got me promoted. Naturally, I felt that this was my role as a leader, and that somehow I was better at getting things done than others. As part of my tool kit to minimize any delays, I would give speeches and advise my team on how much we had to do, how much I was counting on them, and how much others were relying on us. In other words, I was deliberately making it hard for people to call time-out. I was preempting a pause.

By "preempt" here, I mean taking action to prevent something else from happening in the future. In this case, I made comments with the aim of keeping the team in redwork and making the barrier to exiting redwork higher.

The captain of *El Faro* preempts the pause with statements like these:

- "So we'll just have to tough this one out."
- "You can't run [from] every single weather pattern." Then, mimicking a frantic voice, "Oh my god—oh my god."
- A crew member asks, "We're goin' into the storm?" The captain responds, "Wouldn't have it any other way."

These are preemptive statements because they erect barriers to questioning the decision. It probably wasn't the captain's conscious intention to prevent people from speaking up, but that was the exact effect of these statements.

On a cold January morning in 1986, right before the space shuttle *Challenger* exploded just seventy-four seconds into flight, NASA leaders preempted a pause. Among its crew of seven, the shuttle was carrying specialist Christa McAuliffe, the first teacher to go to space. The flight was a big deal for NASA. President Reagan was going to deliver the State of the Union address that evening (he delayed it a week after the explosion) and would probably talk about this major achievement. Nineteen eighty-six was going to be the "Year of the Shuttle," with a launch set to occur every month. But NASA was already in danger of missing that goal and it was just the first month of the year. Delays had pushed the January launch back, now to the twenty-eighth of the month. The launch date was dangerously close to slipping into February.

When the engineers from Morton-Thiokol, the booster's manufacturer, recommended another delay in launch due to the cold weather, NASA officials said they were "appalled." One official exclaimed, "My God, when do you want me to launch—April?"

Exaggeration, hyperbole, exasperation. These NASA officials were succumbing to obeying the clock. They were preempting the pause.

Instead, leaders should take the time during the preamble to decision, start-up, preflight, and presurgery meetings to remind the team that they have time to pause. Here are some things leaders say:

- "We have time to do this right, not twice."
- "You may have heard that this is an important milestone. That is true, but if we can't get this done safely, I'll recommend a postponement and I'll be responsible for it."
- "I invite you to call pause if necessary."
- "You all have yellow cards to signal the need to slow down."

Let's take a look at some typical work situations.

On a construction site, the pre-shift meeting is ending, and a decision has been made to start work on a day when the weather is predicted to deteriorate. As usual, the team feels time pressure from management to meet production deadlines. They know they are already behind because of previous delays in site preparation. The foreman sends the team off, saying:

a. "Let's all have a safe day."
b. "We need to make quota today."

c. "I'll be coming by at twelve to check on you."

d. "Don't be scared by a little snow."

e. "If you see any hazardous conditions developing, please text me."

f. "I'm a bit nervous about the storm. We are going to start work, but we will revisit this decision at twelve. I'd like to learn about conditions on-site at eleven thirty, in support of that decision."

Let's evaluate each of these statements, scoring 1 to 5 for their ability to invite a pause by team members, with 1 being worst and 5 best.

a. "Let's all have a safe day."

Score: 3. This is too vague to be meaningful. It also shifts responsibility for creating a safe environment away from leadership and over to the workers, who may have little control over fundamental safety. The best we can say is that it does not make it harder to escape redwork.

b. "We need to make quota today."

Score: 1. This declaration preempts the pause and pushes the team into production mode and a prove mindset, reducing variability. It makes calling a pause more difficult.

c. "I'll be coming by at twelve to check on you."

Score: 3. Here, it depends on what is meant by "check on." If the foreman plans to monitor progress, it will feel like a judgment and press the team further into redwork.

If the foreman plans to evaluate well-being and the need to exit redwork, it will invite a pause.

d. "Don't be scared by a little snow."

Score: 1. This admonishment makes it harder for anyone on the team to suggest that conditions have deteriorated to the point where work should stop for the day. It's the equivalent of the captain of *El Faro* mocking mariners who would take a detour for "a little weather."

e. "If you see any hazardous conditions developing, please text me."

Score: 4. This line invites the group to share concerns. It lowers the barrier to signaling the need for a pause and provides a mechanism to do so. Also, the foreman invites the group to speak up when they see conditions *developing*. They don't have to wait for an unsafe condition to present itself.

f. "I'm a bit nervous about the storm. We are going to start work, but we will revisit this decision at twelve. I'd like to learn about conditions on-site at eleven thirty, in support of that decision."

Score: 5. The leader's willingness to show vulnerability invites the team to express any fears they might have. Additionally, the leader has built in a secondary decision point, at noon, with a preliminary evaluation beforehand at eleven thirty. So the team is invited to think about the weather conditions and gather information to inform any subsequent decisions. Remember, the shorter the planning horizon is, the shorter the period of redwork.

Let's take a look at another scenario. On a deep-water oil rig, after a decision to shift the well to production mode, the superintendent says to the team:

    a. "Time to get our money out of this rig."
    b. "Pay dirt time, people."
    c. "Let's be aware of any unusual situations."
    d. "How ready are we to shift to production?"
    e. "Let's start pumping and I'll check in in two hours."
    f. "We are heading into a different phase of operations. Let me know about any readings or indications that you are unsure about."
    g. "If you see something, say something."
    h. "What questions do you have?"
    i. "Great getting us to this point. We're set!"

Again, let's evaluate these comments, scoring 1 to 5 for their ability to invite a pause.

    a. "Time to get our money out of this rig."
        Score: 1. The leader is expressing frustration with the sunk investment in the well, urging the team forward.

    b. "Pay dirt time, people."
        Score: 1. This line implies the decision is made and closes the option for debate.

    c. "Let's be aware of any unusual situations."
        Score: 4. The leader is reminding the team they are about to do something different and invites them to look for disproving indications. There is an implication

that the shift into production can be paused. If the statement were more specific to the current situation, I would rate it 5.

d. "How ready are we to shift to production?"

Score: 5. The leader is asking the team how ready they are rather than forcing them into a binary "ready or not" position. This approach reduces stress. By opening with "how," the leader makes it easier for the team to signal any level of discomfort with the plan.

e. "Let's start pumping and I'll check in in two hours."

Score: 5. The leader has set a clear endpoint and secondary decision point, opening the door to keener observation by the team, facilitating a pause.

f. "We are heading into a different phase of operations. Let me know about any readings or indications that you are unsure about."

Score: 4. The leader is reminding the team that today will be different from yesterday and invites their observations. If the statement included clear instructions for reaching out to the supervisor, I would rate it 5.

g. "If you see something, say something."

Score: 3. This is just a general reminder. Remember: the problem is not them, it's the leader.

h. "What questions do you have?"

Score: 3. This question would be worse if it merely invited a binary "yes or no" response ("Any questions?").

But it would also be better if it invited dissent: "What is unclear?" or "What am I missing?" The latter is the best option, because the emphasis is on the leader's gap. The former implies that team members are unable to comprehend what's been said.

i. "Great getting us to this point. We're set!"

Score: 2. This statement closes the door on discussion and implies nothing can go wrong.

You'll find another cautionary tale with Boeing's 787 Dreamliner. On July 8, 2007, the highly anticipated airplane was rolled out at a ceremony attended by fifteen thousand people. Clearly, Boeing was committed to the event happening on that day, and so there would have been a sense of urgency to showcase the 787 on that date.

At the ceremony for the rollout, the head of commercial aviation for Boeing announced, "We are gratified that the 787 has been so strongly validated in the marketplace by our customers. Their response is proof that the Dreamliner will bring real value to our airline customers, passengers and the global air transportation system."

The pressure had been building for some time. In its 2006 annual report, Boeing referred to the 787 program as "the most successful launch in commercial airplane history," even though it had not actually launched yet. The annual report later stated, "The 787 program is moving forward on schedule, with first flight planned for 2007."

At the same time, Boeing's archrival Airbus had beat it to the punch with the next generation of long-haul jumbos. Airbus's A380 had first flown in 2005. The A380 was about to enter service in the fall of 2007 and the 787 hadn't even flown yet.

The plane that Boeing rolled out at the July 2007 ceremony was a

Potemkin village—a facade with missing electronics, temporary fasteners, and wooden parts.

The CEO of Boeing was James McNerney, who had risen at GE under Jack Welch and was once a contender to replace him at GE. Under his watch, a press release at the rollout ceremony announced that the first flight would occur "in August or September"—within one or two months.

The first flight actually occurred on December 15, 2009, over twenty-nine months later. He was off by a factor of twenty.

How was it that the Boeing executives got the date so disastrously wrong? Had they been duped by their employees and suppliers, or had they sent a signal that a change in the timeline would not be tolerated? The Oscars, the *Challenger*, the 787, your company. All too often we preempt a critical pause.

These executives were going by traditional Industrial Age redwork plays. They were reinforcing the importance of production adhering to the stated timeline. They were deliberately trying to set the team into a prove-and-perform mindset in support of making the deadline. But this action also activated a protect mindset in people, and in both cases, prove or protect, the mindset made it harder for team members to state dissenting opinions or raise objections.

2. Give the Pause a Name

When our team goes into a period of redwork, we tend toward a performance mindset (prove or protect). In support of the goal of performing the redwork, we narrow focus, reduce perspective, and work "head down." We might also feel the urgency of the clock and the pressure to get it done. We are locked into the redwork of completing our tasks, like Beatty at the Oscars. Beatty, I believe, was motivated by the less helpful performance mindset—the protect mindset and not the prove mindset—and his actions were motivated by the desire to avoid error, which ironically made the error more likely.

So we need to protect ourselves from being "under the influence of redwork" before we launch into that redwork. Leaders do this by preplanning phrases or signals the team can use to create an operational pause. With the language defined, both team members and leadership can signal a need to escape redwork.

Some preplanned operational pause signals could be:

- Saying, "Time-out."
- Saying, "Hands off."
- Raising a yellow card.
- Pulling a cord.
- Raising a hand.

On the USS *Santa Fe* we used the phrase "hands off." At first, I found that team members were reluctant to call "hands off" on other team members, and even when they did, the person who was told "hands off" often reacted defensively. We overcame this through practice. The purpose of practice is to familiarize the team with the language, destigmatize the act of calling a pause, and allow other team members and leadership to practice reacting to the call for a pause.

Practice means occasionally asking a team member to signal a pause *even when no pause is needed*. The leader must still acknowledge the pause. During operations, I would occasionally plant a pause in a team member to see how the team reacted. The only way to never have an "unnecessary" pause is to avoid calling a pause unless you are 100 percent certain there's a problem. If the reaction to an unnecessary pause (a pause where it turns out that there was no impending problem) is to ridicule or call out that person as being "wrong," then people will be reluctant to call a pause in the future.

We call a pause "practicing resilience," and it doesn't matter whether the pause identifies a problem or it turns out there was no problem. This means that in truth, there are no unnecessary pauses. Regardless of whether it turns out the pause was justified, every pause is necessary to establish a culture in which people are comfortable raising their hands when there is less than 100 percent certainty, which is to say, all the time.

Over time, the team is trained to use the code words, and the leader learns how to respond to the code words. The practice removes anxiety over calling the pause.

At Toyota they use the Andon cord.

Andon is the Japanese word for a traditional paper lantern. At Toyota, manufacturing workers pull an Andon cord when they encounter a problem in the production system. The cord turns on an indicator light.

Before Toyota made cars, they made sewing machines. Sakichi Toyoda, the founder of Toyota, designed one of the first automated loom designs, which immediately stopped the machine when the needle broke. This prevented wasted material and defective product.

When Toyota started building cars on the assembly line, the managers wanted a similar system, whereby workers could signal that they needed to stop production, thus avoiding unnecessary waste. So the plant designers installed pull cords that illuminated lanterns (*andons*). A worker simply pulled the cord to light up the *andon*, letting a supervisor know there was a problem at the production station. Hence the term Andon cord.

The Andon cord allowed the worker to escape from production work, redwork, and shift to problem solving, bluework.

As soon as a light flashed above a workstation, it was mandatory for a supervisor to check out the problem. Upon arrival, the supervisor first thanked the worker for pulling the cord. This gratitude was unconditional.

If the problem could not be resolved within the time the worker normally had to complete his task, then the production line stopped. They controlled the clock, removing the time pressure of the continuously moving assembly line from the worker, and allowing the worker and supervisor to collaborate on a solution.

Later, Andon cords were installed for the first time in a Toyota factory in the United States. The CEO, Tetsuro Toyoda at this point, noticed that a worker at this factory was struggling with a particular problem. Even though the Andon cord was available, the worker was doing everything he could to solve the problem and not pull the cord. Finally, someone pulled the cord. After that, Toyoda apologized to the frontline worker. He acknowledged that he had not adequately transmitted through his intermediate management team the importance and conditions under which the Andon cord should be pulled.

As with my team, there was a stigma against pulling the cord. This would be overcome with practice.

What makes many people hesitate about speaking up is the notion of being labeled "the boy who cried wolf." What if they raise their hand, not only calling attention to a potential problem but also to themselves, and they are wrong? They worry that their credibility will be damaged, just like the boy who cried wolf.

Let's review that fable.

A shepherd boy was tending a flock of sheep. Idle and bored, he cried "wolf" to trick the villagers into running up to his field. In some versions of the story, he ridicules them after they arrive. He does this several times, deliberately calling "wolf," even though he knows there is no wolf. When a wolf does appear, the boy's cries go unanswered. The previously tricked villagers do not come. The wolf eats the sheep and, in some versions, the boy as well.

In our Oscars example, Beatty was not choosing between lying and telling the truth. In the fable, the boy cried out *knowing* there was no wolf. His motivation was to trick the villagers into running up to his field. Even though the fable is about the perils of lying, it is often misinterpreted to mean that one shouldn't unnecessarily call attention to an issue.

Now, let us imagine that someone at your workplace raises a hand and asks to stop a process or project to question a base assumption. Upon investigation, it turns out that the base assumption is, in fact, correct, and that the process can proceed without alteration.

How do we react to this stoppage and how do we label it? How does the team react to this person?

In our workshops, groups uniformly describe the stop as unnecessary. They say the person calling the stop was "wrong" or "made an error." This perspective is a cultural barrier that makes it harder for people who "see something" to "say something." It does not have to be this way—we are the custodians of the culture. These people come from organizations that have "safety first" slogans. We need those pauses for safety.

Instead, we should simply call these pauses what they are—pauses. Better, we could describe them as resilient moves or backup. We could applaud those who call for a pause by valuing that questioning attitude.

For the following situations, what signal could we provide so that this person controls the clock?

- A nurse on an operating team notices an indication that the head surgeon seems to be missing.

- An operator at a power plant senses something is not right during the start-up of a generator.
- A copilot on a transpacific flight notices an inconsistent indication as the plane is descending during a low-visibility approach.

This was one of the situations for which Crew Resource Management (CRM), the language that cockpit teams train to use, was designed. CRM gives subordinates the words to voice concerns. In aviation, copilots use CRM to force a pause and collaborate with a pilot to solve a problem. One of the CRM practices is to start with an opener or attention getter, addressing the individual by name or position—"Hey, chief" or "Dr. Smith." Next, the subordinate states the concern. For example, "I'm concerned we may run out of fuel if we go around one more time." CRM enables someone to share a concern, even though they might not be certain it is a problem—while it is still only a potential problem.

Still, any approach that puts the onus on the subordinate to speak up will have limitations. Not only does the signal need to be sent, it also needs to be received.

3. Call a Pause

If you are on the team and see something unexpected—like Mr. Beatty saw when he opened the envelope—it's also your responsibility to call a pause. But it's hard for team members to call the pause.

Here's why:

1. The team might be lost in redwork because of the stress of the clock.

2. The team might be lost in redwork because of the intensity of focus.

3. The team feels the pressure of obeying the clock most acutely.

4. Calling a pause is likely to be calling attention to a problem, or a possible problem.

The first reason has to do with how stress affects humans. We know that stress handicaps the prefrontal cortex, where we do our higher-level thinking, bluework. This is one of the key differences between redwork and bluework: stress takes a much bigger toll on the latter.

Imagine you are running a hundred-meter dash. It's a short, physical, individual task. Everyone in the stadium is shouting at you. This is a stressor. How does this affect your performance? Likely, it will not have a negative impact. It might even make you move faster. Once the gun goes off, you run.

Now consider instead that you need to make a complex decision, one that involves multiple assessments of a current condition, navigating uncertainty, and making predictions of future conditions. Again, you have a stadium shouting at you. Does the stressor have a negative effect? Without question.

Stress is dangerous because it *inhibits your ability to recognize when you need to exit redwork*. This is why it is unfair and unreliable to depend on the person or team in redwork to call a pause.

The second reason has to do with allowing team members to immerse themselves in their work. You have probably been in a situation where you were so deep in production mode and focused on a task that you lost track of time. In 1975 psychologist Mihaly Csikszentmihalyi called this feeling "flow." It is a sense of being totally absorbed in our work. How wonderful! But only if the work we are doing is appropriate work. If we are off on the wrong track, then we need a signal. When we are deep in redwork, we have a narrowing of focus and perspective. This focus helps us achieve our task but limits our self-regulating mechanisms. We lose track of time. We can even forget to eat. We persist when it may be wiser to stop and reflect on choosing another path.

Knowing that someone else is watching the clock and will call a time-out enables us to go deeper into the redwork. We don't need to worry that something will sneak up on us. We're able to fully immerse ourselves in our work, with the likely result of being more effective, creative, and productive—and happier.

This is why leadership that urges those in the red production work to get better at controlling the clock will only get an organization so far. The mindset that optimizes a team in redwork (the prove mindset) views delays as bad. Therefore, it is the leaders—who can remain aloof from the day-to-day demands of work—who will be in a better mental state to see the need to control the clock. It is the responsibility of leadership to call the pause for the team.

Further, leaders have the responsibility of creating a culture that accepts and invites pauses from the team and of providing the team with the mechanism—like the Andon cord— to call a pause.

One reason it's hard to call a pause is because it's most likely called to identify a problem—and some people don't like to hear about problems. Barings Bank, a 233-year-old City of London bank, was brought down directly as a result of a culture of fear in which people didn't speak up. Faced with an error made by a member of his team, Nick Leeson, the star trader of the bank's Singapore operation, chose to cover up rather than speak up. He used an account, numbered 88888 (eight being a lucky number in Chinese culture), to hide the error, and when the cover-up worked, he used the account to hide his own growing losses until the amount reached an astonishing £827 million—twice the bank's trading capital—and the whole institution collapsed.

Leaders need to be sensitive to signals from their teams that it is time to call a pause, even if the team does not use the exact right code. Remember the hesitation, the double-checking, the furrowed brow and downturned face of Beatty at the Oscars? An attuned leader would recognize these signs of distress and call the pause. Remember the tortured language from the officers of *El Faro*, trying without a clear signal to send a clear signal? An attuned leader would recognize these signs of distress and call the pause.

In the following situations, a team member is not using agreed-upon words to signal a pause, but is signaling a pause nonetheless.

- On a construction site, a foundation worker asks, "Are you sure you want us to start pouring concrete?"

   How could the foreman call a pause?

- On a software team, a coder states, "These features are going to really add a lot of complexity to the testing process."

   How could the team leader call a pause?

- On a manufacturing team, working on new-technology electric vehicles, a junior engineer muses aloud within earshot of the supervisor, "I don't know about these new batteries. The performance numbers aren't as good as we had hoped."

   How could the supervisor call a pause?

- On a firefighting team, upon entering a burning building, the person carrying the hose yells, "There's something strange about this fire, not sure what it is."

   How could the fire chief call a pause?

- On a hospital team, after checking on a patient, a nurse remarks to the head shift nurse, "There's something about this case that has me wondering if we've got the right diagnosis."

  How could the head nurse call a pause?

- In a sanitizer manufacturing facility, when starting to mix a new ten-thousand-gallon batch, a junior line operator states to the line supervisor, "This valve lineup looks different to me."

  How could the line supervisor call a pause?

Each case calls for statements that invite the team to take a time-out, raise their heads, and exit redwork. Then they can shift into bluework, decision mode.

You probably came up with lines like:

- "It seems like you think we might not be ready. What are you thinking?"
- "Let's get the team together and revisit our decision."
- "We might need to reevaluate our supplier. What is the evidence?"
- "Let's hold here and take a look. What does everyone think?"
- "I can see you aren't sure. Would you like to show me what you see?"
- "Tell me what's giving you pause."
- "Is there anything else?"

But this shifts the burden of recognizing and calling a pause from the team to the leader. What if the leader does not notice? There is one more way.

4. Preplan the Next Pause

We can safeguard ourselves against the tendency to get carried away with redwork by preplanning the next pause. This could be as simple as setting a timer to go off in forty-five minutes to allow a break or planning a more formal pause for the project every two weeks. Another strategy is to incorporate less frequent events, like annual strategic reviews.

In psychology, there is a concept called "metacognition," or thinking about our thinking. By preplanning the next pause phase, we free all of our cognitive resources for execution rather than holding some back for process monitoring. In other words, knowing that a pause is coming allows teams to focus 100 percent of their efforts on the work and allows leaders to resist the trap of becoming "good idea fairies"—showing up unexpectedly to offer unsolicited advice for a better way to do something, then leaving their people to figure out how to implement the idea.

Agile management is an effective tool for this purpose. Used by many software development teams, agile management structures teamwork in sprints. These sprints are commonly two weeks long but could be longer or shorter. The sprint is bookended by bluework—collaborating on what to include during the next production increment at the beginning, and testing and reflecting at the end. Because the length of the sprint is determined ahead of time, there is a planned exit from the redwork. This allows the team to focus deeply on the production work right until the next pause happens.

While teams are in production, designing and coding software, one of the key rules is that leadership is prohibited from redirecting or interfering with a team's work. If leaders have a new idea, they add it to a backlog for discussion at the next sprint planning meeting.

The end of the sprint includes bluework. The teams present and celebrate what they have accomplished. They reflect on their work practices from the previous sprint and feedback they have received on the product. Then they decide what to take on for the next sprint cycle. This is bluework. The sprint can be represented as /blue-red-blue/ and the continuing sprint cycle would look like this:

/blue-red-blue//blue-red-blue//blue-red-blue//blue-red-blue/ . . . and so on.

We frequently have that opportunity to schedule the next period of bluework. Whenever a team gets permission to start or go on with the next phase of a project, the question could be, "When will we pause and evaluate where we are?" This is different from an update. An update occurs as part of redwork and provides information on how the team is doing. An update does not invite interference by management to change priorities, scope, or schedule.

Let's review.

- During a repair period at a power plant, following a decision to try a new approach for repairing a pump, what could a leader say to preplan a pause?
- On a software team, following a decision to add several features that are expected to take two weeks, what could a leader say to preplan a pause?
- In a trucking company, following a decision to shift the advertising budget, what could a leader say to preplan a pause?
- On a pipeline operational pumping station, following a decision to commence pumping after a test, what could a leader say to preplan a pause?

IN SUMMARY, TO CONTROL THE CLOCK

1. Instead of preempting a pause, make a pause possible.
2. Instead of hoping the team knows what to say, give the pause a name.
3. Instead of pressing on with redwork, call a pause.
4. Instead of relying on someone to signal a pause, preplan the next pause.

Now that we have controlled the clock, we have the opportunity to open up our prefrontal cortex. We feel safer sharing our ideas, even when we might not be 100 percent sure they are right. We are ready to . . . collaborate. Which brings us to the next play.

CONTROL THE CLOCK

Control the clock is the start of the cycle. Control the clock is when we exit redwork and shift to bluework. The Industrial Age has programmed us to obey the clock, which tends to keep us in redwork, feeling the stress of time pressure.

Controlling the clock is about the power of pause; the power of our ability to control the clock rather than obeying the clock; being mindful and deliberate with our actions; and broadening our perspectives.

Teams in redwork want to continue in redwork.

Since people who are engaged in redwork often have a performance (prove or protect) mindset, it is difficult for them to call time-out on themselves. Because they want to get things done and are penalized for any delays, they do not want to be the source of interruptions to the work. This responsibility lies with the leader.

The team relies on the leader either to preplan the length of the redwork and the moment of exiting redwork or to spontaneously call a time-out during a redwork period, in essence, an audible when needed.

Historically, the fundamental reason bosses needed to coerce teams was because the boss decided what the team needed to do. The deciders and the doers are different people in Industrial Age organizations.

Controlling the clock sets us up to collaborate.

Into the Bluework: Collaborate

The Industrial Age obey-the-clock play drives us to get the team moving forward. Since we've separated the deciders (blueworkers) from the doers (redworkers), the deciders need to convince, cajole, bribe, shame, or threaten the redworkers to do work they had little or no part in choosing.

The appropriate verb is "coerce." Coerce is what Faye Dunaway is doing to Warren Beatty with "You're impossible!", scowling at him, placing her hand on his arm, and saying, "C'mon."

We don't use that word often in polite society, it's ugly. So we label it with other words like motivate, inspire, or collaborate. Often "collaborating" is really coercion in disguise. I've been guilty of this myself. You've probably done it, too.

The root cause of this is the separation of roles into redworkers and blueworkers. The solution can be summed up as follows: **let the doers be the deciders.**

As we saw in the previous chapter, when leaders attempt to collaborate with their teams to make decisions, they often end up skipping the divergent part ("What does everyone think?") and jumping straight to the convergent part ("Here's what I think. Does everyone agree?").

This represents the language of too many brainstorming and decision-making meetings, where the boss states an opinion and others fall in line. Bosses try to be compelling, not curious. They ask leading and self-affirming questions. They suppress dissent and push for consensus. This is not collaboration. This is all coercion disguised as collaboration. This is why Fred, stuck in making redwork happen all day, feels so depleted—he spends a lot of time coercing people.

Coercion, as I am using it here, means using my influence, power, rank, talking first, talking more, or talking louder to bring people around to my way of thinking.

Here's what we don't want as a decision-making model: the boss decides and seeks validation from the group. Those kinds of meetings exist only so that the boss can say later on, "Well, you all were there. You could have said something."

After the captain on *El Faro* decided that they would take the Atlantic route, he ridiculed the imaginary mariners who would deviate for every storm. He was preemptively shaming anyone on his crew who might question his decision to take the Atlantic route.

NASA officials in the space shuttle *Challenger* disaster did the same thing, bluntly telling the engineers they were wrong about the danger of low-temperature conditions during the launch. At one point, a NASA official said, "Take off your engineering hat and put on your management hat."

When I hear bosses say things like "get everyone on board" or "build consensus," that's coercion. That's trying to convince people "I'm right, and you need to change your thinking."

We don't need anyone in the group to change their thinking. As long as the group supports whatever decision comes out of the meeting with their behavior, leaders are happy if individuals think differently from them. Otherwise, they're just in an echo chamber of their own ideas. There is power and resilience in a diversity of ideas.

Do you believe that? I mean, do you *really* believe that? If history is a guide, you think you're special.

Here's how I know. In another workshop activity, we give people a scenario in which they are rushing past a person in distress. They are on their way to a meeting and have been told they are already late. We ask them, "What's the chance you would help even though you are running behind?" Response: high numbers. Typically, 70 percent.

Then we ask people to answer the same question about the other people in the room. "What's the chance they would help?" Response: low numbers. Typically, 30 percent. How can this be? Each of us thinks we would be much more likely to help than the people around us. We think we are special.

We judge ourselves by our intentions, but we judge others by their behavior. If we fall short, we come up with external reasons to explain what prevented us from acting in a way that is consistent with how we think of ourselves. When others fall short, we tend to blame them as people and discount the environmental barriers that might have been in the way.

For me, it's good enough that I wanted to help but couldn't, but I have no sense of the other person's desire to help. I only see the behavior of not helping. Then I judge.

This bias gets in the way of collaboration because collaboration is based on the belief that others have something to offer.

HOW TO COLLABORATE

The objectives of our COLLABORATE play are to broaden our perspectives, embrace variability, and make visible the collective knowledge, thoughts, and ideas of the group.

Here are four ways to run the COLLABORATE play.

TO MOVE FROM COERCION TO COLLABORATION

1. Vote first, then discuss.
2. Be curious, not compelling.
3. Invite dissent rather than drive consensus.
4. Give information, not instructions.

1. Vote First, Then Discuss

In *The Wisdom of Crowds*, Surowiecki tells the story of Francis Galton, a polymath who lived in England in the 1800s, who was intrigued by a contest at the county fair where people would guess the weight of an ox—the closest guess won the animal. After the contest, Galton collected the tickets and indexed everyone's vote. It turned out that the group—independently, diversely, collectively—had a closer guess than all but a few people. He repeated this experiment several times. Each time, only a handful of people were able to guess more accurately than the collective average of the group.

To expose the greatest diversity and variability of thinking, invite participants to express what they think independently first, before anchoring the group by discussion.

Here are a few ways to put that principle into action.

Conduct anonymous blind electronic polling. With a large number of participants or when psychological safety* of the group is low or unknown, anonymous electronic polling is a good way to go. This allows people to share what they think without social and hierarchical

---

* Psychological safety means the degree to which we feel we can share our thoughts and feelings in an environment like our workplace without being judged or evaluated. When people feel psychologically safe, it makes it easier for them to share "what-ifs" and partly formed ideas and to share their anxieties about projects. Psychologically safe environments allow people to be vulnerable. See books and research by Harvard professor Amy Edmondson on psychological safety.

pressure to conform. You'll get perspective from the crowd without singling people out. It is key to avoid showing people the poll as it develops so as not to anchor a decision prematurely. We've seen a good variation in responses quickly become more uniform once results-in-progress are revealed. This happens even when a poll is anonymous. Such is the power of wanting to conform to the group.

Ask probabilistic questions instead of binary ones. Instead of the binary "Is it safe?" or "Will it work?" ask "How safe is it?" or "How likely is it to work?" The idea is to invite thinking that considers future events as a range of possibilities, not as will-happen or won't-happen choices. This means starting the question with the word "how." We like practicing this with most questions about feelings, assessments, and even descriptions. For example, instead of "Did you like the movie?" or "Do you speak Spanish?" consider "How much did you like the movie?" or "How well do you speak Spanish?" Encouraging others to respond on a scale rather than with a simple yes or no allows you to bring more nuance and information into the discussion.

Probability cards are a helpful tool to facilitate this in meetings. This is a set of cards that display the following percentages: 1, 5, 20, 50, 80, 95, 99. We want to focus on the outliers, the team members with the strongest positive and negative feelings.*

Imagine you're in a meeting and it's time to decide whether to launch the software product or delay to do more testing. You have good knowledge of your piece of the project, but maybe have limited

---

* We also avoid using 0 and 100 because one of the things we are doing is nudging people toward probabilistic thinking and inoculating ourselves against the arrogance of certainty. Not giving people the option to say it is 0 percent or 100 percent helps with that. This works for assessment questions as well, such as "How well do you know Spanish?" Almost everyone knows a couple words, like *salsa* and *siesta*, and no one knows anything perfectly. Also, you could have people write any number from 1 to 99, but having the preprinted cards makes things faster, especially once people have used the cards once or twice. When writing down numbers, people will spend time deciding between, say, 60 and 65, which really does not matter that much.

knowledge about the project as a whole and how it fits into the business strategy. You, along with the other twelve people in the room, are asked to vote on "How strongly do you believe we should launch on time?" A vote of 1 means you totally disagree, it's vitally important to delay launch; and 99 means you totally agree, it's vitally important to launch.

You all have the same seven cards. Each person picks a card and slides it to the middle of the table, facedown. Once the votes are in, flip the cards. Invite the outliers (the people who chose 1s and 99s) to speak, sharing their ideas with the group. Questions I like to ask the outliers are "What do you see that we don't?" or "What is behind that vote?"

I attended a meeting where people were asked to vote up or down on whether they supported a proposed course of action. When the vote was over, each of the down voters (there were only a couple) was asked, "What would make you turn your down into a yes?" This did not have the intended result because it put them on the spot, placing them in the position of blockers, with the implication that everyone was expected to get on board. The message was "We are going this way, how can we overcome your objections?" not an honest "Is this the direction we should go?"

When psychological safety is middle to low, it is sometimes better to ask the group to rationalize each outlier's position. This has the benefit of not putting outliers on the spot and exercises our ability to view things from another's perspective. If outliers know they will be put on the spot, it will reduce the tendency of people to take outlying positions.

For particularly sensitive questions requiring high trust and vulnerability but where electronic polling feels like overkill (for example, with groups of fewer than eight to ten members), use blank sticky notes or four-by-six-inch cards. People can write their responses on

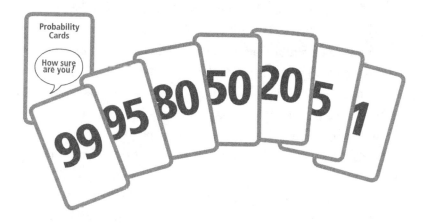

Probability cards

the cards and slide them in facedown. This makes it harder for people to backward analyze who voted what and may make it easier for people to vote honestly.

Use simultaneous open probability cards (requires good psychological safety). This time, we just hold our probability cards up for all to see rather than putting them in the middle of the table. In the discussion that follows, we invite the outliers to speak.

Use dot voting or multiple voting (requires good psychological safety). When the group is trying to select from among several options, the probability cards won't work, and you need to narrow the options. In this case, people could vote on their preferred options. Give people about one-third as many votes as there are options—for example: ten options, three votes. See which options collect the most votes. This can be done openly, along a wall, or electronically.

Use fist-to-five voting (requires good psychological safety). With fist-to-five, we just use our hands to vote: zero to five fingers. It is a public, simultaneous vote, but it is fast and we use the tools we have: our hands. I much prefer fist-to-five over one-to-five because in a large group, distinguishing one finger from two is hard, but the fist votes really stand out. So do the full-hand votes. That is what you want. Again, make most visible the strongest feelings, positive or negative.

This simple tool can be used when two factors are clear: the decision we are trying to come to is not a big decision needing lengthy discussion, and the people involved feel psychologically safe enough to express their opinions, ideas, and thoughts openly.

We use this as a quick check at a construction site meeting, at a morning huddle, at a medical operation premeeting, or prior to equipment start-up. Questions should again be probabilistic ("How safe is it?" or "How ready are we?") as opposed to binary ("Is it safe?" or "Are we ready?").

We tend to use fist-to-five to get a quick sense from groups ("How ready are you for break?") or as a final check before transitioning from bluework to redwork ("How ready are we?"). Times when we can use this:

- Just before a construction crew goes to work.
- Just before a hospital operating team commences a procedure.
- Just before a flight crew takes off.
- Just before a power plant team starts a turbine.
- Just before a ship gets under way.

It also works during project status updates and at the end of a project. One creative company in Scotland uses a double fist-to-five to summarize project status. One hand rates the health of the project, and the other rates how happy they are to be on the project. The managing director told me that the conversations around the fist-to-five voting are more valuable than the lengthy updates that precede them.

A meeting or conversation might start like this:

- "Before we anchor everybody's thoughts, what do you think the number should be? Write it down on the index card in front of you."
- "Before we discuss this, I'd like everybody's best estimate. What day will we ship the first product? Text your answer to the meeting app."
- "I'd like to make it as easy as possible for people to tell us if we're not on track here. On a scale of 1 to 99, how enthusiastic would you be about the idea we're proposing? Use the cards in front of you."
- "This plan is based on the following critical assumption. Before we move forward, I'm curious what you think the probability is that this assumption is true."
- "Before I tell you what I think we should do, what would you do if I weren't here?"

Here's an example of how this was used. In a recent meeting with the US leadership team of a global company, the CEO presented the new vision to colleagues in order to gauge levels of support and engagement from the team. He was originally going to use fist-to-five. But this was a critical question for the business and the team was meeting for the first time—would people feel completely at ease to show what they really felt?

After a quick adjustment, the CEO asked the team to score their support for the vision on sticky notes with a range of 1 to 99 (a version of anonymous blind probability cards), which were then gathered and analyzed. The results showed that most people were supportive, but a small and important minority were not quite on board yet, so the CEO invited them to approach him after the meeting. The CEO could move forward with the knowledge that most people were in support but better informed of the need to listen, and acknowledge, the whole team's perspective.

A team holds the probability cards in response to a "how" question.

Asking dissenters to discuss their concerns with the leader in private has some advantages and some drawbacks. The advantages: it allows people who might not feel safe speaking in front of the larger group to voice their opinions and it saves time for the group. The downside is that it reinforces the hierarchical position of the leader as the decision-maker and deprives the group of hearing dissenting viewpoints unless the leader comes back to the group with them. In one case where this was a consistent practice, I noticed that one person regularly had additional advice for the CEO, to discuss with him in private. After a while, it became clear that this person just wanted time and attention and was finding reasons to act special. Leaders need to watch out and correct for these drawbacks.

Overall, however, this approach is far preferred to asking the question in a self-affirming way—"Are we all on board?"—and having the dissenting opinions lie dormant. Not only would the CEO and group be deprived of potentially critical information, but those dissenters, not having felt heard, will find other ways to sabotage the program.

Here is an example of how this works. Let's say the company

needs to decide whether to launch the product or delay launch. There has been a public announcement that the product will come out five days from now. There are several arguments for launching on time: keeping our promise; early testing and feedback from the market; a sense of completion and celebration. There are also arguments for delaying: an important feature has not been fully integrated; testing has indicated that there are some minor bugs.

The decision is binary (launch on time or don't), but the input on the decision is not binary. This is another opportunity to use the probability cards: ask the group how strongly they support not launching (a lower vote) or launching (a higher vote). There are ten people voting. Six vote strongly supporting a launch, and four vote strongly against a launch. What next?

Embrace the outliers. Start with the smaller of the two groups—in this case, the four who voted against the launch. It becomes harder for the minority to speak after the majority has spoken. In an environment of good psychological safety, where the group has become accustomed to inviting and listening to the outliers, we might be able to ask directly: "I see we have some 1 votes. Can we hear about them?"

Keep in mind, the people who vote do not know they will be the outliers until the votes are revealed. They might need a moment to reflect on this before they are ready to explain what they see and what they know. Additionally, if every time they vote a 1 or 99 they get "called out," people will eventually stop voting that way. It's only by being truly curious about the outliers' observations or information and making it safe for them to speak that we will continue to get good variability of expression.

If the minority is small in comparison to the majority—say, only one or two people out of a group of ten—and I am worried that they might be reticent to talk about their position, I would ask the question this way:

"What might be behind a vote like this?"

"Let's come up with some reasons why this might be right."

"What could explain this vote?"

"What does a person who voted this way see that we don't?"

This removes the idea from the person and invites the group to think from the perspective of another. We're inoculating ourselves against the arrogance of thinking we are right.

2. Be Curious, Not Compelling

Once you discover people in the meeting who see things differently than you, your next play is to be curious about what they see that you don't see and what they think that you don't think. The programmed Industrial Age response is for people to defend their own positions. There is a time and place for that, but the overriding mindset of the leader should be one of curiosity.

Stephen R. Covey, author of *The Seven Habits of Highly Effective People*, considered this concept of "curiosity first" so important he titled his fifth habit "Seek First to Understand, *Then* to Be Understood."

LEADERS SPEAK LAST

Part of the behavior behind being curious, not compelling, is withholding your own opinion until later. The higher you are in the organization, the more important this is because the more likely it is that people will want to align to your position. You speak last not to prove you're the leader, but because speaking last allows others to freely voice their opinions first.

Idea Swap

Have people argue for the opposite position. Break up the meeting into small discussion groups and invite people to talk to someone who voted the opposite than they did to learn what was behind that vote. This will allow them to practice being curious instead of compelling. They can practice asking curious questions and open-ended questions. This is a mechanism for getting people to listen carefully, nonjudgmentally, and nondefensively to another point of view.

Using this exercise, we often see groups come to an agreement or compromise without needing the boss to act as a decision-maker. This is because it trains your brain to think considerately about ideas other than your own—and opens your perspective on what the situation might actually be.

Additionally, it allows those outliers to feel heard. Even if you do not ultimately agree with them, feeling heard will minimize an outlier's likelihood of sabotaging the decision afterward.

I had an experience that taught me the power of practicing this— or, in this case, the pitfalls of not practicing this. In the early 2000s, I served as a military liaison officer escorting several prominent New York City businesspeople to a meeting with the Joint Chiefs of Staff in the Pentagon. These are typically cordial and uninteresting sessions.

At the time, the United States was debating what force size to use in the upcoming invasion of Iraq, if it were to happen. President Bush and Defense Secretary Rumsfeld had signaled that the force level going into Iraq would be low, maybe 150,000 Americans, and the generals were publicly supporting that force level. I call this the "cheap and easy" story line, in which a risky decision is justified by promising that it will be "cheap and easy." In the case of the Iraq invasion, a larger force size would have required mobilizing the reserves, which would have contradicted the "cheap and easy" story line.

One of the businessmen I had escorted to the Pentagon had earlier served in the cabinet of a Republican president, and I could sense his skepticism about low force strength. When he asked about the planned force levels, one of the generals defended the small force size. He talked about what the United States had learned in the 1991 Gulf War and gave other compelling reasons for why the low number was the correct number. He defended the party line.

The former cabinet secretary then pointed out that General Shalikashvili had argued that the invasion would need a much higher number. General Shalikashvili had served as the chairman of the Joint Chiefs of Staff under former president Clinton, and had been making public statements that the United States should be cautious about going to war, and that if it did, it would need a force strength significantly higher than what was currently being considered.

"How did General Shalikashvili come up with his numbers?" the former cabinet secretary asked. "And why are they different from yours?" I leaned forward, eager to hear the answer.

Instead of answering his question, the general simply repeated the same arguments we had just heard in defense of a low troop number. I looked around the room. Most people were starting to look perplexed. Our questioner did not show any frustration, and when the general was done, he asked again: "I'm not asking how you came up with your numbers, I'm asking how General Shalikashvili came up with his."

Again, the general repeated the same arguments. By now, the room was visibly frustrated, and as a representative of the military, I started to feel embarrassed. When the general was done, we went on to other matters. I wondered if the general simply couldn't or just wouldn't state the arguments for the higher troop levels. I never did find out.*

---

* As an aside, I think the explanation was that the military's numbers were based on the military campaign only, whereas General Shalikashvili's numbers were based on maintaining control of the country after a successful military campaign. It would have been a good debate to have.

The Seven Sins of Questioning

Being curious about what someone else thinks is the foundation of asking good questions. There is such a thing as a bad question: one that is less curiosity driven than others. Here are some examples. We call these the seven sins of questioning.

1. Question stacking

Example: "So, how much testing has been done? I mean, do we really have all the bugs identified? Yeah, I just really think it's important to know that—are we good to go?"

Question stacking is asking the same question repeatedly in different ways or drilling down a logic tree you think defines the problem. Just ask one question once, then button it.

We observed a meeting where an executive was prone to question stacking. It went something like this: "We really need to understand why clients don't buy this service, and what our team is doing to address this, whether it's to do with our communications, or is it because they don't have the skills which are needed, or do they think it's not important and if we asked them what would they say, and what are our measures of success for this anyway, and who is leading on this?" By the second or third question everyone had turned off and tuned out, and he ended up getting really frustrated that people didn't respond.

Put a question mark on it. Then go silent. This takes practice because you have to think of the question before you start talking, and then resist the urge to step in after two seconds. Rest comfortably in the quiet.

2. Leading questions

Example: "Have you thought about the needs of the client?"

A leading question comes from a place of thinking the person is wrong, or that you have the answer. I hear this a lot from people who think they have the right answer but don't want to just say so, so they try using the Socratic method as a "teaching moment." It's annoying and arrogant.

Instead, have a learning moment for yourself. Ask questions that assume the other person might be right, not you. An easy start is the neutral, "Tell me about that." Temporarily set aside judgment, and then be curious about what they see that you don't see and what they think that you don't think. Since it is temporary, you can immerse yourself in that belief, and when it is over, you do not need to agree with them or approve the action.

Another approach is to start the question with "how." Ask, "How would that work?" or "How does that align with our objectives?" This is the "inquisitive how." The inquisitive how sounds like "How does ____ affect ____?" or "How do you see that?"

3. "Why" questions

Example: "Why would you want to do that?"

This type of question puts people on the defensive and reveals that you think "that" is a bad idea. In such cases, it's best to reserve judgment and simply say, "Tell me more about that." Another option is to ask, "What is behind your decision?" or "How do you see the issue?"

4. Dirty questions

A dirty question is like a leading question but does not overtly carry the message that the other person is wrong—but it does carry subtle and often unconscious biases and anticipates a particular answer. The phrase "dirty question" comes from Clean Language, a way of speaking and asking questions in psychological counseling that eliminates the counselor's biases from the question and allows the patient to develop his or her own response.

Clean Language was devised by David Grove in the 1980s and has been expanded since. A good book to read on the subject is *Clean Language: Revealing Metaphors and Opening Minds* by Wendy Sullivan and Judy Rees, published in 2008.

Here's an example: Let's say a colleague has expressed frustration with another colleague and said that they are at a dead end when it comes to getting the other person to complete work that a project depends upon. You ask, "Do you have the courage to stand up to them?" That is a dirty question.

It's "dirty" because that question presumes your friend should confront them by speaking up, that the metaphor is "stand up to" instead of, say, "partner with," and finally, that the needed resource for your friend is courage. It also implies that it is your friend's responsibility to get this person to do their job.

A clean question would eliminate those biases and would sound like this: "What do you mean by dead end?" or "What do you want to have happen?" The structure of the clean question is designed to remove your biases and preconceptions.

Clean questions are a technique specifically designed for therapy when there is a lot of time and dedicated listening resources. We rarely have the luxury of this at work, but paying attention to the biases that might be present in your questions will make your everyday questions much more collaborative. For me, listening to my own questions reveals just how much I picture what the other person has told me (and what we should do about it) based on scanty knowledge.

5. Binary questions

Examples: "Are we good to launch?" or "Will it work?"

Binary questions narrow the available responses to two: yes or no. They are convenient for the one asking, but put the one answering in a bind. In a sense, it is getting the receiver to take responsibility for a successful launch by eliciting a "yes." We hear these all the time. Another is "Is it safe?"

Instead, start your question with "what" or "how." This makes it impossible to ask a binary question. For example: "How safe is it?" or "How ready are we to launch?" "What" versions of the question might sound like "What might go wrong?" or "What do we need before we're ready to launch?"

We have found the simple rule of starting a question with "what" or "how" significantly improves the questions and the quality of the information coming from the team.

When we use "how" in this way, we call it the "probabilistic how." We are using "how" to invite a response that sees the future in terms of probabilities, not a deterministic yes/no.

Now think about share of voice and how it captures the difference between these two conversations:

CONVERSATION 1

 BOSS: "Is it safe?"

 TEAM MEMBER: "Yes."

Word count is three to one.

CONVERSATION 2

 BOSS: "How safe is it?"

 TEAM MEMBER: "I'd guess 4 out of 5."

Word count is four to six, with the leader speaking fewer words than the team member. This inverts the typical pattern. The share of voice is more even and the Team Language Coefficient is lower, 0.20 for the second conversation and 0.50 for the first conversation.

6. Self-affirming questions

Self-affirming questions are often binary questions with a special motivation: to coerce agreement and make us feel good about the decision we have already made.

Example: "We're good to launch, right?"

As I've already reported from the transcript, the captain of *El Faro* provides us with several examples:

- "You know what I'm saying?"
- "It's going to be between these two, right?"
- "Does that make sense?"
- "Everything good as far as RPM [speed] goes?"

Self-affirming questions seek to prove what we want the case to be. The purpose is to make the asker feel good rather than to reveal the truth of the situation.

- "Right?"
- "Does that make sense?"
- "You have what you need?"
- "All good?"
- "Is everything tasting great tonight?"
- "Did you have a wonderful stay?"

Instead, seek enlightenment by asking questions that make it easy to bring up challenging information. I call this "self-educating," not "self-affirming." Some examples would be:

- "What am I missing?"
- "What would you like to hear more about?"

- "What could go wrong?"
- "What could we do better?"

When Captain Sullenberger was piloting an airplane that had lost both engines and he was attempting to land in the Hudson River, he asked the copilot, "Got any ideas?" Notice he did not ask, "So, we're good, right?"

7. Aggressive questioning
Example: Straight to "What should we do?"

This might be too aggressive for some people because it provokes them to make assessments about the future before they are ready. When inviting someone to share their thoughts, start from a place where they feel secure, and move gradually toward areas of uncertainty and vulnerability. One way to do this is with a technique I call "pause, rewind, fast-forward."

Start with pause. This invites simple observation of the situation. "What do you see?" "How do you see it?" Description feels safe because the part of our brain used for description is not connected to emotions. It also feels quite "knowable."

Once you've gotten them talking about what they see, the next phase is rewind. Rewinding is about reviewing how we got here. "How did we get here?" or "What happened before this?" The past has more uncertainty, but it is still bounded.

Finally, fast-forward to the future with what will happen next or what everyone should do. This requires assessments about what is least knowable and is therefore most likely to be wrong—and so requires the most vulnerability. Jumping straight to "What should we do?" might get an "I don't know" response.

Instead, try moving from less vulnerable to more vulnerable with pause, rewind, fast-forward.

SEVEN WAYS TO ASK BETTER QUESTIONS

1. Instead of question stacking, try one and done.
2. Instead of a teaching moment, try a learning moment.
3. Instead of a dirty question, try a clean question.
4. Instead of a binary question, start the question with "what" or "how."
5. Instead of a "why" question, try "tell me more."
6. Instead of self-affirming questions, try self-educating questions.
7. Instead of jumping to the future, start with present, past, then future.

---

3. Invite Dissent Rather Than Drive Consensus

What if there are no outliers to embrace? What if the group is consistently clustered together? That's when you need the next play: don't drive consensus, invite dissent.

The wisdom of the crowd can be undermined in several ways. Anchoring and social conformity are two of those ways.

In our earlier exercise, the number stated by the first person to speak anchors the group, whether they want to be anchored or not. Others may argue to adjust the number up or down –but it will always be in comparison with the initial anchor point. People whose inclinations were far from where the group was will adjust their comments or say nothing, and the group will be deprived of their divergent thinking.

Once a majority starts to form an opinion, it becomes much harder for those in the minority to voice their dissent. In one landmark study, psychologist Solomon Asch invited college students to come in for a "vision test." In groups, participants were shown a straight line on a card. Then they were shown another card with three other lines of varying lengths. The question was, which of those three lines matched the length of the first? One by one, each participant would give his or her best guess. The twist was that only the last participant was actually in the study—the others were stooges who selected the same, wrong answer. Asch wanted to study the power of conformity: Would the final participant, with the correct answer clear as day, go with the group or stand alone? One-third of the time, eyes lost out to ayes.

When the participants were asked why they gave the answer they did, they said things like, "I thought I was wrong," and "I thought the group knew something that I did not." The same rationalization will happen in your business meetings. Since all innovation starts as an outlier thought, driving consensus is bound to suppress innovation.

Asch also repeated his study with one interesting variation: all the stooges chose the same wrong answer except for one, who would dissent by choosing another wrong answer. When this happened, the spell on the participant was broken. In almost no situations did the final person, the subject of the test, then conform with the group. What was important was not that someone else had selected the right answer, but that someone in the group had dissented safely. Once that bridge was crossed, participants felt comfortable selecting the answer they considered correct. They felt safe to dissent.

The lesson here is to make it safe and easy for people to dissent. This might require deliberately introducing dissent. You could ask someone to state an opposing opinion, share why the whole group might be wrong, or just prime them to disagree once it seems the group is coalescing on an answer.

At my organization, we use black and red cards. We call them dissent cards and use them in a ratio of five to one. Five black for every one red. We shuffle the deck and people take a card. Here's the rule: if you have a red card, you *have to* dissent, and the card makes it safe and necessary to do so. You're not being a jerk—the card made you do it.

If you have a black card you can still dissent if you want to, but you don't have to. The black cards have reminders on them for how we should respond to the dissenter—by being curious, not compelling.

The dissent cards are a tool used to change the practices of a group. They are used during the period when we are moving from "hard to dissent" and low psychological safety to "easy to dissent" and high psychological safety. Once dissent is a regular part of meetings, and being curious—not compelling—in response to dissent is a habit as well, the cards are no longer needed.

I saw the amazing power of dissent in an exercise I was running with a group of executives in China. Forty executives, all men, were sitting at four tables of ten. After watching a short video, their task was to determine, as a table group, how many sails an old-fashioned sailing ship in the video had up. They had two minutes.

I observed the tables. Not knowing the language, I focused on who spoke in what order and the body language. The tables were close together, but I did not observe any cross talk between tables.

When it was time to share their answers, an executive from the first table stood up, gave a nice speech about having a "harmonious conversation," during which everyone's voice was heard, and asserted that there were five sails.

At each of the next three tables, an executive stood up, gave a variation of the same speech, and said the exact same number, five.

The answer was eight sails. Every table had it wrong.

We then passed out the dissent cards—two reds and eight blacks to every table—and had them repeat the exercise. The people with the red cards *had* to dissent from the group. And here's the key: I did not show them the video again, so they could not revise their answer by looking more closely. The only new information they had was that their previous answer, five, was wrong.

After two minutes, it was time to share their results. This time there was no speech, but the answers were seven, eight, seven, eight. I could not believe it. By introducing nothing but a dissenter, we got the groups much closer to the truth, to reality.

The point is that we do not want a "harmonious conversation." What we want is an accurate picture of reality. Harmonious and wrong means out of business or dead people. Harmonious means thirty-three dead on *El Faro*, seven dead on the space shuttle *Challenger*.

The fear is that dissent equals disharmony and is to be avoided. But in organizations that practice dissent, where people are dissenting with the best interests of the organization in mind, and where people respond to the dissenters with curiosity, dissent does not feel disharmonious. Dissent creates a sense of excitement and energy—a leaning forward, a rubbing-the-hands-together feeling of "This could be the start of something interesting and new."

The behavior of the group toward the dissenter is important in sustaining the practice of dissent. Here, the group should practice the suggestions above for how to be curious, not compelling. Instead of arguing with the dissenter and explaining why that person is wrong, members of the group should ask curious questions.

These curious questions sound like this:

- "What's behind what you are saying?"
- "Can you tell us more about that?"
- "What are you seeing that leads you to believe that?

. . . and any of the questions from the previous tactic of "be curious, not compelling." With time, this practice will become a new group habit, and the culture will be changed. The group will be more resilient, more robust, and better able to make decisions. Lives will be saved.

Leaders, your job during any meeting is to scan the room and pay close attention to those who remain quiet. These people will often hold differing opinions that they don't feel comfortable voicing. Leadership at moments like these sounds like this:

- "Liz, I notice you haven't said anything. How do you see things differently from the rest of us?" If Liz seems particularly uncomfortable speaking in front of the group, you invite her to speak after the meeting.
- "Paul, you've presented your case. I'd like to invite someone to challenge that position."
- "We seem to be coalescing on the view that we should do this. Now I'd like to flip it and assume it's actually a bad thing. What would be the case for that?"

In other words, if you are running your meeting properly and divergent thinking still isn't happening, your responsibility as a leader is to go looking for it. An absence of dissent is never a guarantee that you're on the right track. Your confidence in a decision should directly correlate with the amount of divergent thinking that went into it.

Now that you have all the information, a decision can be made. In some cases, the group might decide by voting, and in other cases, one person will need to decide. The key is that all voices will have been heard. When more information, more points of view, more ideas are heard, decisions are better.

However, there is no obligation to stop action or give dissenters what they want. This would give too much power to dissenters to derail action. There will almost always be people who see things differently and don't like a particular decision. That's fine, and actually a good thing. There is no need to convince these people they are "wrong" if a decision does not go their way. All we need is that the team members support the decision with their actions and behaviors.

4. Give Information, Not Instructions

All around us, we have signs telling us what to do, like "Wash your hands" or "Keep this door shut!" Telling people what to do is hardly conducive to collaboration. By now, you recognize that as the old Industrial Age play of coercion.

What's the alternative? Provide information. Inform people of the consequences of their behavior and let them choose. This works best when they experience the consequences. If someone else experiences the consequences of your bad behavior, the feedback loop is broken.

I ride with a bike group on Saturday mornings at 8:00. We leave at 8:00. Not 8:02. Not 8:01. Even if someone is pulling into the parking lot at 8:00, we don't wait. The person will spend a tough morning trying to catch the group. Is that mean? Hardly. Because everyone knows the group is not going to wait, almost no one is ever late. Waiting for late people is short-term compassionate, long-term cruel. And it is supremely discourteous to the people who made it on time. Waiting for late people results in more late people, which results in more waiting. We call it "rewarding bad behavior."

The practice of telling people what to do is so pervasive that we barely recognize it when we do it:

- "Park there."
- "Go ahead and submit the proposal."
- "Add these user stories."
- "Double-check the numbers."
- "Be back at 10:00 a.m."

That last one was me. I was leading a workshop, and as I put the group on break, I gave the standard "Be back at 10:00 a.m." instruction. This followed an activity about how often we tell people what to do without even realizing it. At least one person was paying attention. He came up to me and said I was a "big fat hypocrite." (And we hadn't even gotten to the feedback part of the workshop.)

My first reaction was to be defensive, but then I asked, "What do you mean?" in the most neutral tone I could muster.

"Well, we've just spent half an hour on giving information, not instructions, and you just gave us all an instruction. Try following your own advice."

Now I say, "I will start at 10:00 a.m.," and I do.

Another time, I was giving a workshop in Medellín, Colombia. The seminar host warned me about being "too militaristic, too Americano" with my schedule. "This group likes to be late."

I tried my trick. It worked. The first time, there were a few people milling about the coffeepots, but I started exactly at ten. No lectures, no admonitions. After that, we were locked on schedule. He was astounded. He'd never seen it before.

Give information, not instructions.

- Instead of "Park there," try "I see a parking spot there."
- Instead of "Go ahead and submit the proposal," try "I can't see anything I would change."
- Instead of "Add these user stories," try "The product owner has some new user stories for our product."
- Instead of "Double-check these numbers," try "It is important these numbers are correct, and I see something that doesn't quite add up for me."

A fun, everyday way to practice this is by helping someone park a car. Typically, you might wave someone forward, forward, forward, then abruptly say, "Stop!" This is you giving instructions.

Because it is binary—go, then stop—the driver has no warning. They are not slowing down as they get closer, and they might overshoot. The driver is reduced to a robot. They don't need to think or be engaged.

What does giving information look like here? Hold your hands apart to reflect the distance to the obstacle. Gradually move your hands together as the distance gets smaller. This provides a natural feedback loop. The driver will stop exactly where they want to. By the way, this is how they park airplanes, and it is how we teach people to park heavy vehicles in the army. Now the two people are collaborating, working together. The driver is thinking and active.

Give information, not instructions.

ESTABLISH THE RIGHT HYPOTHESIS

Collaboration is used for several purposes. We collaborate to get a better sense of reality. This is the pause button on the video. What is the situation right now? Where is the hurricane? What is the status of the lube oil system?

Collaboration is used to understand how we got here. This is the story we tell ourselves about what preceded this event. This is helpful for understanding cause and effect.

Collaboration is used to make better decisions. This is where we take what we think is true and commit to a course of action. Should we take the Atlantic route or the Old Bahama Channel?

But one of the most powerful purposes of collaboration for teams is to establish your hypothesis before launching into the next period of redwork.

The bluework-redwork-bluework cycle is about learning and advancing the organization. Better than thinking about the decision as something to *do* is knowing that the decision is something to *test*. In other words, the decision is a hypothesis.

Consider every phase of redwork an experiment. Experiments help us learn and improve. By definition, an experiment starts with a hunch that can be tested. We call this hunch a "hypothesis." The primary purpose of every bluework phase is to establish the hypothesis. The primary purpose of every redwork phase is to test whether the hypothesis is valid. In addition, a well-designed experiment:

- has an end, at which point we reflect on what we have learned;
- is fully documented, so others can verify your results and build on them;
- is conducted under controlled conditions—for example, by changing one variable at a time to avoid conflating the effects of multiple changes.

Of course, purely scientific experiments have no obligation to produce anything beyond a test result, whereas work experiments need to achieve a production output as well. Let's look at the case of *El Faro*. How would an experimental approach to redwork have altered the outcome?

After getting under way, the first key decision occurred at the north end of the Bahamas: whether to take the exposed Atlantic route or the protected Old Bahama Channel. Normally, this isn't much of a decision because the exposed Atlantic route is shorter and more efficient. There's no trade-off. This time, a hurricane threatened the Atlantic route. The hypothesis could have been stated like this:

We are taking the Atlantic route. Our hypothesis is that the storm will (a) not slow us down and make the trip less efficient and (b) not become powerful enough to threaten the ship. Because this is a hypothesis, I need everybody to look for information confirming or disproving this hypothesis over the coming phase of redwork: wave size, wind speed, degree of pitch, etc. We will reevaluate at the Rum Cay cutoff point.

A hypothesis is more than just a decision point. It builds upon a decision (taking the Atlantic route) with a rationale (we don't believe the storm will be too strong) and an endpoint (the Rum Cay cutoff), and it establishes how we will measure our results (wave size, ship's responsiveness, and other metrics of storm intensity). During each experiment, we compare current conditions with predicted conditions. This is why it's important to establish the metrics we expect to see before we begin. By deciding these things ahead of time, we remove sunk-cost decision-making and prevent an escalation of commitment.

By establishing the hypothesis this way on board *El Faro*, we have invited the crew into an improve mindset that seeks learning and growth. Rather than simply trying to execute the task of driving the Atlantic route in the most efficient and effective way possible, they will also be questioning whether the Atlantic route is still the right route to take. They will be more observant of the wind, the seas, and the barometric pressure in ways that facilitate a future decision.

Finally, a predefined endpoint when this original hypothesis will be reevaluated—in this case, the Rum Cay cutoff—opens the door to questioning the route without having to tell the captain he is wrong. For the crew, the benefit is that they will be more observant and more willing to share what they see and think, and that they will provide relevant input on the need to alter course when appropriate. For the captain, the benefit is that he will have inoculated himself against the tendency to stick with a previous but losing commitment, hear the results of the experiment, and ultimately change course.

With coercion, the best we can hope for is compliance. With compliance, we get effort, but not discretionary effort. The output of collaboration, however, is a commitment to move forward. This commitment signals the end of bluework (embracing variability), and the start of redwork (reducing variability).

TO MOVE FROM COERCE TO COLLABORATE

1. Vote first, then discuss.
2. Be curious, not compelling.
3. Invite dissent rather than drive consensus.
4. Give information, not instructions.

COLLABORATE

The COLLABORATE play is initiated after controlling the clock.

Industrial Age organizations assigned deciding and doing to two groups of people: blueworkers and redworkers. Blueworkers (management) needed to get the redworkers to follow the decisions the blueworkers decided for them. Blueworkers achieved this through coercion.

Coercion seemed like an ugly word, so instead we used words like coaxed, goaded, prodded, influenced, motivated, and inspired. Language patterns in the coerce play are highly skewed toward the leader's voice.

For collaboration, we need to let the doers be the deciders. There is still bluework and redwork, but there are no blueworkers and no redworkers.

Collaboration requires us to share ideas, be vulnerable, and respect the ideas of others. Collaboration happens through the questions we ask and requires that we admit we don't have the whole picture. Deep down, we need to believe others can contribute to our thinking and understanding of the world.

With collaboration, we ask questions starting with "what" and "how." We invite dissent. We practice being curious before being compelling.

The leader's obligation is to listen to the dissenters, not to stall decisions until each is convinced of the new direction. Always stopping action because of dissent gives too much power to dissenters. It will invite blockers, inhibit bold decision-making, and delay action.

Language patterns in the COLLABORATE play are evenly spread across the team. Share of voice among team members is more equal and the Team Language Coefficient is lower.

Collaboration is a core process of bluework. When we resort to coercion, we get compliance. When we engage in collaboration, we get commitment, which is our next play.

Leaving Bluework Behind: Commit

I t's time to help Sue, stuck in blue. We need to reduce the barrier to moving from contemplation to action. This is the transition out of bluework into redwork. If we collaborate effectively, the result is commitment. If we coerce, the result is compliance.

Commitment comes from within, whereas compliance is forced by an external source. Commitment is more powerful, because it is an intrinsic motivator. Commitment invites full participation, engagement, and discretionary effort. Compliance invites doing just enough to get by, get through, or get it done.

This is true even when you're talking to yourself. Let's say you decide you no longer want to eat sweets, yet at the end of a long day you are faced with a bowl of sweets. You can consider two options for self-talk. You can tell yourself you *can't* eat sweets or that you *don't* eat sweets.

Turns out that telling yourself you *don't* eat sweets is more powerful. You'll end up eating fewer sweets with "don't" than "can't" because, by using the word "don't," the motivation comes from within. "Don't" identifies you as "a person who does not eat sweets." It allocates the power to you.

When you use "can't" the imposition comes from outside. You are the kind of person who eats sweets, but an external force is preventing you from eating them (even though you really want to). An argument from an external force is weaker than one from internal power. At the end of a long day, when you are tired and hungry, the weaker argument won't be strong enough to stop you from the behavior you are trying to avoid.

If you want to keep your commitments, try using "don't," not "can't."

- "I don't buy product insurance," not "I can't buy product insurance."
- "I don't miss deadlines," not "I can't miss this deadline."
- "I don't spend my time that way," not "I can't spend my time that way."

The moment we commit to an action is the moment we choose to dedicate time and energy toward that particular objective. The word stems from Latin, combining *com* (with) and *mittere* (release, send). The word "mission" is also derived from the Latin *mittere*. Thus, "commit" conveys "going forth with a sense of mission." It's this sense of mission that is missing when we see low engagement scores, people just going through the motions, paying lip service to company policies and projects.

To commit is more than a decision. We may make a decision that one course of action is better than another but leave it at that, without action. Commitment attaches action to that decision. Commitment turns bluework into redwork.

Businesses need to get stuff done. We hear a lot from clients who aspire to create an entrepreneurial culture, where people have a bold bias for action and engage in thoughtful, risk-embracing behavior. They envision a culture of deliberate decision-making, an energetic bias for action, a focus on achieving excellence rather than avoiding errors, and personal ownership and accountability for outcomes. This is why we must reduce the barrier to exit contemplation (bluework) and move to action (redwork).

The key is that there must be choice before there is commitment. If a person has no choice but to say yes, then what we have is compliance. So while "inspire" and "empower" are common workplace mantras that employers hope will spark action and commitment within employees to carry out the desired company goals, unless there is choice there will, at best, be compliance.

Sometimes we do want compliance. There was a tragic case in the construction of a New York skyscraper where a craftsman working near an elevator shaft was not wearing a harness. When a piece of the flooring unexpectedly broke away, he fell and died. A supervisor had seen him without his harness earlier in the day, in violation of safety regulations, but the supervisor did not order the craftsman to put his harness on. I'm not sure why, but sometimes there is a sense that telling people what to do is bad—it's bad sometimes, but it is appropriate sometimes. This is one of the benefits of red-blue thinking—understanding that sometimes we need to say, "Do this in accordance with the procedure," and sometimes we need to say, "How do you see it?" This was a case where compliance would have saved a life. Seat belts. Wear them. Compliance.

Individuals make commitments. Groups do not. Commitment is personal; it comes from within.

CONSEQUENCES OF COMPLIANCE

In the traditional Industrial Age structure, the doers do not have choice over what, when, how they work. Therefore, there's no commitment, only compliance. Compliance takes a toll in the workplace.

Gallup conducts an annual survey of US workers to measure their level of "engagement." Gallup defines an engaged worker as one who is involved in, enthusiastic about, and committed to his or her work and workplace. In 2018, Gallup's poll showed the highest level of "engaged" workers since it started the survey in 2000. The percentage of engaged workers was 34 percent, meaning 66 percent of workers were not engaged or were actively disengaged. The low level of worker engagement is a result of cultures of compliance.

Compliance gives us a pass on thinking. Compliance only requires a person to follow rules, instructions, and actions that someone else has determined. It is easy because it relieves a person of the messy process of thinking and decision-making. Worse, compliance gives a pass on responsibility. When it comes to many corporate and operational errors, the common refrain is "I was doing what I was told." The message is this: I am not responsible. Someone else made the decision. Compliance.

Compliance also does not require a lot of context.

"Do this."

"Why?"

"Because I'm telling you to."

"Uh, OK."

It relieves bosses from the time-consuming and messy work of having to explain what is going on. But the lack of context creates a fragile situation.

I had an experience early on as captain of the USS *Santa Fe* where I told the midnight team where the submarine needed to be in the morning. I did not give them context about why we needed to be there or the costs of not being there. In other words, I asked for compliance.

When I got up in the morning to check where we were, I was shocked to see we were out of position. Why? Things came up. A fishing boat got in the way. Then a merchant ship came by. One thing led to another. The watch officer was doing his best to *comply* with my instructions, but without context he was not *committed*.

Compliance makes following procedure the guiding star. Commitment makes achieving the intended objective of the procedure the guiding star. Compliance is what Warren Beatty was coerced into doing with the Oscars card.

Compliance sounds like this:

- The second mate of *El Faro* to a junior crew member: "We're the only idiots out here."
- The third mate of *El Faro* to a junior crew member: "I trust what he's saying. It's just being twenty miles away from hundred knot winds—this doesn't even sound right."

Other common compliance phrases you may hear:

- "Because I was told to."
- "Because it says so."
- "I just do what they tell me."
- "I'm not paid to think."

HOW TO COMMIT

While compliance was the natural consequence of the Industrial Age division of people into deciders and doers, commitment is what we want now. Compliance may have worked for simple, physical, repetitive, individual tasks, but it does not work for complex, cognitive, custom, team tasks. Compliance only gets minimum fulfillment of requirements, whereas commitment invites discretionary effort.

Here are three options for executing the COMMIT play.

TO MOVE FROM COMPLIANCE TO COMMITMENT

1. Commit to learn, not (just) do.
2. Commit actions, not beliefs.
3. Chunk it small but do it all.

1. Commit to Learn, Not (Just) Do

We ended the COLLABORATE play with the idea of developing hypotheses to test rather than making decisions to execute. Developing hypotheses requires making decisions not only about what to do but what to learn. The idea of a hypothesis is that it puts us in a learning and improving mindset. It frames the upcoming period of redwork not as redwork for the sake of redwork but redwork with the idea that we will learn something.

Setting the stage for learning at the point when we depart bluework and dive back into redwork will help in several ways in the future. First, we will be more interested in the redwork itself. In the case of *El Faro*, since the officers felt little control over the ability to adjust the decision on the route, observations of the wind and seas were of limited interest. They may have affected the detailed positioning of the ship but were not going to be key inputs to a future decision. It's the feeling of a sense of control that heightens our senses ahead of time, since we know that what we sense will matter.

Second, a learning and improving mindset at the beginning will be reinforced when we exit redwork and go back to bluework, because we will want to invoke the IMPROVE play, not the prove play. The traditional Industrial Age playbook for how to treat redwork is prove. Prove that we know what we are doing, prove that our product works. What we want, if we want to create agile, adaptive, and resilient organizations, is the IMPROVE play—but this will conflict with the prove play. Setting our sights on learning at the outset of the blue-red-blue cycle will make the IMPROVE play, when it comes, more effective.

Another benefit of setting a commitment to learn is it will help us avoid reacting badly to setbacks and detours.

Focusing on a learning goal lowers the barrier to transition out of bluework to redwork. It is ironic, but having a performance goal actually makes it harder to get into production. Remember Sue, stuck in blue. Sue is prone to rumination and debate and is hesitant to make a decision, a commitment to start doing. One of the things that scares Sue is that she is viewing the upcoming commitment to redwork as a period when she will need to prove something, prove that she made the right decision, prove that the team can get the job done. This is daunting. It is holding her back.

Instead, if she thought of the next period of redwork as the doing part of the learning cycle (make a prediction, then test the prediction by observing what happens, then reflect upon our observations with respect to our prediction), then it would be easier for her to make that transition out of rumination and planning into action.

The reason that it is easier to commit to action when we put ourselves in a learning mode, and the reason we are more resilient in action when facing setbacks, is that it taps the way our brains are wired. Humans, and mammals in general, like to explore, discover, and learn new things. Our brains are wired to respond positively to the novelty of seeing what is around the next corner or over the next mountain ridge. Psychologists call this the "seeking" system. When we set ourselves into a period of doing, and we have a playful curiosity about what might happen, we are activating this seeking system—and life is more fun and interesting.

The opening words of the hugely popular series *Star Trek* (the first episode was in 1966!) tap into this desire.

Space: the final frontier. These are the voyages of the starship
Enterprise. Its continuing mission: to explore strange new worlds,
to seek out new life and new civilizations, to boldly go where
no one has gone before.

So, the question to ask at the end of a bluework meeting would be not
only "What are we going to do?" but also "What are we going to learn?"

2. Commit Actions, Not Beliefs

When we make commitments or look for team members to make commitments, one mistake is to try to get people "on board"—in other
words, trying to get people not only to align their actions and behaviors
but also to make a mindset change. The better way is to simply commit
actions. For any significant decision, you are likely to have people who
would have chosen a different path. What the organization needs is for
the entire organization to align behind the actions needed to support the
decision. Trying to convince people that they need to align their mindsets too adds a burden that delays moving forward and requires them to
admit "they were wrong." Since the action happens immediately after
the decision was made, we do not know who was wrong, if anyone.

Imagine you have to make a decision on an employee proposal.
Your colleague has stated that he or she intends to change an advertising campaign in a certain way. The moment you hear about the proposal, you experience a negative reaction. Your personal experience is
that this is a bad idea. You believe you will lose sales, say, or waste
resources. It is not an ethical issue and no one will die, but it's just not
the best thing for the organization. Still, since this will play out in the
future, like all decisions, you are not 100 percent sure.

The commitment you can make, as a leader, is to support the decision with your actions and see what happens. You do not have to

believe it is a good idea, only that there's enough of a chance that it is a good idea to risk what limited resources will be spent on it. You are also weighing the learning impact for this colleague and the organization. This is good enough for the company.

The same principle holds true if the situation is flipped. If you have asked your team to execute a particular decision, and there are people on the team who don't believe it is the best way to go, you do not have to convince them that it is. You should let them hold on to their ideas. As long as they commit to supporting the decision through actions, the goals of the organization are met.

Once the decision is made, don't try to convince dissenters and outliers that their thinking is wrong. No one can know if the decision is correct—or not until after the period of redwork, during which time you will test the hypothesis on which you based the decision.

Ella's Kitchen is an organic baby-food company outside London. The leaders have worked to build a more collaborative culture where people contribute their ideas. One of the ideas from the product team was for a gum-able breadstick-like food called melty sticks that children as young as seven months could manage. Toddlers would enjoy sticking this in their mouths and feeling it melt away as they gummed it.

Technically, it was a tough product to make—make it too hard and it would be scary and sharp, make it too soft and it would melt into nothing too fast. Additionally, it required special packaging. This drove up the costs of packaging and shipping the product.

For that reason, leadership did not think this was a viable product. But the leaders had made a commitment to build this more participatory culture, so they reasoned that they needed to fulfill their side of the deal and let the team try their ideas. Viewing it as a learning opportunity, leadership approved production.

A year later, melty sticks had become the company's number-one-grossing product.

3. Chunk It Small but Do It All

Imagine you have a bowl of seven-layer dip in front of you. You have (for some reason) made a commitment to eat it all. How do you do it?

One bite at a time—but there are two ways to do it. You could first eat all the olives off the top, then all the cheese, then the salsa, and so on. But now you've transformed the process from eating a seven-layer dip to eating a one-layer dip seven times. Instinctively, you know that to get the full experience you'd rather take a deep scoop, touching all seven layers but in a thin slice, so you can manage to get all layers in one bite.

This is how to think about "chunk it small but do it all."

Here's how it might have played out on *El Faro*:

As we know, the captain made the decision even prior to leaving Jacksonville, Florida, to go the entire route to Puerto Rico using the exposed Atlantic route. He did not think about the trip as a series of smaller increments of redwork divided by bluework decision points.

Operational actions, such as driving a ship from Jacksonville to Puerto Rico, tend to have certain naturally occurring decision points determined by geography, the laws of nature, timing, and the interaction of other organizations. For *El Faro*, the geography of the eastern side of the Bahamas created natural decision points where the bluework should have happened. In between those decision points were periods of redwork to keep the ship moving as planned.

Thinking about the journey in terms of one continuous stretch to Puerto Rico meant that any possible decision point was burdened with the default answer that they would continue on the exposed Atlantic route unless deterred. This also meant that deciding to take the Old Bahama Channel would feel like a change in plans that would call for additional justification.

For significant decisions like this one, it would be better to have both plans debated as equally likely so that a decision is made based as much as possible upon the conditions and expected conditions at sea, not the expected conditions in our minds. This helps us inoculate ourselves against another mental trap—escalation of commitment.

Innovations, new product design, and improving manufacturing processes might not reveal the natural bluework pauses like an operational action does. In this case, we need to deliberately chunk the improvement cycle into discrete, small, bite-size pieces, but each one should result in a complete product—testable in the market.

Here's the rule about the blue-red-blue cycle length: shorter periods of redwork increase learning but reduce production output, and vice versa. Therefore, in environments and under conditions of high uncertainty and unpredictability, we need to shorten redwork periods. As the product or exterior conditions become more defined, we can extend the length of the redwork.

Making a commitment to a small increment also frees us up to be completely absorbed in the work, but for a short period of time. We do not need to reserve part of our brain to monitor whether we are on track, because we know we will have a preplanned interruption soon enough.

We want to make an emotionally strong commitment to a short burst of activity—redwork—for the purpose of learning something. We want to commit to a small increment but do it all.

Sometimes I think of it like an expiration date. We are making a commitment to a period of redwork but there is an expiration date. At that point, we need to check that we're on track.

WHAT DO COMMITMENT STATEMENTS SOUND LIKE?

- "I intend to start the next phase of the project. Our next bluework pause will be in ten days."

- "We are planning on moving forward with option 1. We will pause and reflect on the fifteenth."
- "We are starting the next production run. We will run ten thousand units and then set up a meeting to review our data."

The commitment statement should include a resolve to do the redwork and a plan to shift back to bluework based on meeting some condition or after some duration of redwork.

Inviting a commitment statement from a team member might sound like this:

- "What are you planning on doing?"
- "When will you launch back to redwork?"
- "How long will you be in redwork before your next pause and reflection period?"
- "What will trigger a pause to this next phase of the project?"
- "How will we know if our hypothesis tests out?"
- "What's the expiration date on this commitment?"

In the COLLABORATE play, I discussed the power of starting questions with "what" and "how." There was the probabilistic how and the inquisitive how. The probabilistic how sounds like "How sure are you?" or "How likely is that assumption to be true?" The inquisitive how helps us ask neutral, open, curious questions without judgment. The inquisitive how sounds like "How does ____ affect ____?" or "How do you see that?"

Here's a third, useful "how," the "aspirational how." Here we use "how" or "what" to convert bluework into a resolution that we can fully commit to. The aspirational how is used like this:

- "How could we start?"
- "How could we test that quickly and cheaply?"

I find that the aspirational how shifts people's thinking from worrying about obstacles and barriers to considering what we can do with the time and resources we have. This shifts the focus from what we can't do to what we can do. The aspirational how gets us there.

"What" also helps here:

- "What is the smallest slice we could make?"
- "What can we do?"
- "What would that look like?"
- "What would a first step look like?"

COULDA, WOULDA, SHOULDA

Here's one more tool for getting a person or team to move out of bluework to the action phase of redwork. It is useful if it seems like we have had enough planning, meetings, and discussion about something, and it is time to commit—leaving bluework behind and starting the action phase of redwork.

When having conversations about commitments, there's a natural sequence of could, would, and should, and it goes in that order. This is because we move from could (what is possible) to would (a conditional) and finally to should (which conveys a sense of obligation).

Here are some team members coming to talk about an idea for a new product. The hypothesis is that there is a market for a new product that our customers will feel is consistent with our brand. The team may be debating what to do and you want to help them move to committing to action.

You ask, "What could we do first?"

"Well, we could build a web page and put some pictures up and see if we get any orders, or we could run a poll to see how many people would be interested in a product like this."

Then, "What would you do if you were me?"

"I would make the web page because that is testing actual orders, and we could get it up today."

"OK, then what should we do?"

And they take it from there. If the team members sound stuck in bluework, like our friend Sue, listen to the language to see where they are in the could-would-should path and invite them to take the next step.

This is one of the few cases where the word "should" won't get you in trouble. In general, I find "should" to be used in many unhelpful ways. For example:

- "It should be ready."
- "It should work."
- "You should do it like this."
- "You shouldn't feel that way."
- "The company should give us better chairs."

IN FOR A PENNY, IN FOR A POUND: ESCALATION OF COMMITMENT

Another reason we want to increment small and break up the redwork into a series of small pieces is that commitments tend to be self-reinforcing. This is why the captain's pre-underway decision to take the direct Atlantic route gained so much weight as time went on and became so hard to overturn. Once we commit to a small step, humans have a tendency to continue to commit in that direction. They do not make full use of the bluework period to evaluate whether the next step *should* be taken. Instead, they cherry-pick information that supports their previous decision. What is behind this?

The answer lies in a psychological phenomenon called "escalation of commitment." Escalation of commitment means that once we select a course of action, we stubbornly stick to it, even in the face of evidence that the course of action is failing. Escalation of commitment is why investors hold on to losing positions too long. It is why companies continue to put money into failing products. It is why governments pursue failing policies. This is the phenomenon that results in people justifying decisions gone awry by redefining success after the fact.

Escalation of commitment works like this: We are faced with a decision and we make one. Now we feel responsible for the outcome of the decision, but things do not play out like we had hoped. Evidence builds that the decision was wrong.

The rational thing to do in this case would be to pause, reevaluate, and change course, but this is not what many humans do. It turns out that humans will persist in trying to turn the losing decision into a winner. This is sometimes laudable—for example, when you have a high degree of control over the outcome—however, in cases where the decision is based on factors largely out of your control, this is not the most effective approach. You have to be careful here, because overestimating your ability to control a situation will invite you more readily into escalation of commitment. Escalation of commitment can also feed a sense of futility among team members about the value of speaking up and can erode their autonomy and control.

In 1974, professor Barry Staw ran an experiment to investigate whether and why people would invest more in a losing decision. He was troubled by the decision-making process that led the United States deeper and deeper into an entanglement in Southeast Asia and the Vietnam War. He wanted to understand the psychological basis for the flawed decision-making.

The Vietnam War was in its eighteenth year, and America had ended direct military involvement just the year before. The war was highly disruptive in American society and politics, and the escalation and continued involvement in the 1960s was thought of as an example of pouring good money after bad.

George Ball, in a memorandum to President Johnson in 1965, stated the case for escalation of commitment:

> Once large numbers of U.S. troops are committed to direct combat, they will begin to take heavy casualties in a war they are ill-equipped to fight in a non-cooperative if not downright hostile countryside.
>
> Once we suffer large casualties, we will have started a well-nigh irreversible process. Our involvement will be so great that we cannot—without national humiliation—stop short of achieving our complete objectives. Of the two possibilities I think humiliation would be more likely than the achievement of our objectives—even after we have paid terrible costs.

Ball's memo was released with the Pentagon Papers in 1971.

Dr. Staw devised a clever experiment to test this hypothesis. MBA students were put through a simulation where they needed to make an investment decision. They were executives in a manufacturing company that was seeing flattening sales and declining profits. They were responsible for dividing a $20 million R&D investment between two divisions of the company: a consumer products division and an industrial products division. As part of the simulation, there had been a similar decision five years earlier, and the students had the data from the results of that decision. Half the students had data showing that the previous decision had been successful, and half had data show-ing that the previous decision had not been successful.

But here was the other wrinkle. They then split each group in half again. Half of the students simply read about the previous decision, whereas the other half of the students were selected because they had actually made the previous decision as an earlier part of the study.

When faced with evidence of a poor decision they had personally made, the MBA students poured an average of $13 million, or two-thirds of the available funds, into the money-losing division. As to the students who simply read the previous decision, they split the money more evenly, favoring the winning division and allocating an average of $9 million to the losing division.

When Professor Staw published his paper in 1976 in the *Journal of Organizational Behavior and Human Performance*, he called it "Knee-Deep in the Big Muddy"—a reference to the Vietnam War, which soldiers referred to as "the Big Muddy."

Although the story is still playing out, there's evidence that British prime minister Theresa May was captured by escalation of commit-ment while dealing with managing the Brexit process. She reacted to criticism of her approach by attempting to be compelling—saying, "Brexit is Brexit," and that Britain would leave on March 29, 2019, over and over again.

Then, when faced with strong evidence that her approach was not working (the biggest defeat in the history of Parliament), she simply doubled down on her commitment.

In a redwork world, escalation of commitment sounds like:

- "We started this; we're going to finish this."
- "I've made my decision."
- "We're doing this. Resistance is futile."
- "Come on, let's go."

- "We're burning daylight."
- "Failure is not an option."

On board *El Faro*, escalation of commitment statements sounded like this:

- "So we'll just have to tough this one out."
- "You can't run [from] every single weather pattern."
- "We are gunna be fine—not should be—we are gunna be fine."

In response to a comment that they are heading into the hurricane: "I wouldn't have it any other way."

- "Should (all) work out OK."
- "This ship can take it."
- "Oh. No no no. We're not gunna turn around—we're not gunna turn around."
- "Well, this is every day in Alaska. This is what it's like."

The captain even talks about taking the Old Bahama Channel on the return leg in an email to corporate operations to get permission. He also mentions it a couple times on the bridge to the crew. So what makes it so easy to talk about taking the Old Bahama Channel on the return leg but so hard to change to the Old Bahama Channel on the outbound leg? It's escalation of commitment.

In another example, Kodak invented digital cameras back in 1975. Polaroid had also developed the technology in the 1990s. But in both cases, digital cameras threatened the robust revenue stream the companies enjoyed from selling film. All the earlier decisions added weight to the commitment to film. Both companies missed the transition, and both ended up going bankrupt.

Salesmen have known for a long time the impact that escalation of commitment has on people, and they use it to encourage potential sales prospects to sign up or participate in something small in order to "hook" them into something bigger.

To protect against escalation of commitment, reframe these periods of redwork as opportunities to learn as well as to do. The idea is to make it as easy as possible for a team to exit redwork that they've determined to be erroneous or potentially erroneous.

SEPARATE THE DECISION-MAKER FROM THE DECISION-EVALUATOR

Ego threat—the idea that others will view us (or we will view ourselves) as incompetent—is the biggest culprit in escalation of commitment. In a 2013 article in *Psychology Today*, Adam Grant, author of *Give and Take*, states that one way of inoculating ourselves against the tendency to escalate is to separate the decision-maker from the decision-evaluator. This removes the decision-evaluator from the emotional investment that the decision-maker had in the decision.

This is what Intel's Andy Grove and Gordon Moore achieved in an emotional way when they conducted a thought experiment in which they had been fired and other people were determining the future direction of the company. At the time, they were running Intel—and had become rich and successful building memory chips. But the market for memory chips was becoming saturated and margins were under pressure. Their bluework decision was whether or not to bet the company on a new product—microprocessors. The thought experiment allowed them to separate themselves from their previous decisions, giving them the ability to let go and move in a new direction. It was the psychological separation from themselves as current decision-evaluators from themselves as the original decision-makers (to originally build memory chips) that inoculated them against sticking with their old ways. It worked.

Corporate rotation programs, where executives rotate among positions, also help to reduce the likelihood of escalation of commitment. The new executive, not having any attachment to the decisions made by the previous executive, is more likely to be able to walk away from a project that is unlikely to succeed. A study of managers at a bank in California that was dealing with failing loans found that the tendency of managers to continue to lend money to people who couldn't pay their previous loans was reduced when managers were rotated more often.

A practical way to separate the decision-evaluator from the decision-maker is to have the senior person in the organization act as the decision-evaluator and one of the junior people act as the decision-maker. This is not the way most organizations are designed, and in many organizations, it is the senior person who normally evaluates and makes each decision.

In the case of *El Faro*, the captain was both the decision-maker and the decision-evaluator. He decided to take the Atlantic route. After the decision was made, the location, path, and strength of the storm did not match what was assumed before the decision; building seas and winds, and the ship's response to the rough weather, started giving clues that it was a bad decision. However, the captain, as the senior person on the ship and the one who evaluated whether the decision was good or not, found himself having to evaluate his own decision. Psychologically, it would have required him to admit his previous decision was wrong. While people can do this—some more easily than others—it adds a barrier. A more resilient structure would have a junior officer "make" the decision, and keep the captain solely in an evaluative role. The captain, presented with information that his previous decision to take the Atlantic route was a failing course of action, was unable to change routes.

Further, we saw how tough it was for the other officers to challenge the captain on a decision he had made because of the authority of the captain position and a culture that was working "against the clock."

What does the alternative sound like in organizations? It rests on the word "intent." In these organizations, junior people come to their leaders and state what they intend to do. The junior person also explains the rationale behind the decision, including the safety and technical components of the decision and the purpose and alignment of the decision to the organization's goals. They invite feedback from colleagues and allow senior leaders to veto the decision, but, in the absence of a veto, the junior person moves ahead.

A product owner considering the trade-offs between launching on time and delaying to add one more feature (especially if the feature is one the leader wants) might report: "We intend to launch the product on time." And then give the rationale.

A production supervisor, upon finding unexpected defects in an outbound product sample, may report, "We intend to delay shipping in order to conduct a second inspection." And then explain the rationale.

A buyer for a manufacturing company, dissatisfied with the products from one supplier, may state: "We intend to shift to a new supplier for these parts." And explain the research the buyer has done among other suppliers.

A salesperson, seeing the opportunity to open up a new market, may state, "I intend to give this client a better sales discount than normal."

Is it important to recognize that the initial intent statement is just the start of the conversation and is incomplete without the rationale behind the decision. Several of the results of doing business this way are that junior decision-makers feel a strong sense of ownership, they start thinking like the senior people, and there is a bias for action because simple decisions are not held up in committees.

Now that we've committed to action, we can immerse ourselves in redwork until we COMPLETE the next period of redwork. Our next play is COMPLETE.

TO MOVE FROM COMPLIANCE TO COMMITMENT

1. Commit to learn, not (just) do.
2. Commit actions, not beliefs.
3. Chunk it small but do it all.

COMMIT

Collaboration sets us up for commitment. Coercion results in compliance. Commitment is better than compliance because it releases discretionary effort in people. For complex, cognitive, custom teamwork, discretionary effort is everything.

Just as teams in redwork will have a tendency to stay in redwork, teams in bluework will have a tendency to stay in bluework. That transition point is when we run the COMMIT play.

At the same time, we need to inoculate ourselves against escalation of commitment, where we tend to attach ourselves to past decisions and continue to invest in a losing course of action.

The three ways for executing the COMMIT play are designed to minimize barriers to action and inoculate our organization against escalation of commitment.

Commitment comes from within; compliance is imposed externally. Commitment is linked to intrinsic motivation, whereas compliance is linked to extrinsic motivation.

Following commit we can immerse ourselves in the redwork until we COMPLETE the next period of redwork, which is our next play.

CHAPTER 6

The End of Redwork: Complete

Henry Ford revolutionized human mobility with the introduction of the Model T in 1908. The Model T established many elements of a car that are familiar to drivers today. Powered by a four-cylinder, oil-lubricated gasoline engine, the Model T had pedals on the floor in front of the driver, four air-filled rubber tires, two headlights, a windshield, and a steering wheel. Within days of its introduction, Ford received fifteen thousand orders. Over fifteen million Model Ts would be sold over the next two decades.

Ford's thinking when it came to organizing his production teams was heavily influenced by Taylor, who we discussed in chapter 2. Again, the idea was for leadership to come up with the One Optimal Way to mass-produce the One Optimal Design. The subsequent production run would then be continued for as long as possible. This approach reduced redesigning, retooling, and retraining costs. It successfully produced cars so efficiently that even the people building the cars could afford to buy them. In 1908, this was a revolutionary idea.

Ford was highly successful at supervising the design and production of the Model T. His disciplined approach drove the price of the car down from $825 when it was first introduced to $260 by 1925. By that time, Ford's assembly line could produce a Model T in ninety minutes. For a couple of years, Ford produced more cars than every other manufacturer combined.

In Ford's day, the pace of innovation was nothing like it is today. James Watt invented the first viable steam engine in 1776. Eighty-three years later, in 1859, Étienne Lenoir developed the first commercially successful internal combustion engine. It was yet another twenty-seven years before Karl Benz patented the first automobile in 1886. Benz's car looked more like a carriage with an engine strapped to its back than today's modern automobile. It took *another* twenty-two years before Ford achieved the Model T.

Contrast that timeline with a modern example: in 2008, Tesla proved the market for attractive, sophisticated electric cars with its Roadster. Within a decade, essentially every major manufacturer had rolled out a viable electric vehicle.

Ford's designers and engineers worked on paper, laboriously sketching and resketching their designs. There were no tools like CAD to make the work easier for the designers. What's more, retooling the factory to improve any aspect of the vehicle was a long, costly effort. It made sense to lock in the design and continue it for as long as possible, minimizing any interruptions to the manufacturing process. In Ford's view, the best approach was to launch into redwork and let the redworkers focus on their jobs, with no planned pause, until it became literally impossible to continue.

But the world was changing. Consumer spending power ballooned during the Roaring Twenties, driving the demand for cars with modern appointments and flashy looks. By this point, Alfred Sloan had been appointed president of General Motors Corporation. In addition to refining the assembly line process, Sloan experimented with introducing annual updates for his vehicles. Consumers strongly preferred more up-to-date models to the by-then tired look and feel of the Model T.

Sales of the Model T peaked in 1923 with 2 million units sold. Then, in both 1924 and 1925, sales dropped, even as overall automobile sales continued to increase. The market had shifted. Finally acknowledging the problem, Ford shut down his assembly lines for six months—halting redwork—to retool. But it was too little, too late. Ford's pause gave GM the opportunity to catch up and then pass Ford altogether, overtaking what had once been an unassailable lead.

Today, the combination of a rapidly changing world with reduced design costs means that the emphasis has shifted from production (do, or make, what we know) to learning (what is needed to be done or made?). While in redwork, we benefit by having a prove mindset. However, our overall mindset guiding the redwork-bluework rhythm is one of improve. When preparing for redwork with an overall improve mindset of learning and growth, we are able to extract the maximum possible amount of useful information from each production phase to fuel subsequent innovation.

Ford's plays here included the following:

- Obey the clock, not control the clock.
- Divide the organization between doers (workers) and deciders (management).
- Focus the workers on doing, not thinking.
- Once in red production work, stay in red production work, which we call . . .
- Continue. Continue uninterrupted production. Continue, not complete and reflect.

Today, most cars undergo fundamental redesign every four to six years.

Recall poor Fred, our overbusy executive; he has inherited Ford's playbook. Like Ford, Fred runs around obeying the clock; he's focused on getting his people to do things, has a prove-and-perform mindset, and works to keep everything going. Unlike in Ford's time, however, innovation and change are happening faster than ever, and the people he is managing are much more educated than Ford's workforce was. Additionally, the work Ford trained his people to do—simple, repeated, physical, individual tasks—differs greatly from the complex, ever-changing, cognitive teamwork that Fred's company needs.

Fred needs our new playbook, along with the next play, COMPLETE.

OUR PLAYS SO FAR . . .

CONTROL THE CLOCK, not obey the clock.
COLLABORATE, not coerce.
COMMIT, not comply.
And now . . .
COMPLETE, not continue.

Completion marks the end of a period of redwork. Running the COMPLETE play means thinking of work in terms of smaller chunks of production work (redwork) and frequent intervals of reflection, collaboration, improvement, and hypothesis creation (bluework). Complete means . . .

- We are done taking data on that experiment. Now we analyze it.
- We are done with that operation. Now we reflect on how we did.
- We are done with that manufacturing run. Now we improve it.
- We are done with that software release. Now we invite feedback.

- We have reached the expiration date for that decision. Now we revisit it.
- We are done with that phase of the project. Now we celebrate.
- We are at the end of a period of recurring work (for example, at the end of a quarter, during which we execute a recurring process each week). Now we celebrate and improve it.

COMPLETION IS CRUCIAL

The Industrial Age playbook was designed to maximize the time the team spent in redwork, in production work. Imagine the assembly line running uninterrupted for as long as possible. That's why the management plays we default to today all follow the same patterns: first, obey the clock, then coerce people into doing what we need them to do, get them to comply, and continue the redwork for as long as possible. Maximize production per unit time. Any stoppage of the assembly line, any pause in redwork, meant idle time and wasted resources.

An aid to maintaining those long production runs was to erect barriers to interruptions. Those barriers are the answer to the questions "What's in the way of Beatty and Dunaway stopping the Oscars?" and "What's in the way of the *El Faro* officers from diverting to the Old Bahama Channel?" This aversion to stopping the clock spills over to an aversion to complete.

We are programmed to continue—continue the work, continue on to the next task. In a production line, even when a unit is completed, the work continues. The task is endlessly repeated. There is no sense of completion, ever. Continue.

In a service organization, a team member brings the boss a mock-up for a new marketing pamphlet. After looking through it, the boss's words are: "Good, here are some edits." Continue.

At a retail company, the team works hard to develop a prototype feature for the website. After making it available to a small subset of customers, the boss asks, "When can I expect the next iteration?" Continue.

An employee takes the initiative to offer a client an innovative solution to a long-standing problem. The effort makes the client happy and earns the company significant goodwill. The response from management is deafening silence. Continue.

What's the problem with that? Why do we need complete instead? Three reasons.

First, failure to treat completion as a deliberate step in the process translates into a failure to see the work in discrete elements; this failure carries risks. One risk is escalation of commitment because we see longer production runs, longer operational cycles linked to one original decision. This makes the organization less likely to change course when needed. Continuing to produce the same car like Henry Ford did, continuing with the launch like NASA did, continuing to read the script like Beatty and Dunaway did, and continuing the Atlantic route like the crew of *El Faro* did are the kinds of errors that stem from failing to complete. Viewing the work as one long, continuous action means that any intermediate change needs to overcome the inertia of the old plan before being a viable option. Legitimate options at interim decision points are handicapped. They are not competing on a level playing field against the previous commitments.

As the redwork continues, it begins to diverge from the optimal because the world around it changes. This is what happened to Ford. Customer tastes change, technology changes, the weather changes. Long continuation cycles, lacking opportunities for completion, carry the risk of spending time, energy, and resources on suboptimal activities.

Second, failure to complete also takes a toll on the humans in the organization. No completion moments mean no celebration moments. One hour merges with the next, one day into the other. Without completion, we do not feel a sense of progress for what we've accomplished or learned. There is no opportunity to tell the story and no opportunity to reinforce the behaviors that allowed us to be successful. Humans will become dispirited and lose interest. Behaviors that support the organization will tend toward extinction.

Finally, complete serves to proactively control the clock, exiting us from redwork and launching us into bluework. Controlling the clock gives us the operational pause we need to reflect and improve upon our processes. (IMPROVE will be our next play.) Further, the psychological detachment from our previous efforts that comes after a sense of completion, and after celebration, sets us up to successfully run the IMPROVE play. Unless we feel secure in leaving behind our past efforts, our attachment to those past efforts will impede a full exploration of how we can get better.

The COMPLETE play replaces the Industrial Age play of continue.

KEEP ON ROLLIN'

We saw the CONTINUE play with Ford. We saw the CONTINUE play on *El Faro*. The captain saw the journey to San Juan, Puerto Rico, as one long continuous action—and once that action was set in motion, like Ford's production run, the cultural playbook erected barriers to stopping the work. Had the captain and culture had a playbook that included the COMPLETE play, not just a CONTINUE play, they would have thought of the work in terms of multiple decision points where the plan would be deliberately reevaluated. The rhythm of redwork-bluework would have included:

1. Bluework. Decision. When and whether to depart port.
2. Redwork. Leaving port and going to the north end of the Bahamas.
3. Bluework. At the north end of the Bahamas, decide whether to take the Old Bahama Channel or the Atlantic route. Develop a hypothesis that the weather will support the Atlantic route.
4. Redwork. Drive from the north end of the Bahamas, along the Atlantic route to Rum Cay, gathering information to support the next decision, which is . . .
5. Bluework. At the Rum Cay cutoff, inviting the team to collaborate on the decision to take the Atlantic route or take the Old Bahama Channel. Then . . .
6. Redwork. Drive from Rum Cay to San Juan along the desired path.

In the description above, I used deliberate wording for the decision at the Rum Cay cutoff to give both options equal weight. If thinking in terms of the continue play, we might say, "Determine whether to continue along the Atlantic route or divert to the Old Bahama Channel." This subtly biases the decision toward continuing the existing plan.

What happened on board *El Faro* was that the captain framed the original decision as taking the Atlantic route all the way to Puerto Rico. This meant that a turn to the protected Old Bahama Channel felt like it was a deviation from the plan. This created a larger barrier to overcome. The officers would need to convince the captain to alter the predetermined plan. Thinking of the smaller chunks of the voyage with more decision points works to inoculate ourselves from the escalation of commitment I talked about in chapter 5.

Making decisions while in continue means that when we reach a fork in the road, we do not recognize it as a fork in the road. Instead, it seems like a straight road (continue) with an exit (change of plans). The change in plan must be justified, whereas simply continuing what we are doing does not need justification. Continuing will be what we do if we do not come up with a reason not to do it.

Imagine your daughter is driving off to college. You live in Tampa and she is headed for Austin. That's a trip of 1,144 miles. You ask her what her plan is. She could respond in one of two ways. Response 1 is "I'm driving to Austin." Response 2 describes the trip in shorter chunks. "I'm heading for Austin but I'm going to start by driving to Pensacola, then Baton Rouge, then Houston, then Austin. At each of those points I will evaluate how tired I am and whether or not I should stop for the evening."

In this second plan, the driving is the redwork, and the stopping and reflecting on her fatigue level is the bluework. It's a better plan because it is prestructured to include periods of bluework. It is more likely she will stop when fatigued.

Here is what the Industrial Age play of CONTINUE looks like:

For Mr. Beatty and Ms. Dunaway, continue the awards show.
For Kodak and Polaroid, continue producing film.
For Blockbuster, continue renting DVDs.
For Ford, continue the Model T production run.
For the crew of *El Faro*, continue along the Atlantic route.

This desire to continue what we are doing is not confined to workplaces of the past. I worked with a global technology hardware leader. The managers told me a story. They had continued producing millions of units of a technology product that was no longer selling, even after it was apparent to "everybody" that the market had shifted to a different format. Now they were faced with disposing of the obsolete units.

They paid to make them, paid to ship them, paid to store them, and ultimately paid to get rid of them. Fortunately, the strength of their other products carried the company through that slump. Not everyone is so fortunate.

If every day at work (or in life) feels the same, like it's simply a continuation of what you were doing yesterday with no clear end in sight—then you are stuck in continue mode. How much does this describe your work? What about for people lower in the organizational hierarchy? Our phrase in the navy was "SSDD." Same stuff (ahem), different day.

HOW TO COMPLETE

The COMPLETE play is the moment we exit redwork and head back to bluework. The COMPLETE play is closely linked to control the clock. In some cases, it serves to control the clock in a planned and pre-programmed way. Planning the length of the redwork periods and the frequency of bluework interruptions is a key operational tempo design element for organizations. To bias toward learning and growth, plan shorter redwork periods with more completes. To bias toward production, plan longer redwork periods with fewer completes.

Complete serves to reset ourselves mentally from our past decisions. Celebration is a key part of the completion play. Celebration gives us a sense of closure on previous activities and, feeling good about what we've done, allows us to move on. This psychological detachment serves to safeguard us against escalation of commitment and is critical for setting the stage for critical self-reflection and improvement.

Here are four ways to execute the COMPLETE play.

> **TO MOVE FROM CONTINUATION TO COMPLETION**
>
> 1. Chunk work for frequent completes early, few completes late.
> 2. Celebrate *with*, not *for*.
> 3. Focus on behavior, not characteristics.
> 4. Focus on *journey*, not *destination*.

1. Chunk Work for Frequent Completes Early, Few Completes Late

Early in a project or new product development when there is a wide array of options in decision-making, the redwork-bluework rhythm should be biased toward the bluework, emphasizing learning. This means many bluework interruptions to the redwork and a focus on growth, learning, and improvement. As the project continues, the decision space closes down. There are fewer options. Emphasis should now shift toward doing—and the redwork periods can get longer and the bluework interruptions less frequent.

Imagine your work as a long set of stairs, not a moving walkway. The flat part of the stair is the tread. The tread is the moving forward part, the redwork part, the getting things done part.

The vertical part of the stair is the riser. The riser is the improving part, the bluework part, the getting-better-at-getting-things-done part. We don't diffuse the focus of redwork on trying to do bluework, and we don't contaminate the bluework by trying to get redwork done. Perfectly level treads, perfectly vertical risers.

As the redwork-bluework rhythm shifts from bluework heavy to redwork heavy, the treads get longer and the vertical risers less frequent. So the stairway is not uniform throughout the course of a project

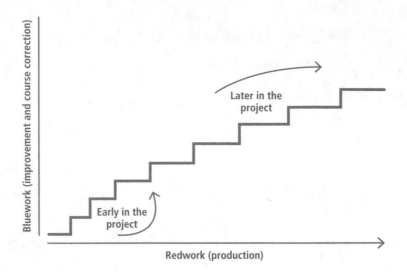

At the beginning of a project, you want shorter redwork periods and more frequent bluework periods to bias toward learning and improving. As the project matures you want to extend the periods between bluework and allow more time in redwork production.

or program or life. It is steep at the beginning and then begins to flatten out, like an arched bridge.

At the same time, the predominant mindset during the life of a project shifts: from an improve-and-grow mindset early, to a prove-and-perform mindset later. Neither mindset is monolithic, but there is a lot of improve and a little prove early, and a lot of prove and a little improve later. Following the end of the project, we then have a larger period of bluework, thinking about improving the project as a whole.

The leader has a role in tuning the redwork-bluework rhythm to appropriately emphasize bluework early, redwork later.

I'm guessing you've probably felt this during a project. Early on, the product can go in a number of different directions—then, later on, you just want to be left alone to finish the work.

Frequent to few, that's when to run the COMPLETE play.

Complete Invites Celebrate

Complete allows us to celebrate. Without a feeling of completing—that phase, that milestone, that project, that product, that quarter—there's just a feeling of continuing and there's nothing to celebrate.

But "Why should I celebrate?" is a question I frequently encounter. "After all, they are only doing their job—they can celebrate when they see their paychecks." People thinking this way are influenced by their Industrial Age structures and language. In the Industrial Age, this was the boss's thought process. Work was transactional, so why would you stop to celebrate your team's work, especially if that would interrupt them from working more?

Done right, celebrate does several things for us—it gives us a sense of accomplishment, allows us to detach from the past and move on to the next thing, and, done right, it reinforces the behaviors that allowed us to be successful.

In today's workplaces, where thinking, creativity, innovation, and decision-making are so important, it would be easy for people to feign that they've done their best—and you as the leader would have no way of knowing. If we want people to be fully invested, we need to reward the behavior we want, and this means celebrating that investment.

At a leadership training event, four executives wearing virtual reality headsets participate in an immersive leadership simulation. OK, it's actually a *submersive* leadership simulation, because they are in a submarine on a rescue mission. Working together, they successfully save the passengers of a sinking ship. But there is no cheering, no clapping, no celebration of any kind in recognition of the team's efforts. As soon as the mission is completed, they simply continue to the next one.

At a large tech company's leadership conference, the CEO makes an announcement: the company has won a major award for quality. The announcement is met with silence. After a moment's pause, the CEO continues on to other matters at hand.

At a small consulting company, an employee texts her boss an idea for a new product, along with some sketches. Her boss, currently traveling on a different continent, quickly texts back, "Great, but what about . . ." and then suggests three improvements for her product. The interaction sputters out shortly thereafter.

At a global tech company, a thirty-two-year veteran who lives, eats, and sleeps for the company is retiring. The company holds the reputation of being a top place to work, with enlightened leadership and founders who care. But the founders left long ago. Through an oversight, HR omits his name from the list of departing employees for the all-hands meeting celebrating company moves. There is no award or certificate of appreciation handed out. In fact, no mention is made of his departure whatsoever. His bosses and colleagues, either clueless or unwilling to interrupt the proceedings, say nothing to fix the problem.

These are just a few examples of the ways we routinely fail to celebrate our accomplishments at work. I'm guessing you have seen examples of "failure to celebrate" as well.

You may be much too courteous and respectful to let a colleague's retirement go by unremarked, but consider how you react in more everyday situations: What is your typical response when someone on your team shows you the work they've done on a project? Is it a pause to observe and celebrate or are you anxious to move on to the next thing?

What gets in the way of celebrating?

Three things.

First, the pause to celebrate takes time away from the production work, reducing efficiency and creating waste. Second, we worry that our team will turn complacent and not be motivated to continue on to the next phase. Third, we don't see the components of the work in chunks, we see it as one long conveyor belt. Hence, we never get to the end of anything, and there is nothing to celebrate because "we're not done yet."

Pausing to celebrate is an interruption to redwork. And what if, during the pause, workers might decide something didn't make sense, or they might get ideas about how to do things differently when they return to redwork? There's no time for that on the factory floor! When leaders operate under the old mentality of obey the clock, coercion, and compliance, participation from their subordinates in the decision-making process might undermine their sense of authority. Hence the relentless sense of urgency on the part of leaders, the drive to constantly obey the clock. No time for thinking or reflection, only doing. What redworkers need is constant exhortation to keep their noses to the grindstone.

In the industrial era, when there was a clear distinction between doers and deciders, this made sense. The cost of managing by metrics, goals, and deadlines, however, is that workers seek to meet only the minimum requirements. Because there is no personal satisfaction in work—because work is already a series of unpleasant tasks to be completed—why go one inch above or beyond what's required? When all you know is redwork, you become expert at predicting exactly how fast you need to go to achieve the bare minimum at the last possible moment. You learn to keep your head down and meet the quota.

As the ratio of bluework to redwork increases for doers and deciders—and as the boundary between both types of jobs continues to blur—this failure to celebrate no longer makes sense. How do you define the minimum effort in bluework or determine whether that minimum has been met? In construction, you can count the bricks in a wall and know the job is done. But how do you know whether an employee has generated enough ideas or insights, or whether they chose to share all the ones they did have?

A pause to celebrate will cost a certain and immediate amount of time out of redwork for the team, and the benefits will be uncertain and in the future. When pressed, the immediate, certain cost supersedes the future uncertain gains. When we pause to celebrate, though, we acknowledge the work we do see, and workers feel valued. Our team feels better about work, and that translates to better engagement, more creative thinking, and reduced turnover. Feeling valued motivates people to contribute, so we set up a positive future. Celebrate validates both bluework and redwork; it's a vital component of a healthy workplace.

How Celebration Affects Behavior

In Aubrey Daniels's book *Bringing Out the Best in People*, he analyzed the structure of what causes behavior changes. He described it this way: ABC.

A = Antecedent. What happens before the behavior.

B = The behavior itself.

C = Consequence of the behavior. This follows the behavior.

What Daniels discovered is that only consequences affect long-term behavior change. Unfortunately, many people, parents, and leaders spend their energy on the antecedents. For example, if we want our child to clean their messy room, we cajole, threaten, manipulate, promise rewards, or use other tactics ahead of the cleaning. It's what happens after they clean their room that matters. If it's just a cursory, "Great, you finally did it," then the behavior will tend toward extinction. That is, the frequency of that behavior will diminish over time. Your child will stop cleaning their room. The same thing will happen at work. If we don't see and recognize the behavior, those good behaviors will also tend toward extinction.

Daniels's work went further. He classified consequences along three dimensions:

- immediate or delayed
- positive or negative
- certain or uncertain

It turns out that immediate, positive, and certain rewards are the most powerful for establishing and maintaining a behavior. This explains, from a neurological level, why smoking is so addictive. The nicotine high that comes after smoking a cigarette is immediate, positive, and certain. Although smokers know logically that smoking increases the risk of cancer, that consequence is delayed, negative, and uncertain.

As leaders, the way to get out of the cajole, manipulate, plead, and hope for certain behaviors game is to focus on immediate, positive, and certain psychological rewards after we observe the behaviors that are useful and effective in the business.

I've seen this firsthand. When I took over as captain of *Santa Fe*, the officers and crew looked like the worst in the fleet. They wore their uniforms sloppily and most did not wear their nametags. Wearing nametags is part of the uniform but feels unnecessary, since of course we know one another's names. Day one at our morning meeting I singled out the one officer who was wearing his nametag and thanked him for it. The next day, several officers wore their nametags. I thanked them. Soon all the officers were not only wearing their nametags, but their uniforms were clean and pressed. Then, like magic, the chiefs (the next level in the hierarchy) started to emulate the officers. And within a month or so, the entire crew was looking professional. Then I would pick something else to recognize (like being proactive and stating intent) and we would change that.

I am naming celebration as the positive consequence your people will experience that will cause them to maintain the good behavior. But celebration is more than a simplistic "good job" comment.

2. Celebrate *With,* Not *For*

Even when an accomplishment isn't ignored or taken for granted, even when there is an acknowledgment, it is usually cursory and followed almost immediately by criticism. I'm sure at some point you've heard, or even said yourself, "Great job! Now here's what I'd change . . ." There are several problems with this kind of typical celebration: It does not rest long enough on the accomplishment. It does not invite the person to tell their story, including any struggles involved, or what they might see as the next steps. It does not unearth any useful observations. It comes from a place of authority rather than collaboration. Finally, the celebration is done *for* someone, not *with* them.

Celebration does not mean "praising." Too many of us have been conditioned—often by our parents—to be external people-pleasers. In fact, traditional praise is unhelpful at work because it is controlling, manipulative, and condescending.

- "Good job."
- "I'm so proud of you!"
- "You've really outdone yourself here."

These are examples of celebrating *for.* The reason these are celebrating *for* is that I am appropriating the good feelings of the celebration (parents do this), and I'm setting myself up as the judge. There's a transference of the reward to us rather than leaving it with the person, such as "I'm so proud of you." I'm appropriating your psychological reward—it is I who feel so proud. That's my good feeling. For the target person, it makes the motivation extrinsic not intrinsic. Instead of having internal joy because of the accomplishment itself, the target person's satisfaction comes from an external source: making their parents or boss happy.

Further, these kinds of remarks assume that a manager or leader has the right to judge. Furthermore, the clear goal of these statements is to increase the frequency of the praised behavior. This is manipulation, and it only encourages a people-pleasing mentality.

To celebrate *with*, not *for*: *appreciate*, don't *evaluate*; *observe*, don't *judge*; and *prize*, don't *praise*.

Celebrating by describing what you have observed and signaling appreciation for the behaviors can sound like this:

- "I see that you've organized the presentation into three sections—I've got your points organized in my head now."
- "It looks like the product will launch on time. Your team has done the coordination with all the departments."
- "I saw that the proposal went out yesterday. Thank you. That will allow the client to look at it before the weekend."

Descriptive statements can start with "I see," "I noticed," and "It looks like."

You can practice this right now. Put the book down and walk around your office or house. Find something that someone else has done and tell them what you've noticed. For instance: "I noticed that the email you sent to the client offered a clear path forward for the project," or "I see you filled the car with gas, which helps me because

I won't have to do it tomorrow morning before the airport run." Be specific and leave judgment and evaluation out. Just describe the action and how that made things better.

Appreciate, don't evaluate. Instead of saying, "You showed great leadership getting your team to deliver on time," say, "I saw you coordinating frequently with your team to deliver on time; it looked like a disciplined delivery process." The first statement presents the person's behavior as being "great leadership"—as evaluated by you. It encourages the individual to try to repeat the same behavior in the same way to earn more of the same praise. It is also an evaluation of them through your eyes and something they have zero control over. The second statement empowers the individual, stimulating learning and risk-embracing behaviors. This statement also labels a behavior—effort—that *is* in their control.

3. Focus on *Behavior,* Not *Characteristics*

Psychologist Carol Dweck found that praising someone for an attribute—"You're so smart" or "You're so talented"—leads them to identify with that attribute. Once it becomes a part of their identity, they tend to avoid scenarios that challenge that attribute. Essentially, it has the opposite effect from what was intended.

In Dweck's landmark study, five-year-old children were asked to complete a puzzle simple enough for all ages to solve. When they succeeded, half were praised for their intrinsic ability to solve puzzles ("You are a good puzzle-solver!") and half were praised for their behavior ("You worked hard to solve that puzzle!"). Then they were asked if they wanted to work on another easy puzzle, like the one they'd just finished, or a more challenging one. Of the group praised for their intrinsic ability, less than half selected the harder puzzle. But among the children praised for hard work, over 90 percent opted for the challenge.

Adults are no different. In short, if we are conditioned to think of ourself as "the smart one," we will avoid challenges that actually test our intelligence and its limits. Of course, taking on such challenges is the only way we can learn and grow. Therefore, the wrong kind of praise becomes stultifying, sapping our willingness to hone our greatest strengths.

As a leader, you need to be conscious about how even positive feedback can have negative consequences if it's delivered improperly. So as a general rule, acknowledge the behavior that is controllable—such as dedication in the face of obstacles, careful review prior to action, inviting others to provide early feedback on an idea—rather than praising someone for an intrinsic characteristic or ability like being a "deep thinker" or "natural leader."

To improve performance, celebrate what people can control—their efforts—and not the things they can't—outcomes. For instance, let's say a team of software developers completes a period of redwork. Instead of saying, "I'm proud you guys got it done," try something like, "It looks like it took difficult cross-department coordination to deliver this product."

When a manufacturing team stops the line because material defects are causing misalignments in a product, don't fall back on phrases like, "Great job stopping the line," or worse, "What is it this time?" Instead, say, "Thank you. Detecting that misalignment and calling for a pause will help us solve the problem properly once and for all."

4. Focus on *Journey,* Not *Destination*

One requirement for stating the observations is that you saw enough of the internal struggles to make the observation.

Typically, parents and coaches often have the benefit of direct observation of the child or client, allowing them to comment on specific behaviors rather than outcomes. In today's workplaces, teams may be distributed, and individuals may work remotely or in different locations. Simply because of the nature of bluework, we may not have a direct line of sight into what the individual did during their period of redwork. So, how do we find out? Well, we ask.

Pausing to celebrate gives us the opportunity to invite the other person to tell their story. Simply paying attention as the individual describes the actions they took—making a phone call, conducting research, collaborating with colleagues—sends a powerful message.

Here are some specific questions to invite someone to tell their story:

- "Tell me what key decisions you needed to make."
- "What were some of the hurdles your team had to overcome?"
- "How did you come up with that idea?"
- "What was the toughest part of this project?"
- "What made this project fun or rewarding?"
- "What were some of the inspirations you used when working on this project?"
- "Tell me more about . . ."
- "How did you overcome that?"

When people are telling their stories, try to detect turning points in the process. Listen for key phrases like "So then we decided to . . ." or "We came to a crossroads" or "We hit a roadblock. The prototype wasn't working, so we . . ." That's your cue to dig deeper and ask further questions, such as:

- "What kind of roadblock was that?"
- "What led to that action?"

- "What happened next?"
- "What worried you?"

Again, start your questions with "what" and "how." Keep them short—make sure to leave room once you've asked your questions in order to open the door to a full response.

It's the Journey

The Biggest Loser is a show that follows sixteen contestants over thirty weeks to see who can lose the most weight. We watch as these people live in a camp where they sweat and starve themselves into a new shape. (The season eight winner lost an astonishing 239 pounds.)

The entire focus is on the endpoint—meeting the goal and being the one who loses the most weight. Even though we see some of the behaviors that result in weight loss and see how the contestants are immersed in a different and supporting environment, the statistic we are updated with is, first and foremost, the weigh-in. It's an entirely redwork exercise coupled with a prove mindset.

At the show's finale, there is a huge celebration. Confetti rains down on the winner in a TV studio, millions cheer along with them, and they get jetted off to New York to meet celebrities.

Sadly, most of them regained the weight. A study in the journal *Obesity* followed up with fourteen of the sixteen contestants from season eight of the show. The season ended in 2009 and the study was published in 2016. Of the fourteen contestants, thirteen gained weight and only one weighed less than when the show ended. Four of them weighed more than when the show started.

What happens after people meet a goal? In general, in business and in life, we *want* to continue the behaviors that resulted in us successfully reaching our goal, but that is not what happens. It turns out that, with this information, we can help other people and ourselves.

When we think of reaching the goal as a journey, and think about the behaviors that allowed us to reach the goal, we are more likely to continue those behaviors with the result that we will continue to maintain our goal, as in body weight. When we think about the goal as the endpoint, a destination, the way the TV show primes us to think about it, and the focus is on the weight number itself, then the likelihood of maintaining the behaviors that resulted in reaching the goal are less likely to be continued. We end up regaining the weight.

Inviting people to tell the story of how they achieved their goal primes people to think about the goal attainment as a mile marker in a greater journey rather than the final milestone. When people think of their achievements in terms of mile markers in a journey, they are more likely to continue the behaviors that resulted in them reaching that goal. This is another lesson from *The Biggest Loser* study.

It is also supported by research.

In a study conducted at the Stanford Graduate School of Business, professors Szu-Chi Huang and Jennifer Aaker followed up with 106 graduates who had completed an executive education program in the African country of Ghana. Immediately following the graduation exercise, participants went through an "exit interview" that was a disguised study intervention. Some were asked to talk about their achievement using a journey metaphor, whereas others talked about their achievement using a destination metaphor. There was also a control group with no metaphor priming. The journey metaphor is what is primed by the "tell your story" approach. The destination metaphor is what is primed by the *Biggest Loser* approach. These interviews were limited to thirty minutes.

Six months later, the researchers concluded that "when executives were guided to describe their attained goal as a journey, they were more likely to continue goal-aligned behaviors." They were more likely to actually have changed some of their company processes to align with successful global business and as taught by the course.

In *The Progress Principle*, Harvard Business School professor Teresa Amabile and researcher Steven Kramer describe research confirming the efficacy of celebrating small wins. They analyzed twelve thousand daily diary entries to determine what drives work satisfaction. One of the key drivers was the reward of completing a task and celebrating its accomplishment. This can't happen if leaders are unwilling to acknowledge and celebrate completion and always respond to accomplishments with, "Great, and here are three things I'd change," before going back to what they were doing.

I call this leadership action "observe and celebrate" because it's so important to pause, say thank you, and signal appreciation before moving on to describing that effort, let alone deciding on next steps or possible improvements.

In another study by the Stanford professors Huang and Aaker, 386 people participated in a 14-day walking program followed by a post-program monitoring period of 3 days. The goal was to walk a total of 100,000 steps over the 14 days. Participants completed a survey which asked them questions about the program using either a journey metaphor or a destination metaphor. As before, thinking about the goal as part of a journey was more effective in helping people continue the behaviors. Those who were primed toward the journey metaphor walked over 50 percent more steps during the additional 3-day monitoring period.

But this study added another variable. They varied the time at which people were primed to think of the program in terms of goal or journey. When the survey came near the end of the program but before the participants had met their goal, the journey metaphor did not have the same effect. This was the "not yet" group, the people who were close to their goal but had "not yet" attained it.

At work, this is the feeling we get near the end of a project where the focus shifts toward completion and the duration of redwork periods relative to bluework periods increases.

For leaders, managing the frequency of the completion play by controlling the length of redwork periods and frequency of the bluework periods allows us to take a proactive approach to controlling the clock. If we have made a thin slice for a commitment and planned the completion of redwork, we have protected ourselves to a large degree against the continued expenditure of time and resources on a losing course of action. We have set the stage for the next period of bluework. This is just another way to think about the CONTROL THE CLOCK play of preplanning the next pause.

Completion gives us not only a sense of accomplishment, but also psychological separation from our previous activity. Closing the books on our previous period of redwork allows us ego detachment from those activities. It also allows us to dedicate cognitive resources that would have been assigned to this project to a different project or a new project altogether. Think of it as rebooting your computer, allowing a clean reset, clearing out unwanted memory, and starting afresh. Having celebrated the previous accomplishment, recalling the journey and behaviors that made us successful, and the ego detachment that comes from the sense of completion all serve as key preconditions for making the next period of redwork better . . . which brings us to the next play: IMPROVE.

TO MOVE FROM CONTINUE TO COMPLETE

1. Chunk work for frequent completes early, few completes late.
2. Celebrate *with*, not *for*.
3. Focus on *behavior*, not *characteristics*.
4. Focus on *journey*, not *destination*.

COMPLETE

Complete marks the end of redwork and is the signal that we go back to bluework. Before we get to the collaboration of bluework, however, we rest and celebrate.

Completion is about a sense of progress and accomplishment. Progress feeds progress. The COMPLETE play also lets us test our hypotheses and the decisions that we've made thus far.

When we celebrate, we want to be careful not to manipulate or to make praise be the purpose of the celebration. The sense of accomplishment should come from the completion of the task itself.

When celebrating, avoid expressions like, "Great, but . . ." because they do not allow enough time for anyone to feel like their efforts were appreciated.

Instead, we need to hear the story behind the achievement. This allows us insight into the behaviors. Without understanding behaviors, we are tempted to praise, not prize, and we are tempted to shortcut our observations toward characteristics rather than the behavior. Praising attributes like intelligence or leadership ability tends to program people toward risk avoidance, when we often want the opposite. Instead, observe the actions, efforts, and behaviors that resulted in the desirable outcomes you're celebrating.

This means that when celebrating we . . .

Focus on *behavior*, not *characteristics*, and

Focus on *journey*, not *destination*.

Executing the COMPLETE play also gives a sense of psychological detachment from our previous actions. This sense of "moving on" and "letting go" enables us to look dispassionately at our past actions and decisions with an eye toward getting better. Executing the COMPLETE play sets us up for the IMPROVE play.

Completing the Cycle: Improve

The team working on *Frozen* was in distress. They'd just conducted a test screening of an early version of the film. The feedback was unsparingly negative. The animated movie, based on Hans Christian Andersen's tale "The Snow Queen," told the story of Elsa, an evil and calculating villain in this version, facing off against Anna, a plucky heroine of no relation. It wasn't working. The creators didn't have much time to diagnose and fix the film, either. Disney had already announced a release date less than eighteen months away.

After assessing all the feedback carefully, Disney's chief creative officer, John Lasseter, paused the clock for the producer and creative team: "You should take as long as you need to find the answers." He didn't say the deadline didn't matter, but by using these words he had called the CONTROL THE CLOCK play. He gave them permission to leave redwork and engage in bluework, which does not respond well to time pressure.

Considering the timeline and the stakes, no one could blame the team for despairing about the situation, getting defensive about the good work they'd already done, or simply becoming paralyzed by indecision. Some teams would be tempted to call the Industrial Age prove play. The prove play is about proving your competence, proving you are a worthy person and deserving of your job and paycheck. The team would explain earnestly why they made the decisions they had made, logically justify why they did what they had done, and waste time rooted in the past, blocking forward progress. Regardless, none of these things would help turn a bad movie into a great one.

The next morning, *Frozen*'s producer, Peter Del Vecho, addressed the team: "Instead of focusing on all the things that aren't working, I want you to think about what could be right. I want you to envision your biggest hopes. If we could do anything, what would you want to see on the screen?" He was not wasting time with the prove play, he was calling the IMPROVE play.

"Does Elsa have to be a villain?"

"What if Elsa and Anna are sisters?"

"What if she is afraid of who she is? And what if she is afraid of hurting the ones she loves?"

Once they had the permission to let go of any anchors to the existing work, the creators became more and more comfortable throwing new ideas into the mix without worrying about stepping on anyone's toes or making more work for themselves. As they considered the idea that Elsa and Anna were sisters, they imagined a three-dimensional character overwhelmed by, or uncertain about, her powers rather than a cardboard villain of a queen doing evil by default. They also rethought the ending, sidestepping the "prince kisses princess and all is well" trope. Freed from the "just get it done" pressure of redwork mode, they were suddenly able to envision a fresh and surprising approach to telling a well-known story.

In this version of *Frozen*, Elsa fears her powers, pushing her younger sister, Anna, away in order to protect her. Anna, energetic but naïve, seeks to restore their sisterly bond, setting up the central conflict. As the new script developed and the themes came together, it became clear that Elsa's journey was all about fear and Anna's was all about love. To explore the sibling dynamic more deeply, the studio invited female employees to share some of their own experiences with their sisters. They even ran a "sister summit" to explore the relationship at the heart of the new script in an attempt to make Elsa and Anna's interactions as credible and relatable as possible.

Once the idea of a villainous Elsa had been abandoned, the songwriters, Robert Lopez and Kristen Anderson-Lopez, saw the opportunity to write her a new showstopper, called "Let It Go," about "a scared girl struggling to control and come to terms with her gift."

Frozen went on to become the top-grossing Disney film of all time. "Let It Go" was a sensation, hitting the *Billboard* charts, selling in the tens of millions, and racking up more than a billion listens online.

Many of the strategies that thawed *Frozen* are components of the IMPROVE play. Improvement—which comes from egoless scrutiny of past actions, and deep reflective thinking about what could be better—is the core purpose of bluework, which is meant to improve redwork. Bluework in isolation is useless. It's relevant only to the extent that it makes redwork better: more efficient, more relevant, more resilient, more responsive. The IMPROVE play requires open-minded inquisitiveness and curiosity from everyone on the team.

Contemplation and self-reflection are key components of learning, creativity, and innovation. But contemplation by itself is not enough. That's why the play is IMPROVE, not contemplate. Remember the story of executive Sue, too long in blue, analyzing data over and over, stuck in endless planning sessions, asking for precise guarantees when none are possible, blocking forward progress. That is why I prefer the IMPROVE play. Improve links the mental activity we do during bluework to the desired outcome—improving redwork.

WHEN TO IMPROVE

To set up the IMPROVE play, we need to relax our minds and remove the pressure of the clock. This is why this play can only be called once we have controlled the clock and called a pause. In production mode, under the pressure of a deadline, it is exceedingly difficult to engage in the inclusive, divergent, diverse, and self-challenging thinking necessary for improvement.

When do we run the IMPROVE play? First, here's when *not* to run it.

Your team is working diligently on a product or project. They are in redwork. As a leader, you will notice potential improvements they could be making while they are in process. You will be tempted to step in and "help"—redirecting focus, adding suggestions and ideas—I mean, how long are you going to let the team work in the wrong direction?

Resist that temptation.

This will lead to redirection, waste, overcontrol of the process, and instability. Instead, maintain your "good ideas" in a log (along with everyone else's) and review them at the next bluework session, once you have taken a deliberate pause. This takes discipline and self-regulation.

W. Edwards Deming, the inventor of the Total Quality Leadership (TQL) program we discussed before, devised an experiment to demonstrate to executives the perils of interfering with the work. Imagine a large funnel on a stand sitting on a table over a target, marked by an X. The objective is to position the funnel such that when you roll a batch of marbles one at a time down the funnel and they drop out the hole at the bottom, they have the tightest possible distribution around the X. The only thing you can control is the position of the funnel. Every marble must be dropped from the edge of the funnel in the same way. (Notice the Industrial Age design objective of reducing variability.)

You launch the first marble. Due to the vagaries of minute imperfections in the marble and funnel it spins down and drops slightly to the right of the X. Do you improve the process by moving the funnel a little bit to the left to compensate?

Even if you move the funnel, each subsequent drop will be off from the X. The result, as you continue to adjust the funnel for these random variations, is to actually increase the distribution of the drops around the X. In other words, your interference degrades the quality of the process by causing a wider dispersion.

What you should do is drop a batch of marbles without moving the funnel. Consider a batch of marbles a batch of redwork. If there is a systematic bias because of a common force (perhaps there's a dent at the bottom of the funnel), then make a single adjustment to counter the bias. Otherwise, leave the funnel in place, positioned directly over the X. The cluster will be smallest, and quality will be highest.

This experiment illustrates the effect of interfering in a process based on small, random variations. Keep it in mind when you are tempted to interfere with your team's redwork process before the batch is completed. Now, the key decision is how many marbles do we drop before we adjust? Too few, and we are interfering with the process; too many, and we live with a systemic error too long.

This brings us back to the importance of the COMPLETE play. If you haven't scheduled the end of the redwork and put the next completion session on the calendar, you will be prone to fretting, worried that the team is not improving and that your good ideas are going to waste. Controlling the clock, scheduling the completion of redwork, and the subsequent IMPROVE play are the activities that allow us to rest easy with the certainty that our ideas will be heard, in time, but at the same time prevent interference with the team while in redwork.

Run the IMPROVE play after a planned end of redwork. You will also want to run the IMPROVE play after a significant error in the process that needs to be understood. In the submarine force, we called these "critiques." They tended to be tough sessions to run because people felt they were, well, being critiqued. And while it's true that their actions were being critiqued, we found that if the team got used to running the IMPROVE play as a matter of routine, whether the last round of redwork went well or badly, then they built up the muscle to be more effective during the critiques.

There might be a bit of this going on in stuck-in-blue Sue's mind. Even before she and the team launch into a redwork period of action and doing, she can think of ways that it will fall short or could be improved. The thing that would help Sue reduce the barrier to action is to view the transition to redwork as simply one step in the learning process that will be repeated—and to realize that until they actually do something, they won't know how good the ideas are.

AIM FOR DISCONTINUOUS IMPROVEMENT

In this vein, I think the term "continuous improvement" does not accurately describe how improvement happens. Improvement happens in batches, in increments, just like the dropping marbles. We have repeated, incremental periods of improvement—the bluework—where we change the process or change the product, like adjusting the funnel over the target. And we follow these with periods of testing and experimentation—the redwork—where we interact with the world and observe the results. The correct image of the improvement process (the learning process) is a stairway, not a ramp.

I have hampered my team with my own eagerness for "continuous improvement." You may have done this yourself. We call people acting this way "good idea fairies" because they appear unexpectedly to offer suggestions for improvement without much regard for how that improvement should be made to the ongoing process. I noticed that I had been acting as a good idea fairy when I launched my team into redwork on a project without specifying the exit from redwork (which would have been as simple as asking, "When will you want to show your first results?"). No expiration date assigned. Soon after the team started, I got a new idea at a conference where I was delivering a speech. This new idea struck me as compelling and urgent, and I thought my team needed to hear it right away. I banged out a note to my team telling them of this tremendous idea.

This was not a singular occurrence. I had a pattern of setting the team off on a mutually agreed course of action, only to then interrupt them with what I thought were helpful ideas and suggestions.

The team did not share my sense of excitement. They felt whipsawed by these ideas. They perceived it as indecision, lack of focus, and confusion. What I should have done was hold all my ideas in a backlog until the next period of bluework, then (after celebrating the progress we had made) look at these ideas with the team, in the context of their own ideas and reflections about the last round of redwork, and let them decide which ones to move forward with.

Scheduling the next period of bluework and the IMPROVE play when we launch into redwork gives us the discipline to hold those ideas in a backlog and surface them when appropriate. This is the idea behind preplanning the next period of bluework in a CONTROL THE CLOCK play and the idea to commit to a thin slice in the next period.

ALL TOGETHER NOW

We've always had the IMPROVE play, but here's the big change: In Industrial Age structures, where we separated work by class—blueworkers and redworkers—the blueworkers were responsible for improvement. They would observe and judge the redworkers. This was the essence of Taylor's work. The redworkers were not asked to evaluate themselves, and the psychological messiness of self-scrutiny was avoided.

When Deming came along with TQL, he suggested, "Hey, let's ask the redworkers what they see and think." This was better, but not enough, because it was ultimately still the blueworker class making decisions about the improvement.

Now we need people to do both redwork and bluework. We are all both redworkers and blueworkers. This requires us to be able to step out of our roles as producers and look back at our production with the dispassionate eye of an improver. This change, where there are no more redworkers and blueworkers but simply people who are engaged in redwork for a time and then bluework for a time, is the tectonic change that is making the old leadership and organizational design models irrelevant.

This is a problem because people are typically attached to their previous work and now we need them to admit it could be done better. We need to help them shift out of their prove mindsets to an improve mindset. We need to leave the prove mindset behind and almost think of ourselves as detached observers of what we have previously done. We call that self that wants to hang on to our previous work, wanting it to be recognized as good, the "be good" self. The "be good" self needs to be tamed in order to activate the "get better" self.

THE "BE GOOD" SELF VS. THE "GET BETTER" SELF

Simply asking people to participate in the IMPROVE play creates a conflict. During this play, we discuss what should be done differently next time.

The damning implication is that, had someone been more foresighted or more competent, it would have been done differently the last time. The improve mindset pits the "be good" self against the "get better" self.

The "be good" self wants to feel competent, effective, credible—a good worker. It wants to protect its reputation, not only among the group but also with itself, in terms of self-esteem. We all have a "be good" self—the part of us that makes us feel good about our work.

Threats to the "be good" self are taken seriously and defended against. People speaking from the perspective of the "be good" self sound like this:

- "I didn't do anything wrong."
- "We did the best we could."
- "I would do it the same next time."
- "I assumed that's what you wanted."
- "We've always done it that way."
- "I've been doing this a long time."
- "You think you know better all of a sudden?"
- "Well, you're new here. You'll learn why we do it like this."

When questioned or even presented with an alternate perspective, the "be good" self goes into defensive mode. Had the *Frozen* team invoked their "be good" selves, they would have defended their existing work.

But we also have a "get better" self. The "get better" self is that part of us that seeks to learn and grow. It is the seeking self. It is intrigued by challenges, is curious about what other people see and think, and has an open desire for learning and improvement. When we embark on exploration and discovery, when we delight in finding a new restaurant, when we compare today's results with yesterday's, we are feeding the "get better" self.

The "be good" self and the "get better" self are not friends. To be effective, the "get better" self must distance itself from previous decisions, beliefs, and knowledge in order to foster learning and growth. If self-worth is tied to past behavior, positive change becomes a form of self-destruction. Since the *Frozen* team invoked their "get better" selves, they were able to see afresh how to improve the movie even though they had been the source of the existing work.

People speaking from the perspective of the "get better" self sound like this:

- "Tell me more about that."
- "How do you see it?"
- "What do you think came before this?"
- "How might we see it differently?"
- "What does this look like from your perspective?"
- "What could we do differently?"
- "How could I have done better?"

The defending behaviors of the "be good" self actively inhibit and crowd out the seeking behaviors of the "get better" self.

To evolve, we need to activate the "get better" self, its behavior set and language. We do this by calming the threat to the "be good" self. We must also play a role in helping the rest of the team lean in the same direction.

Research by Amy Edmondson of the Harvard Business School shows how difficult it is to activate the "get better" self to learn and improve in organizations that do not have a supporting culture. In a 2002 report, she states, "To take action in such situations involves learning behavior, including asking questions, seeking help, experimenting with unproven actions, or seeking feedback. Although these activities are associated with such desired outcomes as innovation and performance, engaging in them carries a risk for the individual of being seen as ignorant, incompetent, or perhaps just disruptive."

People on teams have a choice between protective, "be good" behavior, intended to create an image of effectiveness, and open, "get better" behavior. The risk is being perceived as ignorant or incompetent. If the team as a whole doesn't encourage and reward "get better" behavior, our chances of learning and developing innovative new solutions are diminished. If you recognize a mistake you've made, but no one else notices, it's tempting to stay quiet. You'll probably get away with it.

Edmondson also emphasizes the "iterative trial and reflection" required for learning. The trial she refers to is what we call redwork, the doing, and the reflection is bluework, contemplation. Neither redwork nor bluework alone results in learning. It is the two modes working in concert that drives growth. Framing the upcoming period of redwork as a period of learning rather than a period of achieving actually results in more persistence in the face of obstacles.

A truly free exchange of ideas during contemplation requires people to question the ideas and actions of others as well. In an organization where everyone has embraced the "get better" self, this doesn't create any tension because everyone is grateful for feedback. Unfortunately, this is rarely the case, and, since we all feel the tug of "be good" thinking, we know others feel it as well. Because of this, questioning others is socially taboo. We risk alienation by the group when we do it. Again, being good gets in the way of getting better.

Full participation in an improve session also presents the risk of a loss of autonomy. People worry that admitting to any inadequacies invites the boss to take back control of their job, leaving them with less freedom. Therefore, instead of operating with full transparency, allowing the rest of the team to see into the inner workings of our jobs, divisions, and departments, we tend to reveal things selectively, offering just enough transparency to reassure others that everything is OK and under control.

Our psychological biases cause bad behavior on both sides: Bosses interfere with our jobs if we let them see in. This causes us to hide information so as to avoid future interference and loss of autonomy. When the bosses realize they aren't seeing the full picture, they interfere further, demanding updates and reports, driving employees to be even more opaque than before.

The rhythm of bluework-redwork-bluework is a natural defense against this bad behavior. Knowing that there is an upcoming period of bluework allows the team to hold off on implementing changes until the agreed-upon redwork period is complete. During the next bluework contemplation period, the next batch of "good ideas" can be evaluated, ranked, and decided upon.

How can we motivate our people to adopt the "get better" mindset instead of the "be good" mindset?

OUR THREE EMOTIONAL NEEDS

The separation of the doers from the deciders in traditional Industrial Age hierarchies meant that managers had to use extrinsic motivators to coerce workers into doing work they did not decide to do themselves.

Extrinsic motivation is carrot-and-stick motivation: punishment for poor behavior and reward for good behavior. Extrinsic motivation carries the implicit idea that superiors have earned the right to judge their inferiors.

The "logic" of extrinsic motivation is hardwired into human beings at the most fundamental levels of the brain: harm those who hurt us and reward those who help us. The problem is, this base-level logic isn't effective in a modern workplace. One of the central problems with extrinsic motivation is that it doesn't help people shift to the perspective of the "get better" self, which, as we've seen, is essential to learning and growth.

Once you go beyond simple, physical tasks, people do better when motivated from within. This is because there is so much more to a creative thinking project that we could do. The gap between "good enough" and "awesome" on a creative thinking project is huge, whereas the same gap is small on an assembly line because there is a limited range of expected results from any individual worker.

Intrinsic motivation comes from within. Psychologists Edward Deci and Richard Ryan study the importance of intrinsic motivation in driving healthy human behavior. In their research, Deci and Ryan have identified three fundamental components of intrinsic motivation: competence, relatedness, and autonomy. A growing body of research shows that these are, in fact, fundamental human needs that almost all people feel:

- Competence is the feeling of mastery.
- Relatedness is the sense of connecting with other human beings.
- Autonomy is the sense of being in control of the things that matter in one's life.

Deci and Ryan call it Self-Determination Theory.

Here's why it matters to you. Reflecting openly with your team on how your actions might have been better strikes at the heart of all three of the core human needs underlying intrinsic motivation. Admitting you could have done something better threatens your feeling of competence. Pointing out the errors of others threatens your relatedness to them. Being transparent about what you did and why threatens your autonomy.

Self-Determination Theory explains the importance of intrinsic motivation, but it also explains the power of the "be good" self. It's hardwired into us.

How does it sound when people are trying to meet one of these basic needs during an IMPROVE play?

- "I wasn't trained on that." This externalizes responsibility for a lack of competence.
- "Well, let me explain why I did it like that." This claims mastery of the subject in an attempt to decouple the person's behavior from the negative outcome.
- "Sure, I would have done that, if I'd had enough time . . ." This shifts responsibility for the outcome to a constrained resource, so that one's own competence was not the issue.
- "I know Joe did his best, but . . ." This defends Joe's competence in order to protect one's own relatedness.
- "I think everyone did their best—I like to see the positive." This is an attempt to avoid criticizing others to protect relatedness. We can see others in a positive light without requiring perfection. In fact, if people needed to be perfect before we could think positively about them, we'd have quite a problem.
- "Don't worry about it. We have it under control." This uses vagueness to protect autonomy.
- "All the client needs to know is that we are taking care of it." Again, this is a bid to use vagueness to defend job autonomy.

IT'S MY LIFE

Ultimately, the purpose of learning and innovation is behavior change. If there is no intention of doing anything differently in the future, you can save yourself the mental heavy lifting of learning something new.

A sense of control, which is perceived by people as autonomy or freedom, is positively correlated with innovation, creativity, and learning. Teresa Amabile of the Harvard Business School studied innovation in organizations, looking at both individual and cultural factors that inhibit or promote creativity.

In her research, Amabile found that the number one organizational factor driving innovation is "freedom in deciding what to do or how to accomplish the task, a sense of control over one's own working ideas." In other words, employees with the autonomy to decide how to go about solving problems and achieving goals innovate. Those constrained to operate as their superiors instruct do not.

It makes sense that freedom is closely linked to innovation. First, without the power to change anything, the motivation to develop improvements is removed. Second, environments that lack freedom, in which people are consistently told what to do and how to do it, do not challenge and strengthen anyone's creative thinking. Without autonomy, growth stalls.

The team working on *Frozen* engaged because they were writing the story and they believed their new story would be accepted. If they thought management was going to make a decision about the movie independent of whatever they came up with, the discretionary effort they put into that tough IMPROVE play would have been reduced.

Asda is the second-largest supermarket chain in the UK. In the early 2000s, managers were trying to understand absence rates on the shop floors. These absences were unpredictable and disruptive to the team and production. Conversations with employees revealed that many of the absences were caused when employees were called off to care for sick children or relatives.

The existing plan for shift scheduling was controlled by supervisors who determined who got what shift and when. This determination gave those supervisors power over the shift workers. When it was suggested that the shift workers could self-organize their own schedules, including getting substitutes if needed, these supervisors resisted the plan. After all, it meant a loss of power for them.

Asda persisted with the experiment and it worked. Work absences were reduced and the flexible work practices became part of Asda's culture. They branded it "shift swap." Shift performance improved, workers were happier, and supervisors could focus on other matters. Win-win-win.

OVERCOMING LEARNED HELPLESSNESS

The complaint I hear most often from leaders is that they try giving their people control but their people "don't want it."

There could be many reasons for this, including cultural safety, the size of the change, and prior experience making decisions. But it seems to me that there is a link between our history of command and control leadership—separating workers into tellers and those who are told—that has conditioned many people into believing that resistance is futile. Their early efforts to bring up good ideas and suggestions were ignored. They learned that they were helpless in the workplace.

This is a psychological phenomenon called "learned helplessness," and it was first demonstrated by a pair of psychologists. In one disconcerting study, Martin Seligman and Steven Maier subjected dogs to a series of shocks in various conditions. In some cases, the dog could escape the shock by taking some action. In some cases, the dog could not escape the shock no matter what action it took.

Seligman and Maier observed that the dogs that could not escape the shocks eventually became resigned to their lot in life and lay down and whined. And here's the most appalling part: later, even when they were given a way to escape the shock, they did not. They had learned that they were helpless.

Humans are the same way. If we have no control over our ability to improve, then we learn that any effort to improve is futile and a waste of time. We even resist encouragement to improve when we don't feel we have control, because we know it is just lip service.

Can we teach people to "unlearn" learned helplessness?

Seligman's contribution to science wasn't just about discovering learned helplessness but how to cure it—he's the father of positive psychology. Seligman and Maier discovered a correlation between how thinking about the same event in two different people can cause the depression that comes with learned helplessness in one and not in the other.

The people who tended toward depression thought about negative events as permanent, personal, and pervasive. They were always going to happen, they were happening "to me," and they would happen in any situation. People who thought in terms of temporary, impersonal, and limited tended not to sink into depression. Their approach could be summarized as "This too shall pass" and "It has nothing to do with me."

What can you do as the leader to help your people overcome this trap?

HOW TO IMPROVE

Here are four ways to execute the IMPROVE play.

FOR THE IMPROVE PLAY, USE LANGUAGE THAT INVITES A MENTAL FOCUS THAT IS:

1. Forward, not backward.
2. Outward, not inward.
3. On the process, not on the person.
4. On achieving excellence, not avoiding errors.

1. Forward, Not Backward

There is a strong link between believing we can grow and having control over our behaviors. This is key to invoking the "get better" self. This is why we focus forward during the IMPROVE play.

We can activate this with questions like:

- "What do we want to do differently next time?"
- "How should we change the process during our next redwork period?"
- "What worked well that we want to keep and not change?"
- "If you could go back in time on this, what would you tell yourself?"
- "What do we want to remember about this for next time?"

2. Outward, Not Inward

Focusing on others instead of oneself is another way to short-circuit our instinctive desire to protect ourselves and others on the team from being told how something might have been done better. Here are some phrases that establish a focus on others:

- "If someone else had to take over this project, what would you say to them to make it even more successful?"
- "What changes would the board want us to make here?"
- "What could we do to better serve our customers?"

Finally, the right language can encourage a sense of ongoing improvement, recasting the team's perspective from one of avoiding errors to one of achieving excellence:

- "Let's focus on what's going right here that we can build on."

This is exactly what Peter Del Vecho was doing when he asked *Frozen*'s creators not to focus on what wasn't working but instead to think about "what could be right" and go from there. This helped them adopt the necessary mindset for genuine innovation.

3. Process, Not People

A process focus also dilutes the motivation to get defensive about what was done in the past. It shifts attention from the person to the person's decision or action. Here are phrases that establish a process focus:

- "Thinking about the work itself, what do we think could be improved?"
- "How could this be done better?"
- "What improvements could we make to the process?"

4. Achieve Excellence, Not Avoid Errors

Avoiding errors in organizations results in a bias for inactivity and roots us in the "be good" self. The best way to avoid errors is to avoid actions and decisions. No action, no error. Further, avoiding errors is not an inspiring motivator. Few people are inspired by the negative goal of being less bad at something than before. But people are inspired and moved by the possibility of achieving something great, something excellent.

When pitting the "get better" self against the "be good" self, sometimes the weak motivation to simply not be as bad as before is not powerful enough to overcome the hold of the "be good" self. What we need is the powerful motivation afforded by the possibility of achieving something truly special. Think about the motivations of the Disney team working on *Frozen*.

USING THE TIMELINE AS A TOOL

One of the basic tools for the IMPROVE play is to start with what happened. If there has been a significant operational error, then the IMPROVE play becomes a more formal organizational learning event.

Create a timeline. The most basic timeline is the redwork timeline. For *El Faro*, some of the entries might look like this:

- Day/time. Departed Jacksonville.
- Day/time. Tropical Storm Joaquin upgraded to Category 1 hurricane.
- Day/time. Came right to course 120. Proceeded toward Puerto Rico along the Atlantic route.
- Day/time. Encountered twenty-foot seas.
- Day/time. Helmsman having trouble maintaining ship on course. Disabled steering alarm.
- Day/time. Lube oil system shutdown.

When we write redwork, descriptive timelines, we refer to people by the roles they played, not their names. Another way to think about it is this is the timeline of the redwork and the physical conditions around us.

The next-level timeline is the bluework timeline. The bluework timeline identifies key decisions and who made them. This is a timeline of the results of the bluework, decisions made, hypotheses formed.

- Day/time. Received weather update of a tropical storm in the Atlantic. Captain decided to take the direct Atlantic route from Jacksonville to Puerto Rico.
- Day/time. Chief engineer recommended getting under way with the following material degradations to the propulsion plant: lube oil level low but within tolerance.
- Day/time. Tropical Storm Joaquin upgraded to Category 1 hurricane. Captain decided to continue the Atlantic route.
- Day/time. Passed Rum Cay cutoff point. Captain directed the ship to continue the Atlantic route.
- Day/time. Captain ordered abandon ship.

Sometimes teams have a hard time identifying the decision-maker or they get squeamish about doing it. If the team can't identify who made what decision, that is usually a symptom of unclear ownership roles and muddled decision-making.

Squeamishness about who made what decision is a symptom of low psychological safety and how the organization deals with errors. In an organization that blames people, there will be a reluctance to be identified as the decision-maker. Worse, there will be a reluctance to actually make decisions. In organizations that view the decisions of the people in the organization as the natural outcome of the incentives provided, it will feel less threatening to identify the decision-maker. Still, we refer to position, not person.

Decisions are made by individuals, not teams. Businesses need to be able to move quickly, make bold decisions (hypotheses), and test them. Not everyone will be "on board" with every decision. That's OK. Trying to convince every dissenter that the decision is right gives too much power to those positions to stop progress. It will invite more obstructionism because of the power and attention it brings. It is critical, however, that each person feels as if they were able to freely voice their opinion, and that it was honestly and respectfully considered in the decision-making process.

The final-level timeline is an internal bluework timeline; it describes how the decisions were made. Here's what I would have hoped for as an entry in the *El Faro* timeline:

- Day/time. Received weather update that Tropical Storm Joaquim upgraded to Category 1 hurricane. Assembled the ship's officers to determine which route to take: the Atlantic route or the Old Bahama Channel. Team was split, with the chief engineer and second mate favoring the Old Bahama Channel. Captain decided to take the Atlantic route. Second decision point determined to be at the Rum Cay cutoff point. Expect to reach that position at midnight.

THINKING AS A TEAM

Is all this effort to run a proper IMPROVE play as a team while fending off "be good" thinking even worth it? Can groups truly be smarter than people? Yes, under the right circumstances. To engage in bluework with others, we must all know what each of us knows and all see what we each of us sees. Recall from chapter 4 the game of guessing the weight of the ox conducted by James Galton and told in James Surowiecki's book *The Wisdom of Crowds*. Surowiecki explores various cases when the crowd gets it wrong and when the crowd can consistently be better than almost every individual within the group. Those ideal conditions for thinking in groups include diversity of thought and independent judgment. If you use the right language to establish these conditions for a team, it can often make smarter decisions than any of its members could do alone. By the way, this is also why "vote first, then discuss" is such an important tool to effective bluework.

Let's look at *El Faro* in light of this. Remember when the third mate called the captain before midnight? His language was halting, hesitant, and self-negating. By this point, he was already handicapped because the transit to the intermediate Rum Cay cutoff point had not been framed as a learning activity. Thus, he was confronting all the social norms that prevent people from speaking up when they believe a mistake has been made. Calling it out would threaten the third mate's feeling of relatedness to the captain.

Again, after midnight, when the second mate called the captain, she was handicapped by the same fears. If only one of the officers had exhibited deferential behavior, we would explain it as unique to that individual. Since it was consistent among multiple officers, we need to look closely at the environment established by the captain.

The passage to Puerto Rico was not framed as a learning opportunity, so the team was not primed to collect relevant information for the Rum Cay cutoff decision or to contemplate their current course of action. This does not mean they didn't engage in any contemplation. Only that if they did, it was in spite of the organizational setup, not because of it.

STUDY OF PILOTS SHOWS IT'S ALL TRUE

Researchers at ETH Zürich (the Federal Institute of Technology, Zürich) conducted a study of 1,751 airline cockpit and crew members where they were asked to think of a situation where they did not speak up about a safety-relevant issue and the reason. One captain who'd chosen not to correct a subordinate said, "Sometimes it's hard to know when you are a colleague and when you are the boss. I generally have a trustful and open relationship with my first officers, and I don't want to be the 'four stripes knows it all' type of captain."

This statement is all about defending relatedness. Relatedness is the sense of connecting with other human beings. It is the most frequent cause cited by captains for not speaking up. In fact, relatedness tied into 77 percent of the cases where captains remained silent despite their better judgment.

Meanwhile, a first officer explained why he kept quiet after a captain's mistake by saying, "Yes, we have flat hierarchies in the cockpit, and they all say that we should speak up. But at the same time, many send subtle signals that they don't really want to hear what one has to say."

Of the junior officers, 11 percent didn't speak up when necessary because of power gradient issues. The more junior the person, the greater the power gradient, the stronger the effect: 40 percent of flight attendants cited power gradient as a factor.

In no case did a captain stay quiet because of power gradient issues. Similarly, in no case did a captain stay quiet because of fear of punishment. Meanwhile, that fear played a role with 81 percent of flight attendants. The reason for the disparity is simple: punishment runs down the power gradient, not up.

The researchers used "feelings of futility" as a category of reason for not speaking up. Again, while no captains cited feelings of futility, first officers pointed to this in 33 percent of cases and flight attendants in 51 percent. Feelings of futility map to autonomy and control. In other words: Does it even matter if I speak up? It won't make a difference anyway.

One flight attendant reported: "You know, oftentimes, you are considered a bimbo. It is hard to speak up when you feel you have so little power. I don't even try anymore." Another said, "Of course I know I should always say something—they tell you in training and in every briefing. But when it comes down to it, they either don't want to hear it or think we are 'chicken hearts' and simply laugh at us. I've given up." Clearly, this is not an issue with training or protocol. Every explicit rule allows for correction, but that invisible power gradient still stands in the way of the right action.

A LESSON FROM AGILE MANAGEMENT

As introduced in chapter 2, Agile management practices have a built-in structure that allows for the redwork-bluework rhythm. The end of the cycle includes a retrospective, which is a discussion on how the team could have worked together better. It is an IMPROVE session. Because the doers are the deciders in Agile, this practice pits the "get better" self against the "be good" self. One of the Agile practices to help tame the "be good" self is the reading of the "Prime Directive" at the beginning of these retrospective sessions. Here it is:

> Regardless of what we discover, we understand and truly be-
> lieve that everyone did the best job they could, given what they
> knew at the time, their skills and abilities, the resources avail-
> able, and the situation at hand.
>
> —NORM KERTH, *PROJECT RETROSPECTIVES:*
> *A HANDBOOK FOR TEAM REVIEW*

The purpose of the Prime Directive is to allow the "get better" self primacy over the "be good" self. It makes a retrospective become an effective team gathering to learn and find solutions to improve the way of working.

Sometimes teams recite this, sometimes it is read, sometimes it is posted on the wall. Regardless, the idea is to focus on the future, accept that everyone did their best at the time, but also recognize that there is room for improvement and that our collective intent is to improve. It helps to remind us that there should be an assumption of good intent.

TO MOVE FROM PROVE TO IMPROVE, FOCUS . . .

1. Forward, not backward.
2. Outward, not inward.
3. On the process, not on the person.
4. On achieving excellence, not avoiding errors.

IMPROVE

Improve is a specific play as well as the objective of the redwork-bluework operating system.

Improve is about reflecting on what we've done and making it one better.

Improve pits the "get better" self against the "be good" self. The desire of the "be good" self to defend itself will crowd out efforts to get better. In order to open ourselves for improvement we need to tame the fears of the "be good" self.

Improve happens through collaboration. The output of the IMPROVE play is the next hypothesis to test. Improve sets us up to commit and launches us back into redwork.

The Enabling Play: Connect

Deep beneath the ocean floor, you can find oil, under crushingly high pressure. Extracting it requires serious engineering. It is tough, exacting, and dangerous work.

On the oil rig *Deepwater Horizon*, based in the Gulf of Mexico, workers were preparing the well for pumping. This is not an easy feat. Preventing the pressurized oil from coming up the pipe in an uncontrolled way is a sort of cap: a column of viscous fluid known in the industry as "mud." In order to pump oil, the mud needs to be flushed out and replaced with seawater. The challenge during this part of the operation is that the mud is heavy—it has to be in order to hold all that pressurized oil down. Seawater by itself isn't heavy enough to keep that pressure contained.

If the flushing process doesn't go off properly, oil and highly pressurized gas bubbles start to rise up the well. This displaces seawater and any remaining mud, further reducing the pressure holding the oil down and making the problem worse. As the pressure drops, the gas bubbles expand by a factor of three hundred, further exacerbating the problem. Eventually, the oil and gas erupt from the top of the well with catastrophic consequences.

This is called a "kick."

Oil workers know about kicks and take steps to avoid them. One preventative measure is a blowout preventer installed on the seabed floor. This is a $50 million, five-story-tall valve that can seal the well if there's a problem. If the process of preparing the well goes awry for any reason, inflatable tubes create a soft seal to give workers a chance to rectify the problem. If the tubes don't do the job, the blowout preventer is capable of cutting the well pipe. This emergency disconnect switch, or EDS, is a more permanent solution, used only as a last resort. Activating the blowout preventer on an oil rig is called "EDSing."

During a kick, the well must be sealed *before* the oil and gas mixture rises above the blowout preventer. Once engaged, the safety valve will stop further feeding of the fire, but any gas and oil that has already passed through will reach the surface. Again, with catastrophic results.

On the twentieth of April 2010, aboard the drilling station *Deepwater Horizon*, workers were preparing the well to allow the drill rig to be removed and a cheaper pumping rig to be attached. For this procedure, tests are conducted to ensure the integrity of the well below the floor of the ocean. These tests convinced the operators that it was safe to start replacing the mud with seawater.

As the mud comes up the well during this process, its volume should roughly match the volume of seawater being pumped down to replace it. If at any time the volume of mud exceeds the volume of seawater, you may have a kick on your hands. That's exactly what happened next aboard *Deepwater Horizon*. Measurements indicated that too much mud was coming up the well. The oil and gas had overcome the weight of mud and seawater above it and had begun rising uncontrollably. Alarms started going off. Operators activated the temporary seals, but they weren't strong enough to stave off the pressure.

Time for the EDS, right? But no one activated it.

When the mixture of oil and gas reached the oil platform, it erupted from the well head. For nine minutes, combustible hydrocarbons roared onto the rig. No general alarm was sounded. Finally, when the concentration of gas was high enough to explode, it readily found an ignition source. The oil platform was immediately engulfed in flames.

According to the US government report on the disaster, here's what happened next:

> By now, [one of the Transocean executives] began to wonder why the derrick was still roaring with flames. Hadn't the blowout preventer been activated, sealing off the well and thus cutting off fuel for the conflagration? He headed to the bridge. [The captain] said, "We've got no power, we've got no water, no emergency generator."
>
> [The chief engineer] was still at his station on the bridge and he noticed . . . [one of the operators], standing next to the panel with the emergency disconnect switch (EDS) to the blowout preventer.
>
> [The chief engineer] hollered to [the operator]: "Have you EDSed?"
>
> [The operator] replied he needed permission. [The chief engineer] asked [the Transocean executive] was it OK and the executive said yes.
>
> Somebody on the bridge yelled, "He cannot EDS without the OIM's [offshore installation manager's] approval."
>
> [The senior Transocean rig operator], still dazed, somewhat blinded and deafened, had also made it to the bridge, as had BP's [senior executive].
>
> With the rig still "latched" to the Macondo well, [the senior Transocean rig operator] was in charge.

[The chief engineer] yelled, "Can we EDS?" and [the senior Transocean rig operator] yelled back, "Yes, EDS, EDS."

[The operator] opened the clear door covering the panel and pushed the button.

[The chief engineer]: "I need confirmation that we have EDSed."

[The operator]: "Yes, we've EDSed."

[The chief engineer]: "[Operator], I need confirmation again. Have we EDSed?"

[The operator]: "Yes."

It's unclear why nine minutes passed before this conversation finally took place. Either way, when it was activated, the blowout preventer did not operate properly and failed to seal the well. The subsequent investigation revealed problems with the assembly and maintenance of the device, including dead batteries and mis-wired coils. The delay in attempting to seal the well may have been a contributing factor to the disaster.

With the well unsealed, the oil and gas mixture was able to flow rapidly to the platform, feeding the existing fire. Eleven people died. Over the next four hundred days, 5 million barrels of oil spilled into the Gulf of Mexico, making the *Deepwater Horizon* oil spill one of the worst environmental disasters in history.

Here's the question at the heart of this chapter: How is it that a person could be more afraid of pushing a button without permission than dying in a fiery explosion?

HIERARCHY FIRST

A lot of organizations say "safety first," but the actions of people, such as this crew, reveal that it's really "hierarchy first."

Never underestimate the power of fear to distort common sense in environments with a strong culture of control and compliance. When the organization strictly and repeatedly enforces the idea that people should do as they're told without question or suffer serious consequences, they learn to be absolutely certain that each action is correct before taking it. A suffocating layer of doubt begins to inhibit any proactive behavior.

On a fiery oil rig, an engineer delays taking action.

At the Oscars, Mr. Beatty does not call time-out.

On *El Faro*, the officers continue into the storm.

The point is that they *knew* there was a problem, but the power of hierarchy suppressed the needed action.

On *El Faro*, the officers *knew* they were headed into a hurricane. With their lives on the line, they had the ability to alter course by ordering the helmsman to make a turn. Instead, they suggested the turn to the captain, communicating in a way that was strained, self-deprecating, and ambiguous. If the situation was dire and the need to change plans immediate and pressing, why were communications to the captain so unclear and unconvincing? And this was after the captain told them "not to hesitate" to call him or take action.

What was it about these cultures that prevented action when needed, decisions by the people who knew the issues, and open and direct communication about serious threats?

Again, fear, steep power gradients, and an absence of psychological safety.

The CONNECT play is the antidote to fear. Connect makes it safe to say what we see and think, even if no one else sees or thinks the way we do, even if we are not 99 percent sure that we're correct. Connect creates cultural conditions that encourage diversity of thought and variability of opinion. Connect is what allows us to move from paralysis to action. Connect is the key to effective bluework, effective decision-making—but it is also what moves us from thought to action, so connect also underpins our ability to get stuff done in redwork.

But connect is not in our Industrial Age playbook. Conform is our Industrial Age play. We conform to our roles. I'm the manager; you're the employee. You're the captain; I'm the crew. I'm the parent; you're the child. You're the teacher; I'm the student. We don't necessarily sever connections, but simply avoid and discourage them to begin with. In an environment where we have blueworkers and redworkers, bosses and workers, connection is seen not only as unnecessary, but unwanted. Instead, conform most of all to your position in the hierarchy. If you are in the subordinate position, be a good team player, don't rock the boat, don't bring up the elephant in the room, don't challenge a decision made by the boss. If you are in the superior position, distance yourself emotionally, maintain a detached relationship, use your position and power to coerce people to *do* things.

Bosses of the Industrial Age wanted sterile workplaces devoid of emotions. The manager's only job was to get the workers to do what management had decided they should do. It meant coercing and controlling people and getting them to comply. We don't use those words today, of course. We say things like "motivate" or "inspire." But what we mean is manipulate and coerce.

If you are deciding what others should do, you have to maintain a certain distance from them; connection is counterproductive. The navy is one of many highly structured and hierarchical work environments with strict rules against fraternization. The goal of this rule is to prevent friendship from coloring decisions about work assignments and promotions.

This is another problem for Fred, whose team is stuck in red, and why work feels empty and unsatisfying. He works in a place that has separated redworkers from blueworkers. As the leader, the blueworker, it's his job to get the redworkers to do tasks that Fred has decided on, not the redworkers. This leads him into the Industrial Age play of coercion. Since he will be engaged in that, it will sure be better if he remains aloof from the workers. Better not to get to know them too well. What Fred does all day long is to deny his humanity in order to conform to his role. No wonder he gets home depleted.

Connection had no place in the Industrial Age. After all, you only need emotions if you need your people to think, to make decisions, and to take action—like sealing a well during a life-threatening emergency.

The CONNECT play is about caring—caring what people think, caring how they feel, caring for their personal goals. Instead of judging from a position of power, we walk alongside from a position of encouragement. This does not mean accepting whatever the person thinks or does. It does not mean shielding them from the consequences of their own behavior, but it does mean removing unnecessary and artificially induced workplace inhibitors to feeling safe. People will not feel cared for if they do not feel safe. People can't strive for stretch goals or feel free to say what they think.

When organizations talk "safety first," they generally mean physical safety of workers and equipment, but the path to making a safer workplace is by allowing everyone to see, think, and be free to state differing observations and dissenting opinions. This psychological safety is not created by suppressing challenging statements, differing opinions, and uncomfortable viewpoints, but is designed deliberately to encourage such statements and the ensuing discussions. Safety comes from a culture of cherishing and valuing differing opinions, not judging, shunning, or avoiding them.

There are four options for executing the CONNECT play.

CONNECT IS ABOUT CARING. TO DO THIS:

1. Flatten the power gradient.
2. Admit you don't know.
3. Be vulnerable.
4. Trust first.

Connect is a special play in that it does not fit into the sequence of the blue-red-blue cycle. Rather, it is an underlying basic building block that enables all the other plays. The behaviors that support some of the earlier plays help with connect, like observing and celebrating, and inviting colleagues to tell their story. Others are strongly enabled by connect, like creating the feeling of safety that allows everyone to speak up and to let go of the "be good" self.

The Industrial Age imperative to conform to our defined roles and responsibilities presents such a major obstacle to running the other plays we have discussed up to this point that connecting is the necessary antidote. Connect allows us to be more effective at controlling the clock, collaborating, committing, completing, and improving. In turn, all of the other plays help establish a culture of connection.

1. Flatten the Power Gradient

One of the simple ways to think about connect is through the power gradient. The power gradient is the amount of social distance there is between one person and another. Remember the aircrew safety study in which 40 percent of flight attendants and 11 percent of junior officers did not speak up because of power gradient issues. The steeper the power gradient, the harder it is to tell your boss something they don't want to hear.

This social distance is difficult to measure, but it can always be felt.

Here are several proxies to measure the steepness of the power gradient: salary or pay rate, office size, carpet thickness, physical separation such as reserved parking spots and private dining rooms, access to particular people and inclusion in particular meetings, stripes on sleeves, seating location (distance from the top boss), number and attractiveness of assistants (male or female), amount of talk time allocated, tolerance of tardiness, and whether people laugh at dumb jokes.

But some of the proxies of a steep power gradient are more subtle, and they show up a lot in meetings, from whether the meeting doesn't start until the most senior person shows up, to who chairs the meeting, who sums up the discussion, and who allocates actions. Even who we look at. At something as mundane as a team huddle, does the person speaking look at and talk to the team, or do they look at the "boss." The Industrial Age playbook determines that things like task assignment and the right to ask provocative questions are assigned to the senior leader. An interesting ritual to help understand power gradient is to observe how people interact with a senior executive the day before and the day after that person has been selected to be the next CEO.

There are some boundaries where power gradient is particularly acute: doctor to nurse, partner to non-partner, political appointee to government employee, pilot to cabin crew, owner to employee. If your boss makes a lot more money than you, then you are more likely to feel a steeper power gradient than if you both make about the same amount of money.

Here's the rule with power gradients: the censoring of information is directly proportionate to the power gradient. Have a steep power gradient and employees will carefully censor their communications to the boss. They will edit out bad news, draft and reword emails, and stay silent when the boss has suggested an idea, whether they think it is a good one or not. They will invoke the prove self.

In steep power gradients we are also limited to "one step at a time" communications—where "jumping the chain of command" is a social and hierarchical no-no. Case in point, in the 2003 space shuttle *Columbia* disaster,* people did speak up, but leaders (who were convinced that they had created a culture of openness following the 1986 space shuttle *Challenger* disaster†) did not act. In fact, when Rodney Rocha, who led the Debris Assessment Team, was asked why he had drafted, but not sent, an email that challenged the leaders' decisions not to investigate the damage the *Columbia* had sustained on launch and which was to prove fatal, he said that he did not want to jump the chain of command. Having already raised the need to have the orbiter imaged, he would defer to management's judgment on obtaining imagery. One rung at a time.

This common mistake in organizations comes from treating all communications, orders, and information in the same way. Ideally, orders should follow the chain of command, but information should be able to flow freely throughout the organization.

A flatter power gradient results in less censoring because it feels safer. Employees in flatter hierarchies will speak truth to power, tell it like it is, admit mistakes, and deliver bad news; they will be able to tame the "be good" self in order to embrace the "get better" self. Now, since a power gradient manifests primarily as a feeling, it is possible for people who have significantly more power than you to make you feel valued and relatively equal, thereby making it easier for you to speak up. As leaders, we need to be sensitive to the power gradient and take deliberate steps to flatten it.

---

* The *Columbia* broke up upon reentry in 2003 because a piece of falling insulation during launch had damaged the wing.

† The *Challenger* blew apart upon launch in 1986 because one of the booster rockets burned through a seal.

Note that I said "relatively" equal. I am not advocating a perfectly flat power gradient. Even if it were possible to achieve one (which I have never seen despite claims that they exist), a flat power gradient invites unnecessary ambiguity. People get confused about who has what decision rights, and in the absence of clear guardrails, the normal behavior is to play it safe, not to push boundaries.

I think about it like a river I'd like to canoe on, out and back. If the river is too steep you have heavy rapids, capsizing your canoe and preventing upward movement. Too flat, and you have stagnant water, with no clear sense of direction. And it stinks. What you want is gently flowing water. It's clear what direction the water is flowing, but it is not so fast that you can't paddle upstream.

While flat power gradients pose their own challenges, what we encounter much more often in companies is steep power gradients. If your position gives you more authority or power, then invoking the CONNECT play means flattening the power gradient with those below you.

In the Taylor management world, where the separation of doers and deciders was a deliberate goal, the power gradient was reinforced through various means. Physical separation, executive dining rooms, reserved parking spots, different attire and hard hat colors. Removing such trappings is a good first step to flattening the power gradient.

In 2005, the Royal Bank of Scotland opened its new headquarters at Gogarburn outside Edinburgh, Scotland. The HQ featured an extensive executive suite, which became known as the "torture chamber." Getting inside the RBS executive wing used to be extremely difficult, even for those who had enjoyed a long career at the bank. Security guards were placed outside the entrance under strict instructions to admit only the top executives (physical separation). CEO Fred Goodwin's penthouse-style office on the top level was a staggering twenty meters long (office size).

Within three years, RBS faced collapse and survived only because of a £45 billion bailout by the UK government. Ask any middle manager who worked at Gogarburn during that time and they will tell you that everyone knew the bank was overstretched, long before it needed a bailout. But of course, with such a steep power gradient, no matter how many people doubted the strategy, they were never going to be heard.

Happily, the executive suite has now been converted into a hub for business start-ups.

Share of voice is also a proxy for power gradient. As we saw in the *El Faro* transcript, in every conversation the captain had, he spoke more words than the other person. Then there was a steep drop-off from the ship's officer to the seaman. In one case, the third person on the bridge, an able seaman first class, said only three words in a two-hour period while the captain and ship's officer were talking.

The rules for children in some houses—don't speak unless spoken to, and be seen, not heard—had now been applied to the professional team of adults operating a multimillion-dollar ship.

You may have attended a brainstorming workshop where the facilitator or leader announced that "there would be no rank" in the workshop, that everyone would go by their first names, and that ideas would be evaluated based on their merit and not their source. These practices are a recognition that a steep power gradient is detrimental to the thinking part of work, and they are meant to counteract power gradients that may have built up.

However, these are Band-Aid approaches and probably feel artificial and temporary. A better approach is to consistently flatten the power gradient during routine work processes.

Power gradients are sometimes bluntly enforced, reminding people (as if they needed reminding) that bosses are in a more powerful position than they are. This sounds like:

- "I'm the boss here."
- "It's my decision."
- "It's my company."

Emphasizing one's qualifications or duration of experience is also a way of reinforcing the power gradient.

- "I've been doing this longer than you."
- "I have a degree from a prestigious school."
- "I am a certified technician."

Such statements have the effect of reducing diversity of thinking, reducing variability. Variability is an ally to bluework, so reducing it impairs our team's ability to do bluework.

Another steep power gradient move is to invoke another authority. Within the organization this sounds like:

- "The boss said do it. I'm just the messenger."
- "I'm just enforcing the rules here."
- "It's our policy."

Again, the effect is to reduce variability of opinion, thinking, decision-making, responsibility, and a feeling of ownership. It dehumanizes us.

Instead of reinforcing the power gradient, flatten the power gradient. Here are some ways to do that:

- Instead of creating separation, whether physical or emotional, create connection.
- Instead of doing things *to* or *for* people, do things *with* people.

- Instead of reinforcing authority, reduce it.
- Instead of judging, observe and describe.

For example, instead of saying:

- "I need you to make a decision." (Decision assigned *to.*)
- "I need you to do this." (Decision made *for.*)

Try:

- "We need to decide about this." (Decision-making *with.*)

Another example, from parenting. Instead of:

- "If you don't get your shoes tied . . ." (Threatening to do *to.*)
- "Here, I'll tie your shoes." (Doing *for.*)

Try:

- "Let's get your shoes tied so we can go." (Doing *with.*)

Celebration is an area where I see people, often parents, falling into the *to* or *for* pattern and reinforcing power gradients. For example, instead of:

- "I'm so proud of you." (This is a *to* pattern.)

Try:

- "I saw you skipped the party to work diligently on that project."
- "I bet it feels good to have that exam over with!"

When it comes to reducing rather than reinforcing authority, here are some examples. Instead of:

- "Look, I'm a certified master black belt. What are your qualifications?"
- "I've been doing this for twenty-five years. How long have you been doing this?"

Try:

- "Your opinion matters here."
- "Your fresh eyes will help with new perspectives."
- "You have different experiences that will help inform our decision."

I think it is difficult for a junior person to flatten an otherwise steep power gradient to their senior. People who have developed a steep power gradient have done so for a reason, and it will feel "uppity" or socially inappropriate for the junior person to take steps unilaterally to attempt to flatten the power gradient. Walk into the boss's office without being invited? Slap the boss on the back? (To be avoided in most cases.) Walk into the executive dining room without permission? Show up at a meeting for "senior" executives? Chances are, such behavior will only communicate to your superiors that they need to reinforce the steep power gradient.

If you are the junior person in such a situation, what are your options? Be careful about challenging the power gradient directly. Rather than trying to influence decision-making directly, start by earning the right to be heard, and make it safe for the senior person to hear you out. Giving choice and making the change small are two ways to make it safe.

Consider the case where a boss has typically made decisions about the timing of a product launch by himself or herself. Instead of "I really think we need to delay product launch," which is about affecting the decision directly, try, "Boss, I know you have to make a decision about the timing of the product launch. How helpful would it be if I showed you what the team sees on this issue?" It's a small step, you've given the boss choice, and by reaffirming that it's the boss's decision, you haven't challenged his or her authority.

I would also add, "And the team will support whatever decision you make." This removes the feeling of challenging authority and reaffirms team loyalty. What you are doing is helping it feel safe for your boss.

Still, the primary responsibility for reducing the power gradient rests with the senior, more powerful person in the relationship. This is tough, because the junior people will sense the power gradient more, and the senior people might not even be thinking about it or bothered by it. They might be bothered by the power gradient between themselves and their boss, though. If you are a senior person in a hierarchical relationship, then the best way to understand the power gradient is to ask the people below you how much of a power gradient they feel toward you.

Observe vs. Judge

The Oscars, *Deepwater Horizon*, *El Faro*. The "fear" in the workplace is about feeling judged, assessed, and evaluated by others, especially in a social context. Judgment places one person in a superior position to another, which is why so much feedback does not help and actually has a negative impact. Judgment is a special subset of enforcing the power gradient because the ability to judge is proof of being in a more powerful position.

Further, judgment generally works against our goals.

Judgment sounds like:

- "You should have . . ."
- "I wish you would . . ."
- "You need to . . ."
- "You performed poorly . . ."

Using nouns rather than verbs might take some of the sting out of a comment. Compare "You performed poorly" with "Your performance was poor."* How judgmental does each one sound? If you sense that the former places more emphasis and judgment on the individual, you're on the right track. One way to tilt toward observation over judgment is to opt for nouns over verbs—"performance" instead of "performed"—when discussing any dicey subject. This small shift in language can be powerful when emotions run high.

Take Jerusalem, a city that has been in conflict for over five decades or several millennia, depending on how you look at it. Political lines are drawn deeply and rigidly. Since Jerusalem is holy to Islam as well as Judaism (and Christianity too), some believe the only road to Arab-Israeli peace includes a division of the city itself between the two worlds. This is exactly the kind of fraught topic where language can play a decisive role.

In one experiment, 129 Jewish Israeli students were asked to rate their level of support for the statements "I support the division of Jerusalem" and "I support dividing Jerusalem." When the statement used nouns (division), participants reported less anger and increased support for concessions. Further, when asked how angry they would be if the policy were adopted, anger was tempered when the question relied on nouns. Retaliatory measures were also muted when policies were phrased with nouns.

So, if you must make an assessment, focus on the work by using

---

* I'm providing this example to directly compare the two phrases. I would recommend avoiding even "Your performance was poor" and use an observation instead. If this refers to a meeting with a client, say, "I noticed you jumped around with your points on our offering."

nouns rather than verbs. But better is to try to remove yourself as judge and make observations. Here are a couple examples:

Judging the person: You wrote that report poorly.

Judging the work: That report is poorly written.

Observation: I noticed three spelling errors in the report.

Judging the person: You need to step up your game and make it happen.

Judging the work: The results are not what they should be.

Observation: I saw the percentage of closed deals this quarter was the same as this quarter last year.

Let's say someone shows up late for a meeting. This was disruptive and you have been emphasizing timeliness, of delivery and of meetings. Then one of the team members arrives late, again! Your instinct is to tell them, "I noticed you were late for the meeting and that's unprofessional." The fact that someone was late for a meeting is a fact. Whether it is unprofessional is a judgment because you do not yet know what caused them to be late.

It's much better for the person who was late to make the judgment. Maybe there was a compelling and infrequent reason: "I had a difficult call with a client that went on longer than planned," "I had to find care for my sick child," or, perhaps, "I was unexpectedly asked by another manager to attend a meeting."

Maybe there was no reasonable reason, or more likely, the reason the person had did not seem more important to you than being on time. If you want to create ownership and develop thinking, you still want the other person to think through the situation.

One question you might ask at this point is: "What is in the way of being on time to the meeting?" You want to say it in a way that allows that some of the barriers to being on time might be legitimate reasons. Maybe, maybe not.

You making judgments for (or on) other people means you are doing the thinking for other people and you are pushing your organization away from a can-think organization back toward the Industrial Age can-do organization. You can do it, but recognize later, if there's a paucity of thinking, it was the result of your actions.

2. Admit You Don't Know

It's hard to connect with a know-it-all, and a know-it-all is not going to care what you think. Instead, we get the sense from know-it-alls that all they care about is what they think. For a long time, I made a living being a know-it-all. I was supposed to know all the answers and have all my decisions be correct. I was not rewarded for saying "I don't know," but I have found that leaders who can say these words lead better teams.

When leaders admit they don't know, they allow the team to admit that they don't know. This is particularly important when discussing decisions because there's no way of knowing whether one decision is better than another until afterward, sometimes long afterward. Ironically, a leader admitting they don't know also allows the team or a team member to admit that they *do* know. If a boss says, "I don't know," it might allow someone junior to say, "I know . . ." or "How about this?"

The other thing to remember is that all learning starts with "I don't know . . ." Now, that's not the end of the conversation. It's "I don't know, . . .

> . . . let's look it up."
> . . . how can we test it?"
> . . . let's run an experiment."

But no one ever started a journey of learning and discovery with, "I know all this already."

Here's how a leader might express uncertainty of knowledge or a decision and avoid the arrogance of certainty.

- "I don't have experience with this, yet."
- "We are in uncharted waters."
- "I'll have to say, I'm only 60 percent sure about this. That means there's a 40 percent chance I'm wrong."
- "I can see arguments on both sides."
- "Here's the counterargument for this position, and I'd like everyone to be on the lookout for any signs of these."

Admitting, as a leader, that you don't know or are less than 100 percent certain requires being vulnerable. In the Industrial Age, vulnerability was a weakness because of the fundamentally coercive nature of leadership. Because we divide the world into deciders and doers, and we (the deciders) needed to get the doers to do what we decided they should do, admitting that we may be asking you to do something that might not actually be right would weaken the coercive power of what we were trying to do. Therefore, we were programmed to be invulnerable and to never express uncertainty. This brings us to our next option for executing the CONNECT play.

3. Be Vulnerable

Another tool for reducing the power gradient is vulnerability. Theoretically, being higher up on the ladder makes it less necessary to behave defensively. Ironically, those in charge tend to cling even harder to an aura of invulnerability. Take the captain of *El Faro*. These are a few of the declarations of invulnerability he makes on the transcript:

- "So we'll just have to tough this one out."
- "It should be fine. We are gunna be fine—not should be—we are gunna be fine."
- "We're going into the storm. I wouldn't have it any other way."
- "Should (all) work out OK."
- "Oh. No no no. We're not gunna turn around—we're not gunna turn around."

Only after the captain leaves the bridge does the second mate reveal her anxiety about the obvious disparity between the captain's statements and the actual conditions. She must not feel safe expressing these concerns to the captain. The captain could have established an environment that was safe for others to express their vulnerability by expressing his own genuine emotions:

- "We could tough this one out, but man, I don't know about these conditions. What do you think?"
- "It should be fine, but let's stay alert to the conditions. We may need to alter the plan and take the longer route."
- "We're going into a major hurricane. I'm a little freaked out."

- "How is everyone else feeling about this? I think I'm moving away from excited toward worried."
- "How sure are we that we should persist along the Atlantic route?"

Had the captain shown vulnerability, the other crew members would have felt empowered to chime in and express their own concerns about the danger at hand.

At the 2019 Cricket World Cup, the favorites, England, had stuttered with two successive losses and were on the brink of being eliminated from the tournament. The team got together and talked about what was happening. Crucially, the senior players were vulnerable. They were open and honest about their fears, nerves, and emotions. It allowed everyone to share, which in turn reduced the fear of failure and created a powerful sense of connection. Fast bowler Mark Wood says this was a turning point, and the team went on to win the next vital game against India, and subsequently the World Cup.

Vulnerability is anything but weak. In fact, it's a tremendously powerful tool for creating connection.

I had a client that used the word "exposed" a lot and in a negative way. They wanted to make sure no one felt "exposed." This reluctant exposure is a symptom of low trust and vulnerability and high levels of judgment. They are doomed to mediocrity because they infantalized their employees and no one will risk a new idea. The key is to create a culture where being vulnerable and exposed feels perfectly safe.

4. Trust First

The Industrial Age play about trust needs to be turned on its head in two ways. First, we were programmed to make someone prove themself to be trustworthy before we trusted them. This naturally set up the case for judgment, not observation, and served to increase the power gradient. Now, leaders should trust first.

Second, trust does not mean you are always right. Trust simply means that your actions are being guided to support the best interests of the organization. This does not mean that your actions are always 100 percent in the best interests of the organization. This is important because without this underlying approach to trust, dissent equals distrust, and making a mistake once turns into "We can't trust you."

Assume good intent.

When someone makes a mistake, ask this question: Were they trying to do the right thing and made an error or were they motivated by something other than the best interests of the organization?

Sometimes we find that their motivations were misaligned with the organization. If we have not been clear about what we are trying to achieve, our intent, and they were making decisions based on their best guess of our intent, then that mistake is on us. A simple example of this is looking at the time horizon over which a decision is designed to be optimized. If it is made for a short-term win but will incur significant costs in the long run, and that is inconsistent with our organizational values, then this is an issue of organizational clarity.

Sometimes people just make technically incorrect decisions. These are issues of competence.

But if people are trying to make decisions that align with the organization's objectives, then we ought to trust them. Trust people first because your trust in them will affect their behavior. They will work harder, stay longer, and unlock more discretionary effort when they feel trusted.

We say "Take risk on people, not Mother Nature" because the act of taking risk (trust) will invite a modification of the person's behavior but won't have the slightest impact on the laws of physics.

Because trust means "I trust you are trying to make the right decision," it is OK (and appropriate) to then follow up with "Now take me through your thinking on this decision." Because the decision itself has been separated from the emotional heaviness of trust, the discussion happens more freely.

PATIENT ELLIOT

In *Descartes' Error: Emotion, Reason, and the Human Brain*, neurologist Antonio Damasio highlights the relationship between emotions and decision-making through the story of one of his patients, Elliot.

Elliot had been an intelligent, diligent, socially adept, and capable man with a well-paying job. Then a tumor in Elliot's brain damaged adjacent areas of his prefrontal cortex, areas tied to the formation of emotional states. Post-surgery, people close to Elliot noticed that he'd developed a tendency to get stuck on one task, persisting long after it would have been appropriate to move on to something else. Or he would squirrel off to work on something unimportant instead of tackling something urgent.

When he talked about his health struggles, Elliot's description was flat, lacking any sense of sadness or frustration, both of which would have been appropriate considering his condition. The damage to his brain had affected his emotional core, leaving him unable to properly engage with his work or to connect with other people. This would seem to put Elliot's future happiness and well-being in jeopardy, but while he could recount his own story accurately, he didn't seem to be moved by it.

As Damasio continued to treat Elliot, he developed the hypothesis that emotions are critical to effective decision-making. One might have assumed that good decision-making comes down to some kind of pure logic, but Damasio suggests otherwise: we need to know what we feel in order to weigh the variables and decide what to do about them.

Since Damasio's study of "Patient Elliot," his hypothesis has been validated by subsequent research. Damasio's work with neuroscientist Antoine Bechara and other colleagues shows that our emotions are inextricably entwined with our decision-making faculties. In fact, if we attempted to somehow remove any emotions from our decision-making process, we would find ourselves mentally paralyzed, just like Elliot. Connection is about bringing intuition to work, acknowledging the importance of emotions and psychological safety in decision-making. The idea that emotion does not belong in the workplace is a relic of an era when we didn't need people to exercise good judgment or make important decisions.

Every time you use your senses of sight, hearing, taste, touch, and smell, electric signals travel throughout your body and into your brain, gathering in your frontal lobe (just behind your forehead) to form a perception about the world in front of you. These sensory signals pass through the emotion-creating limbic center just before reaching the reasoning area of your frontal lobe, giving you an emotional, intuitive picture of the world around you. Accompanying these intuitions are physical responses: a lump in your throat for sadness, flushing with heat for anger, paralysis for fear, rapid heartbeat and sweating for anxiety and anticipation. These emotions are finely tuned, sophisticated tools that have evolved over millions of years—ignore them at your peril.

As the need to get everyone involved in the uncertainty of bluework increases, so does the need for emotion in the workplace.

GAMBLING IN IOWA

In the Iowa Gambling Task, developed at the University of Iowa, participants are each given a pot of money and tasked with growing it as large as possible through a card game. Players draw a card, one at a time, from one of four decks. Each card offers a win, a financial gain, or a fine, a financial loss.

There's a twist, naturally. The decks are stacked. Decks A and B are good: win and fine cards are both $50. Decks C and D are bad: win cards are $100 and fine cards are $250. Drawing from either of the bad decks for too long will inevitably clean you out.

To measure the natural physical reactions triggered by positive and negative emotions, the participants are wired up to measure minute levels of sweat on their skin. There's a reason we get sweaty palms when we're nervous—and sweat can be measured as a proxy for distress.

Most participants with healthy brain functions alternate between the various decks until they are able to conclude that decks A and B offer better results than C and D. Here's the interesting part. Their stress levels start spiking when reaching for decks C and D *before* they consciously realize the difference. In other words, they develop an intuitive sense that C and D are bad before coming to the conscious conclusion.

This intriguing finding shouldn't be interpreted to mean that we can rely on gut feeling and intuition in lieu of reason and critical thinking. For example, if you include a deck with lots of tiny wins and a handful of large losses, players intuitively respond to it as a good deck even though it is, in financial terms, a bad one. Our intuition does not weigh the severity of a few large losses properly. We get carried away by the frequency of those small wins, no matter how trivial they are in the big picture. It takes the player's cognitive power to consciously identify what's really going on. This weakness is well-known to casino operators, whose slot machines are programmed to disburse many small gains—our emotions reward us for gambling our money even as our conscious minds can see the vanishing total.

So, yes, logic is essential in decision-making. Emotions can be manipulated. That said, making complex decisions without the benefit of emotion is disastrous. Emotions are a critical tool for making decisions. This is especially true when it isn't possible to arrive at a logically definitive and complete solution to a problem, when choosing between immediate and delayed outcomes, or when subjectivity is involved. This makes emotions a critical source of information for social and personal issues, as well as in scenarios where available information for decision-making is incomplete.

As the need for thinking and decision-making—bluework—goes up, the need for a positive, safe, and vulnerable emotional culture goes up with it.

Before any of these new ways of communicating will work, members of the team need to feel sufficiently safe to speak up. When you operate with a "get better" mindset, you risk exposing inadequacies in competence or the loss of social connection. This is where understanding power gradients is crucial. This degree of power gradient in an organization is no small obstacle to the CONNECT play, and to this book's strategies in general.

Because of the importance of power gradient, I'd like to revisit it here in the context of trust first.

I once worked with a top global multinational with headquarters in Switzerland. The company's senior executives occupied a special part of a special floor. They had special parking spots and a special dining room. Even the carpet there was special, noticeably thicker and more luxuriant than it was elsewhere in the building. They had spent a lot of money to show how special they were. It had its effect.

Other employees who needed to get from one side of the building to the other would go around or even take the elevator to avoid this executive zone. There was no rule against passing through, but the design choices made the power gradient an almost physical obstacle. They would go down one floor, cross over, then back up when they got to the other side.

Major financial papers have described the company as slow moving and not keeping up with nimbler competitors. Its stock was stalled for five years while the broad market increased 50 percent over that time. Several key people departed. These problems and the plush carpet are linked.

Each of us is more likely to be aware of the power gradient going up than the one going down. The people subordinate to you are far more aware of these cues, and if you're not deliberate about smoothing that gradient, you are unconsciously hindering your team's ability to innovate and learn. Whether or not you see the power gradient below you, it's there.

I learned this the hard way. Sometimes I pose thought experiments to explore hypothetical scenarios. In this case, we were negotiating a new relationship with an important training partner. We discussed establishing longer-term relationships with the trainers to encourage deeper investment and higher levels of trust. This made sense, so I decided to test the idea by playing devil's advocate. As a thought experiment, I proposed adopting a contracting approach instead, facilitating quick, short-term relationships, a sort of Uber or Airbnb approach. What might the benefits of that be in comparison?

Unfortunately, the training partner interpreted this thought experiment as my actual intention and revamped the entire proposal. This resulted in a great deal of wasted time and effort in addition to setting our own relationship back. The training partner's team interpreted this as essentially reneging on the original intent, as opposed to a simple miscommunication. If the power gradient had been flatter, they would have clarified my intention on the spot, instead of going directly to execution.

Power gradients exist in *all* relationships, inside and outside traditional organizations. Pretending they don't exist can get people killed. A well-studied example of power gradients is the one that exists between pilot and copilot on board an airplane. A National Transportation Safety Board report from 1994 that studied thirty-seven accidents from 1978 to 1990 found that the accidents occurred with the pilot at the controls more than 80 percent of the time. Why was this? The pilot should be the more experienced operator, after all.

Research indicates that it comes down to the power gradient. Despite long-embedded CRM practices that have positively affected communication and safety, pilots crash planes more frequently because copilots are less willing to correct pilot mistakes than the other way around. Further, the pilot is less willing to listen to a correction from the copilot than vice versa. This speaks to the powerful allure of human nature to hierarchy.

HUMANS AND HIERARCHY

There are several different kinds of power gradients that humans experience automatically. One "default" gradient springs up between newer members of a group and the more established members. When longer-term employees speak of their "experience," they are invoking the social power gradient of "I was here first." Hazing and rites of initiation serve to reinforce this power gradient. It's hardwired and tough to address. And, of course, it exists among other primate species, such as chimpanzees.

In chimpanzee groups, the power gradient follows the order in which the chimps are introduced into the group. The unfortunate reason primatologists can study this is that simply being lower in social status results in more stress, which can be measured by certain markers in the blood. When chimps were introduced in a certain order, the ones who joined the group later showed higher indications of stress. When the group was disbanded and a new group was formed, the researchers introduced the same chimps in a different order. As expected, the stressed-out chimps calmed down if they were introduced into the new group earlier on—that is, at a higher status. They were even more likely to live longer.

The worst outcomes were reserved for those chimps who went the other route, from an early introduction to a later one, with correspondingly lower status. These "fallen" chimps experienced a severely negative impact in terms of stress markers, predicting dire health outcomes.

Again, while power gradients themselves are invisible beyond external cues, like better carpeting or club membership, their effects—on decision-making, innovation, even health—are very real and very powerful.

Language that steepens the power gradient and prevents participation sounds like this:

- "I have more experience."
- "I've done this before."
- "I was in the meeting."
- "The boss told me that he/she wants . . ."
- "Well, you've never done that before."

On the other hand, language that flattens the power gradient and enhances participation sounds like this:

- "Your fresh eyes will be valuable on this."
- "Just because we've been doing this for a long time doesn't mean we can't improve it."
- "When it comes to improving things, different perspectives are helpful."
- "You are the only person who sees what you see."

- "I've done this so many times, it's hard for me to see it objectively."
- "This whole project was my idea, so I'm more likely to get defensive about it than those of you who were more removed from it emotionally."

At the same time, there are other decisions that play a role in establishing or changing power gradients. Decisions that steepen the gradient and prevent participation include:

- Establishing separate offices, dining rooms, bathrooms, and parking.
- Creating physical separation, such as the use of a large desk or putting a glass divider within an open floorplan.
- Using gatekeepers, such as administrative assistants or security people, to reduce accessibility.
- Printing posters and photographs that feature only the CEO.
- Publishing company literature "authored" by the CEO even though ghostwritten by the staff.

Decisions that flatten the power gradient and enhance participation include:

- Increasing proximity by sitting next to each other, coming out from behind a desk, or coming to the subordinate's office rather than having the subordinate report to the boss's office.
- Enhancing accessibility, such as using direct address in emails, being in the same space as the team, either frequently on visits or more permanently with an open, centrally located desk.

- Printing posters and photographs that feature the team.
- Publishing company literature attributed to the actual authors.

If you want a good model for steepening the power gradient, look at the practices of a highly authoritarian leader such as Kim Jong-un of North Korea. You'd think he, his father, and his grandfather single-handedly built the country.

The rule of power gradients is that the steeper the gradient, the more difficult it is for information—think, truth—to flow upward. Amy Edmondson of the Harvard Business School did research based on surgical teams adopting a new technology and showed that teams with flatter gradients among surgeons, nurses, and other attendants had more back-and-forth communication, better error correction, and more learning. This led to a more successful implementation of the new technology than teams that retained a traditional hierarchy had.

It would be difficult, if not impossible, to flatten the power gradient completely. Even if we could, we probably shouldn't. A perfectly flat power gradient confuses people, leaves decisions up in the air, and makes people unhappy. As leaders, however, we should make every effort to flatten the power gradient to the extent we can, especially for the CONNECT play. Using the right language at the start of any brain-storming session serves to flatten the power gradient just enough to encourage the free flow of ideas.

**CONNECT IS ABOUT CARING. FOUR WAYS
WE CAN DO THIS ARE:**

1. Flatten the power gradient.
2. Admit you don't know.
3. Be vulnerable.
4. Trust first.

CONNECT

Connect is the enabling play that makes all the other plays work better. The Industrial Age play is conform. Connect is about caring: caring what people think; caring how people feel; caring about their personal goals.

Connect is not a superficial "friendship" but caring for someone else and wanting the best for them. Connect is love.

The key concept for connect is power gradient. Power gradient is how we feel hierarchy in human relationships. A steep power gradient means my boss seems much more important than me. Salary, office size, and accessibility are proxies for power gradient.

We want a low and smooth power gradient. If the power gradient is steep, it makes it hard for team members to speak truth to power. If the power gradient is flat, the team wastes time and energy understanding decision rights.

Part of flattening the power gradient involves leaders demonstrating vulnerability and being able to admit they don't know.

Trust is the result of practicing transparency over time. Trust means I believe you mean well. Whether or not you do well depends on many factors beyond just wanting to do well.

Applying the Redwork-Bluework Principles in Workplace Situations

It was six hours to game time at Citizens Bank Park in Philadelphia and things were not going well for the development team from Assist.

A few miles from the stadium, I had just sat down at a table for lunch with Shane Mac, the CEO of Assist, when he received a text from the project lead that they were having problems.

Shane and I had collaborated on several projects in the past; I was particularly impressed by the empowering and enlightened way he was running his company. Shane had explained to me that this project was particularly complicated. They were planning to field test a new product that would enable people to scan a bar code on the back of their seats with their iPhones, select the beer or food they wanted, enter their seat number, and have an attendant show up with their order moments later. Payment was handled through Apple Pay. It required interfaces between several company software systems, the service organization at the stadium that would handle physical delivery of the orders, the stadium, and an intermediary. This test was a big deal for Assist. A successful demonstration would raise its value and prove not just that the technology was sound, but that it successfully met a real customer demand. Several other major technology companies were evaluating bringing Assist on board for similar projects—and waiting to see how this experiment worked.

Things seemed to be on track, and then he got the text telling him that they weren't.

Shane called his project lead, a woman with a strong reputation in the technology industry, who was at the stadium working through the issues. At this point, some of the other companies involved were going into defensive mode, getting their excuses ready to blame someone else if the test failed.

At the end of the short conversation, Shane said, "Tell me if you need me to come over." He said it rather emphatically, as in, *You would tell me if you needed me.* There was a pause, then he said, "OK," and hung up and looked over to where the menu was sitting on the table.

I had only heard Shane's side of the conversation, but I had an idea about how he'd phrased his responses to the project lead. I suggested he call his project lead back and rephrase the last thing he'd said: "How helpful would it be if I came over to the stadium, 0 to 5?" He called. Pause. The answer was "5." I was shocked. Shane's eyes got big. He hung up, stood up, threw a $5 bill on the table, and called an Uber to take us to the stadium.

This story has a happy ending: the teams solved the problem well before the Phillies took the field, and the demonstration worked. I think I might have been the first person to order a beer on their system.

Make a statement one way and you'll get one response that leads to one outcome. Say it slightly differently and you'll wind up with a different response and a different outcome.

When Shane said, "Tell me if you need me," it required the project lead to admit she needed help and to give instructions to her CEO. Both of these are hard to do, even for a kick-ass, take-names project owner like the woman leading this development team. If she had been a wilting lily, we could attribute her reluctance to ask Shane for help to that. But she wasn't.

Once he asked, "How helpful would it be if I came over?" it became a request for information. Notice how he phrased the question. He didn't ask, "Would it be helpful . . . ?" That would have been a binary question that again would have made it just a bit harder for her to say "yes."

I'd like to tell you that these language changes have the certainty of a light switch. They don't, but every step you take that makes it just a bit easier for others to feel safe to speak up will result in a higher likelihood that they will. And these little probabilities, over time, over repeated meetings and interactions, will add up to a big change.

A QUICK RECAP OF OUR NEW PLAYBOOK

We have two different work modes. Redwork is the active production work that benefits from reducing variability and a prove mindset, whereas bluework encompasses the reflective, collaborative thinking processes that benefit from embracing variability and an improve mindset. Within these two modes, there are six leadership plays:

Starting in redwork . . .
Transition from redwork to bluework with:
    CONTROL THE CLOCK, not obey the clock.
    COMPLETE, not continue.
While in bluework . . .
    COLLABORATE, not coerce, with the goal to:
    IMPROVE, not prove.
Transition from bluework back to redwork with:
    COMMIT, not comply.

And use the enabling play:

CONNECT, not conform.

These plays exist in the rhythmic dance between bluework and redwork, between thinking and doing, between embracing variability and reducing variability, between improving and proving. When you're in a work situation that seems stuck at an impasse, you want to read the pattern, identify where you are in the dance, and call the appropriate play.

The first question is: "Are we in redwork or bluework?" Remember, redwork is doing, executing, and proving. Typically, it's the work of the organization—operating machinery, making products, serving customers. Bluework is thinking, deciding, and improving. If you are not sure whether you are in redwork or bluework, ask yourself whether the activity you are engaged in would benefit more from embracing variability or reducing variability. If you want more variability—more ideas, different options, decisions made in uncertain times—then you are in bluework. If you want less variability—consistency in a process, production of identical parts—then you are in redwork.

Now figure out how long you want to stay in that activity mode and when you want to transition to the other state.

Let's say you are in Sue's situation. There's too much thinking, discussion, and rumination. You are in bluework, but need to start taking action. You want to wrap up the COLLABORATE play and move to COMMIT, with a plan to CONTROL THE CLOCK that includes COMPLETE and IMPROVE. Spend too much time in bluework, and you may become frustrated by a perceived inability to take action; in worst-case scenarios it can even lead to anxiety and depression. Common idioms reflecting the feeling of being trapped in bluework include "Just do something," "Don't overthink it," "We're in analysis paralysis!"

When you wake up in the middle of the night, dwelling on a situation, unable to go back to sleep, you are stuck in bluework. How can you get out? Commit to a small, very small, piece of action that will move you into redwork. Act, move, do something. Write down your thoughts on a notepad or in your journal. If that doesn't work, get up and start working on the project. (I wouldn't actually send any emails in that state, but you could draft an email, which you could look at again in the morning.) That usually works for me; after ten to fifteen minutes, I'll have gotten the main part of my idea down and I can go back to sleep.

On the other hand, you may feel you've spent too much time in red, like Fred. If you're starting to plateau in redwork, and need to rethink or improve your processes, you want to CONTROL THE CLOCK and then take steps to COLLABORATE and IMPROVE. Too much redwork feels like mindless activity, a lot of motion and noise that doesn't actually get you any closer to achieving your goals. Common idioms reflecting this condition include "We're running in circles," "We're cutting down the wrong forest," "I'm on auto-pilot."

(Maybe you've never heard some of those phrases before. That's OK. They're expressions I've come across in my experiences at various workplaces. Your experience will be different, your people will be different, your cultural norms will be different, and your language may be different. But if these phrases capture some of what you're experiencing, that may suggest you're stuck in redwork.)

Learning to execute the pivot from redwork to bluework or vice versa takes practice. Start really, really small—and start with yourself. Maybe start by avoiding binary questions; instead of setting people up to give you a "yes or no" answer, ask them a "what?" or "how?" question. Try that and see what changes happen around you.

This takes practice because the mental programming to default to Industrial Age plays runs deep—and I am no exception. At a recent conference, I was talking about the importance of not anchoring the group as the leader (see chapter 2) and of avoiding self-affirming questions (see chapter 4). Then, after I put the group into a small activity, I walked over to the stage manager and asked, "I can go to 10:00, right?" I'd violated two of the rules I'd just given them!

Whether it is a conversation with a boss, a peer, or a colleague who reports to you, every conversation is an opportunity to reengineer the way we interact. You can shift yourself into a temporary state of bluework, then pause and reflect on the situation in order to come up with a response that's deliberate rather than automatic. Just ask yourself: What pattern am I seeing? What play is appropriate to run now?

Let's see how this might look in a few common workplace scenarios. These examples are based on our experiences with clients over the past several years. First, we have several scenarios where we approach it from the senior person's perspective, then two from the perspective of a junior person.

INTERFERENCE OR CONTROLLING THE CLOCK: WHEN TO EXIT REDWORK

Situation: Scientists at a global research business are not sure whether to stop a trial early.

Mia is a research supervisor at a global pharmaceutical company that conducts many trials of new drugs. Most of the early drugs never make it to later trials or get to market. Teams of scientists design the trials, and the trials must meet rigorous scientific standards to certify a drug is effective and safe. Once a trial is designed, the company starts testing. Often, the scientists have a "gut feel" early on in the process that the product will not pass, but they seem locked into the entire trial, "just in case."

Mia is frustrated by the inefficiency of a process where she often hears, "We knew it wouldn't work," and resources are wasted on failing products, but she fears cutting a trial short. Often, various trials are associated with certain people's ideas and there is emotional bias to continuing and organizational resistance to cutting them short. What is going on and what should Mia do?

Conducting the trials is the redwork. Designing, evaluating, and deciding which trials to continue is the bluework.

Mia and her team are trapped in escalation of commitment—because they continue trials that they sense will fail anyway. One of the root causes is that they view the trial as one long stretch with no COMPLETE play—going all the way to the end of the trial in the hope of proving a positive. Since the burden of proof for a positive test is high, that demands a long trial.

But the company is a business and there's an asymmetric burden of proof. It should not take much "proving" that it won't work. The reasonable sense of experienced scientists that it won't work should be enough. But to prove a drug works with few deleterious side effects requires a high burden of proof.

The team should design the trials with an "early out" decision point. Here, the trial starts (the redwork) and let's say it is scheduled to run six months. The scientists generally can predict within a month if the trial will fail. So an "early out" bluework meeting happens at the one-month point. The decision to be made: continue the trial, or cut losses and allocate resources to a different potential product.

At the "early out" meeting Mia uses probability cards (see chapter 4). The team members have worked together in the past and there is high trust among them, so she opts for the simultaneous open probability cards method. The question she asks is, "How strongly do you feel that we should stop the trial now?" Everyone offers their input using the probability cards (1 to 99). Now they have made visible the group's thinking, and Mia can make a decision about continuing the trial.

It is likely that people will want to know the rationale behind anyone's vote that is strongly for or against stopping the trial. That would be a useful discussion.

It may turn out that people are uncomfortable committing that level of advice. In that case, she could ask, "What is the probability this trial will fail?" The first few times she runs this, it might be necessary to calibrate her understanding of the votes with questions like, "Jon, I see you voted 95. Tell us what that means to you." Then she could convey how much risk she thinks the group ought to embrace with continuing or cutting short a trial. They may find that even though people think the trial has a low probability of success, they ought to continue because the benefits might be huge.

It is a low-risk decision because the trial can always be reinitiated.

With practice, the team will find it easier and easier to signal the high likelihood of failure and business case to cut short the current trial and begin another.

ENOUGH TALK ALREADY:
MANAGING A CHANGE INITIATIVE

Situation: The CEO/founder wants to announce a new change initiative. How does she do it?

Jen is the founder and CEO of a twenty-five-person software development company in Austin. The company has been successful because

Jen has allowed her software engineers a high degree of freedom over their engagements with clients, their work schedules, and the types of software solutions they develop. However, Jen sees that as her company grows, there is an increasing amount of inefficiency and internal friction because the freedom the engineers enjoy in their work processes also leads to missed communications and scheduling difficulties. She knows that, over the next year, she will need to introduce more standardized processes, and that her team will bristle at what they will perceive as constraints on their creativity.

Jen's software engineers are in redwork, each doing his or her own thing, but they're starting to fall out of sync with one another. She needs to CONTROL THE CLOCK, then COMMIT. If she presents her team with a "change initiative," it will likely provoke fear and stress in them because it sounds like a permanent change they don't have any control over. Instead of working at their own pace, they will feel pressured to perform.

If Jen wants to convince her team to change the way they work, then she should discuss with them the reasons she wants that change, allowing them input in the steps they'll take together to reduce inefficiency throughout the company. Instead of a "change initiative," she can call it an "experiment" or a "beta test" and make plans to review the results with her employees in a month or so (an expiration date). That is, if Jen is collaborating and not coercing.

If the team knows that this is an experiment, and that they will be included in the process of refining the new work processes, they will be less resistant to Jen's proposed changes. They'll engage in learning mode, collecting information that will help them report, when the review session comes up, whether the changes are helping or hindering their ability to do their work.

(This should be a *real* collaborative effort, though, and the review process should be meaningful, with the software engineers' input taken seriously. Otherwise, Jen is just running a variation on the old

Industrial Age plays of coercion and compliance—and if she pretends to listen to them, then dismisses all their suggestions, it will be just as bad as, perhaps even worse than, if she'd dropped a "change initiative" on them at the beginning.)

When it's time for the review session, Jen should invite a small group to work on the problem. Participation in the group should be open and self-selecting, and if Jen ends up leading the discussion herself, she'll want to be careful not to impose her own ideas on the group before they start looking at possible solutions. As Jen calls the COL-LABORATE play, she should ask what people saw during the experimental period, what they thought was going on, and what they should do about it. Eventually, it'll be time to COMMIT, and Jen will be able to make a decision about the company's future work processes that's grounded in what her software engineers have reported based on their experiences.

Here's a similar situation that took place at our company. When we started using Slack, some people were using it to communicate internally, but they were also still using their email, and we ended up with multiple communication paths. In order to improve efficiency, it seemed to make sense that normal internal communications should take place on Slack, with email reserved for communicating with external clients. We believed that shift would lead to more collaborative conversations among our staff, and fewer missed communications.

Instead of handing down a mandate, though, we announced an experiment: "Hey, let's do this for a month and then we'll talk about what we learned and how we like it. If it turns out to be unhelpful, we can reverse the policy in a month."*

---

* We learned that people did check their Slack messages regularly, and it seemed that internally we had a good common view of reality and collaboration. Few things dropped through the cracks and the remote workers felt better connected with the team than before. But even so, the problem only got worse: it turned out that LinkedIn messages were another channel that clients sometimes used, and I even received a speaking inquiry (and booked it) via Twitter!

While not all changes are that easily reversible, the closer you can get to the model of running an experiment, the better—make adjustments to your redwork, establish a quick bluework period of evaluation with a firm endpoint, then finalize the changes to your redwork as deemed most effective.

WE CAN'T STOP, WE'RE GOING TOO FAST: PAUSING TO IMPROVE

Situation: The leader at a global engine repair company would like to do more to improve the firm's work processes.

Henrik is the production supervisor for an engine repair facility in Europe. The facility is attached to one of the major European airlines, but approximately half the workload is generated by repairing engines from other airlines (typically smaller airlines that do not have their own repair facilities). When Henrik took over, the engine repair facility was falling behind in the acquisition of new clients—even though the number of airplanes out in the global aviation industry, with engines that need repairing, has been growing. Henrik has encouraged his team to be bolder in coming up with new ideas for streamlining work and improving quality, but the handful of ideas they've come up with have been either extremely minor or too impractical to implement.

Henrik's company appears to be stuck in an overall prove-and-perform mindset that spans both redwork and bluework cycles. The problem is that prove-and-perform puts a burden on us and our people to be right all the time, and that suppresses the sharing of ideas out of fear of getting it wrong. Additionally, the COMMIT play is likely to be too big; the company is trying to execute major initiatives all at once rather than generating small hypotheses to test, with a focus on learning from the outcomes.

The plays needed are CONTROL THE CLOCK, COLLABORATE, COMMIT, and above all IMPROVE. Henrik will need to schedule a pause in production in order to create an opportunity for bluework. That should generate a lot of ideas, and then Henrik will have to determine how to pick one or two new initiatives that can be implemented and tested when the team resumes redwork.

For example, when engines are being repaired, they are suspended from overhead cranes and workers get on ladders to replace the turbine blades. But that means the workers need safety equipment whenever they go up on the ladders, and the process slows them down as well. If they could lower the engine, then the workers could stand alongside the engine on the floor, replacing each row of turbine blades at an optimal ergonomic height. But digging big holes in the factory floor to create those repair zones would be a big expense. How could they test whether it would actually improve the workflow?

One way would be to buy a circular platform that could be raised around the engine instead of using individual ladders. This would allow the team to test the ergonomic and time-saving benefits without digging holes in the floor. They could run an experiment for sixty days and let different teams try out the elevating doughnut, and with what they learn during those two months, they could make a subsequent decision about whether digging holes would pay off.

It turns out that it was a good idea and now the workers stand on the floor as the engine moves vertically—keeping the work location at the same height. The work is safer, faster, and the team has practiced prototyping new ideas.

ALL QUIET ON THE IDEA FRONT: USING CONNECT TO MAKE IT SAFE

Situation: An assistant plant manager feels differently from his colleagues, but is reluctant to speak up.

Tomás is one of eight assistant plant managers for a paper manufacturer at a large plant in Brazil. Three shifts operate the plant twenty-four hours a day. Managing the large papermaking machine—five hundred feet long and three stories high—is one of their primary responsibilities.

The machine, which the workers have nicknamed "O Bastardo," is designed to run at one hundred feet per second, but Tomás's plant has been running it at sixty feet per second because of inconsistent quality and tears when run at full speed. Small misalignments in rollers and variations in temperature in the drying section have resulted in minor variations in paper quality, mainly measured as thickness. In the final step of the process, the paper is collected on twenty-foot-wide spools. If the paper tears, then 1,200 square feet of paper is dumped out onto the floor every second until the machine is stopped.

The company is pressing the plant to improve productivity, and the group members are discussing how it can be done. Tomás does not think the discussion is helpful, because they're focusing on details like how many tears there have been on Miguel's shift compared with Francisco's and so on. Tomás believes that, although some shift supervisors are able to tweak the machine somewhat effectively, the tears happen more or less at random. In his mind, they need to perform an extended shutdown to resolve some fundamental problems with O Bastardo—to repair its worn bearings, align its fans, and clean the belts.

Tomás can see that the majority of his colleagues are following the plant manager's lead when it comes to how to deal with the problem, and he doesn't think they'd want to hear him out—or that he'd lose social status and risk loss of relatedness within the group if he spoke up.

The managers should be running the COLLABORATE play in this bluework stage, but they aren't executing it properly. Rather than seeking observations and ideas from the group, the plant manager has revealed his bias. These meetings should have started with a pause, rewind, and fast-forward process. The plant supervisors needed to identify the current situation, analyze how things got to this point, and then determine what should be done about it.

Tomás needs to CONTROL THE CLOCK and COLLABORATE. If he hopes to advance a different agenda, he will need to do it with a light touch that's not too disruptive to the group. He can make an observation, trying to avoid judgment. "I see another option that has not been discussed yet. I see the shift supervisors spending a lot of time making small adjustments to rollers and fans while the machine is running. I know that's hard to do. When the machine breaks, we are in a rush to get it going again and do not have the time to analyze and fix the root cause of these problems. Maybe we could get the machine to seventy feet per second or even higher. Then we could have scheduled shutdowns and control the machine rather than have the machine control us."

In the transition to COMMIT, Tomás and the group would want to find a specific objective within his idea that they could test on O Bastardo. Perhaps the shift supervisors could identify the ten rollers that require the most frequent adjustment, allowing the plant to schedule a shutdown to overhaul just those ten rollers, not all 150 rollers.

I'M STARTING TO THINK IT'S YOU, NOT ME: MORE EFFECTIVE COLLABORATION

Situation: A product owner at a bank is frustrated that one of her team members is full of ideas but they seem to be off base.

Jessica works as a product owner at a bank. She has a small cross-functional team, including coders, designers, and privacy and compliance experts, that develops technology backbones and interfaces for customers. The team works together using agile processes and has generally been successful.

Nevertheless, Jessica is frustrated that one of the coders, Jens, often suggests ways of implementing user stories that seem "off" to Jessica. For example, one of the recent objectives was to allow users to pay with the app and Jens suggested a ring people could wear and hold up to a card reader.

Jessica is trying to run the COLLABORATE play, but instead of pinning her problem on Jens, she should reconsider her own attitude. First, she should recognize and celebrate the divergent thinking that Jens brings to the process. This divergent thinking could be the source of innovation and improvement. When Jens makes a suggestion, Jessica should reserve judgment and, instead, explore the idea with curiosity. What if Jens is actually right?

Jessica should assume that Jens is closer to the problem than she is, since he is in the code, and that he has something to offer. Asking "what?" and "how?" questions would help her uncover what Jens sees that she is not seeing. She might ask:

- "What would the next step look like?"
- "How does that align with what the user might need?"

- "How does that simplify the process for the customer?"
- "What assumptions is that based on?"

What if Jens's suggestions really are "off," though? Maybe he has the development criteria wrong. If that's so, it's an issue of clarity. Say, for example, that the bank wants products that are both simple to use and excel at data collection, and Jens consistently comes up with ideas that would enable the products to collect data effectively, but also complicate the user interface? Jessica would need to be clearer about the development criteria so Jens is working in greater sync with the rest of the team.

At the end of the process, Jessica may have to approve one approach or another. It may turn out that Jens's proposal offers the best solution, or it may turn out that his idea won't work. If she does not approve Jens's proposal, Jessica can explain why she chose an alternative solution, but that doesn't mean she should try to convince him his proposals are "wrong." All she needs to do is get a commitment from Jens that he will support the decision she makes about the team's course of action.

GETTING COMMITMENT INSTEAD OF COMPLIANCE

Situation: A senior vice president is ready to respond to questions at a change management meeting.

Matthew works as a senior vice president at a global automobile manufacturer in Europe. His division is responsible for consumer technology, programming the robots used to assemble the vehicles, as well as the electronics in the cars themselves. A year earlier, his predecessor implemented an agile transformation to bring the entire division to agile ways of working, but failed to create any enduring changes.

The CEO and senior management know their company needs to change the way it works if it is to survive the future. They see the challenges of self-driving cars, electric vehicles, and driverless delivery systems disrupting their industry; they know they need to be more innovative—and that means they need to get all of their employees thinking about innovation, too.

Matthew and his core team have reinitiated a transformation process with the goal of being more adaptive and agile, as well as getting new products to market faster. As part of this, Matthew's department will be reorganized and will adopt new practices. There have been six months of workshops involving employees at all levels to work out how the reorganization will happen and what the new processes will be.

Matthew believes that wide involvement and engagement are key to a successful transformation, but the openness of the intended change has allowed some resisters to verbally sabotage the plan before it has even started. Matthew knows he will not get consensus on launching the change program anytime soon, but now he's just hearing the same complaints over and over and senses it is time to move forward despite the objections.

One group of resisters is, ironically, the agile coaches who feel that the new approach, or "operating system," does not go far enough to embed agile processes and governance structures in the company. They insist that only a complete transformation, burning bridges behind them as they go, will produce real change within the company.

A large segment of the middle managers are also putting up resistance. They have asked Matthew a number of questions that, in his mind, are unanswerable until they actually start the transformation process.

Finally, the existing change management team members feel their status has been threatened because in the new operating system, everyone will need to be a change agent. They want to know what their new roles will be.

Matthew's group is stuck in bluework. He feels he has spent enough time talking about things. No new ideas are forthcoming, only reiterations of the old ones. So he calls a meeting and tells all the managers that they will be starting the first phase of the transformation. He starts the meeting with the following statement:

"It's time to launch our new operating system, based on the last six months of discussions and workshops with you and people at all levels in our department. We know this plan is not perfect, and we will learn and adjust as we go. I am asking you to commit to what we have now as a starting point for three months, after which we will have a series of retrospectives and course corrections." He has put an expiration date on the change.

Matthew invites questions: "Knowing that we are moving forward, what makes you uneasy and how can I help?" In a smaller group, a verbal discussion ought to feel comfortable enough for everyone to speak freely. If Matthew feels that many managers will be afraid to state their concerns out loud, he might have them write their concerns on cards and pass them to the front of the room.

He could also ask, "What questions do you think your people will be most concerned about when you go back and tell them that we are moving forward with this change?" This changes the perspective to one of Matthew helping his managers convey the message.

One of the agile coaches responds, "I feel this new operating system is not agile. It does not go far enough and I do not support it."

If he wants to know more, Matthew could ask, "In what ways do you think this does not go far enough?" But his main point is this: "I wish I could wave a wand and we would be instantly agile and innovative, operating with intent and striking the perfect balance between redwork and bluework, but I don't know what that is now. I see this as the first step in a process to help us get better. It will be OK with me if you continue to have reservations about this change, but I hope that you can commit to trying it and using your thoughts and experiences over the next three months to help us move toward a more agile and responsive organization, focused on learning while producing great cars."

A middle manager asks, "Is this the best way to reorganize?"

Matthew responds, "No, it is definitely *not* the best way to reorganize but it is closer to what we need than where we are now, and we will make observations as we implement it and use the retrospective three months from now to improve and work our way toward better. Our approach is not to study forever until we somehow find an infallible solution, but to create a system where we can experiment safely and get better. We are launching into a period of doing, redwork, and in three months we will pause, reflect, and collaborate in bluework sessions. I'm asking everyone to take notes about how it goes—we've given everyone a journal for this purpose—and participate fully in the retrospective."

Another manager asks, "Isn't this just another big reorganization, like the one we tried last year? What's different?"

"It sounds like you are frustrated with the repeated changes here without results. I am too," Matthew says, "but I can tell you, no, it is not the same. We have incorporated a new process advancing from the mistakes we made before. Those mistakes will make this new transition all the better, in fact, because we have advanced our learning, and I appreciate everyone's participation over the last six months telling us what we got wrong and how to do it better."

A person from the change management team speaks up. "Our

team has been excluded from running these kinds of changes," she says. "I've heard you say that everyone is a change agent in this new operating system, but that seems to also be saying we have no role. And, by the way, you don't know how to manage a change."

"It sounds like you are worried about being irrelevant and you want to make sure you have a place in the future organization," Matthew responds. "In conversations with the CEO and senior leadership, we see that change—the ability to learn, adapt, and operate with agility—will become more and more important. Since understanding how humans deal with change is your team's core competency, I don't see how you could possibly be irrelevant. We need your input throughout the process, and in the next bluework retrospective three months from now. You and your team have been invited to the workshops just like everyone else in the department. But you are right if it seems we are not 'running' the change the way we used to do these things."

After the meeting ends, Matthew's managers may still feel uncomfortable and concerned that they cannot answer every question they think their teams will ask them. They can practice "I don't know." They may still have anxiety about what the new organization will look like and what their role will be in it. But through Matthew's leadership, they have committed to giving it a try and have language they can use when communicating with their own teams.

PUT YOUR OWN MASK ON BEFORE HELPING OTHERS

I was in a conversation recently that involved a difference of opinion. I ended up getting louder and louder. I started making accusations. I lost my cool. What I needed to do was to call the CONTROL THE CLOCK play on myself, call my own pause.

How do I prevent myself from falling into that same trap again?

What were the signs leading up to this gaffe? After review, I noticed the following:

- The tempo of both our words started getting faster and faster.
- I stopped listening. I began to formulate my response before the other person was finished; I even started clipping the other person's statement, talking before they were finished.
- My perspective became strictly internal: I felt like I was looking through my own eyes at the other person rather than observing the scene from the outside. I lost the ability for detachment and monitoring.
- My focus narrowed to the other person at the exclusion of other stimuli: I no longer noticed what was happening in the rest of the room and no longer heard the birds outside the window. The conversation got louder, but the world got quieter.

These are typical symptoms of the prove-and-perform mindset that we often get pushed into during redwork. While a prove-and-perform mindset would be appropriate while running a four-hundred-meter race (that's redwork), it is not the most effective one in a business conversation (that's bluework).

If I had another person with me acting as an observer or coach, they could have helped me CONTROL THE CLOCK. But I didn't, and there will be more times in the future when I'll be on my own. I needed—and I will need—to impose the self-regulating mechanism on myself. I know what to look for, and I can reserve a part of my cognitive resources for monitoring the situation in case these symptoms emerge. For me, one of the easiest symptoms to spot is my accelerated speech, so I try to count to at least one before speaking.

AVOIDING THE PITFALLS OF
THE OLD PLAYBOOK

Situation: Public statements by a company reveal lack of CONNECT.

In 2017, Dr. David Dao was dragged off a United Airlines flight when the airline decided to remove passengers from the full plane in order to fly four of its employees to Louisville from Chicago. The incident was videotaped and went viral.

Oscar Munoz, the CEO of United Airlines, issued the following statement: "This is an upsetting event to all of us here at United. I apologize for having to re-accommodate these customers. Our team is moving with a sense of urgency to work with the authorities and conduct our own detailed review of what happened. We are also reaching out to this passenger to talk directly to him and further address and resolve this situation."

The statement is tone-deaf. He apologized for having to "re-accommodate" these customers—not for the violent behavior. He later referred to Dr. Dao as a "passenger," not by name. When Munoz was interviewed weeks later, he said he felt "ashamed" when he watched the video, but that emotional and human reaction did not come through in the statement.

Why? Munoz was using the Industrial Age playbook and conforming to type—the CEO of a major corporation—and, I suspect, coached by attorneys motivated to reduce risk.

First, he played conform, not CONNECT. CONNECT would mean putting himself in a vulnerable state. Instead he relied on a traditional, distancing hierarchy: he's the CEO and they're just "customers" and "passengers," whose names don't even need to be mentioned.

Next, he was in a prove play, not an IMPROVE play. He defended his company and left no room for further discussion. He sent a letter to United employees later that day, stating, "Our employees followed established procedures for dealing with situations like this." He meant to express support for United employees, but his tone equated "following established procedures" with what the viral video showed was an unnecessary overreaction.

I fly a lot on United. I can tell you from personal experience that there are hundreds of dedicated, well-meaning, professional, and thoughtful employees there, but unfortunately the CEO's comments made a bad situation worse.

Later, after a public outcry, he provided a better statement, referring to the "truly horrific" event and stating United would do better. Those are the CONNECT and IMPROVE plays he should have called from the start.

USING RED-BLUE THINKING TO CONTROL SITUATIONS BETTER

Situation: A colleague gets ambushed into overcommitment.

Andy is a set designer at a small film studio in London that creates video content through multidisciplinary project teams assembled to serve a client's needs. These project teams vary in size from four to seven people and are not fixed. It is a cross-functional and matrixed organization.

Andy tends to say yes too readily, and his overcommitment leads to stress. When multiple scheduling conflicts result in work that's not as good as he knows he's capable of doing, he feels bad. Sometimes it gets to the point that he feels physically ill and just stays home.

He doesn't want to say no, though, because he's afraid he'll get a reputation for not being helpful and that people will refuse to help him when he needs to ask for their assistance on his own projects.

One situation that tends to set Andy up for overcommitment is the ambush. Here's an example: A colleague asked Andy to coffee to "tell him about her project," and then—boom!—she asked if he would be willing to be the set designer. Even though Andy was already quite busy, he heard himself agreeing to help and almost immediately regretted it, feeling even more stress as he walked out of the coffee shop.

The problem Andy faces is that he's being drawn into a redwork action mode without any time to do bluework reflection. In effect, he is the victim of his colleague's coercion play. He complies, then he conforms to the role of helpful assistant. The plays he wants to run against her manipulative behavior are CONTROL THE CLOCK, COLLABORATE, and COMMIT.

How can Andy CONTROL THE CLOCK? Even though he feels like he needs to respond immediately, Andy does not need to make a commitment to his colleague right then. It is perfectly appropriate for him to say, "I would like to hear more about what you are expecting from me on this project. How many hours do you think you will need from me, and when does that work need to be done?"

Additionally, he could also say something like, "I cannot say yes right now. Let me think about it for a day before I make a commitment." (I don't think he needs to make an excuse, or have a reason for thoughtful consideration, before the decision—not even to say, "Let me check my calendar." All he needs to tell his colleague is that he'll consider the project.)

If the person presses him for an immediate answer, Andy can simply say, "It sounds like you need a commitment now, and that's not possible for me. I think you will need to find someone else."

If Andy's colleague expects a clear and immediate commitment from Andy, I would advise Andy to be particularly wary of working with someone who operates like this, as ways of behaving are generally consistent. In other words, I would expect a lack of transparency or advance planning throughout the project. Instead, you could look forward to more coercion, with an expectation of compliance and conforming. It would most likely not be a fun project to work on.

Depending upon your relationship with the person, it would be appropriate to point out the ambushing behavior. If Andy felt capable, he could confront his colleague and explain to her how he felt about how she had tried to manipulate him. It might sound like this:

"When you invited me to coffee, you told me it was to catch up and tell me about your project. You did not say anything about asking me to work on your project. I feel ambushed, like I am being rushed into a commitment, and it gives me pause. I need to think about it before I make a decision."

If Andy does agree to COLLABORATE on his colleague's project, he can still make his commitment time-bounded. For example, he might say, "Based on what you are telling me, it sounds like you need four to six hours in the next two weeks. I can commit to three hours next week, and three the week after that. The rest of my time is already committed to other projects, and after that, I have full-time commitments to other projects, so if your project carries over, you will have to find another set designer. How well does that work for you?"

That way, if Andy does COMMIT, it will be on his terms, not his colleague's.

MAKING IT SAFE FOR MY BOSS

Situation: The boss tells the maintenance crew what to do, and he's wrong.

Sarah works as a maintenance supervisor at a nuclear power plant in the midwestern United States. Her boss is fifteen years older than she is and has worked at that plant for almost thirty years. The plant is periodically shut down to allow the machinery to be inspected and repaired; each shutdown lasts about two weeks. Most of the machinery comes with recommendations from the manufacturer for how often it should be repaired—the same way your car manufacturer recommends you change the oil regularly. Sarah's boss is conservative about these repairs; if the manufacturer recommends changing the oil every five thousand miles, he has the oil changed every five thousand miles. After all, it is a nuclear power plant.

There are new ways of measuring equipment performance, though, and it's become possible to estimate the need to "change the oil" more precisely. In many cases, that means the equipment could go longer without repairs. That would save money on parts and contractors, and it would keep the plant offline for shorter periods, because the scheduled shutdowns could be completed more quickly.

Of course, if the equipment breaks or requires repair before the next scheduled shutdown, it would result in a reduction in plant capacity or, worse, require an unscheduled shutdown. Either would be extremely costly in terms of lost revenue.

For the upcoming shutdown, Sarah and her team believe a particular pump could go without its recommended overhaul, even though the low-risk thing to do would be to repair it this time. Sarah is worried that her boss will react poorly to the team's recommendation. The plays she needs to call are CONTROL THE CLOCK, COLLABORATE, CON-NECT, and hopefully COMMIT.

Sarah and her team are caught up in too much redwork, doing what they have always done because that's how they've always done it, without the bluework that would enable them to find more efficient processes. Sarah's play starts with CONTROL THE CLOCK. She will want to pick the right time to discuss the team's proposal. If she directly confronts her boss with a recommendation that contradicts what he has already approved, either specifically or by policy, he probably *will* react negatively. She needs to avoid a confrontation of will and ego that would come from challenging his authority. She needs to find a good time to discuss the issue with her boss and work on gaining influence with him, making herself heard before trying to change his mind.

Once Sarah has found a good time to discuss the maintenance plan, she wants to move to COLLABORATE. She should start by talking about what she and the team have concluded, in a way that doesn't undercut her boss. She could start by saying, "I see the shutdown plan includes overhauling the secondary feed pump. My team has some thoughts about that I'd like to go over with you, but if you still want to stick to the plan, I will let the team know and we will do that in the most supportive and effective way." This takes any possible contest of will and authority off the table, reassuring Sarah's boss that she is a loyal supporter.

Then Sarah can state the team's observations, remembering to pause, rewind, then fast-forward. She should make sure to give the boss a choice first. The most basic choice is whether or not her boss actually wants to hear from her. "Would you like to hear what the team sees here?"

(Sometimes it is better to phrase the question in a way that allows the person you're asking to say no. Giving someone the option to say no gives them a feeling of safety and control over a situation.)

Then Sarah can describe what she and her team have learned about the pump's operation now, and how they've analyzed the data they've collected to determine that, although it's scheduled for a recommended repair, it's actually running fine right now and should continue to work efficiently until the next scheduled shutdown period.

From there, Sarah could say, "So what would you like us to do?" Or she could make a suggestion: "So we recommend deferring the maintenance until the next shutdown." She might even phrase it as a done deal: "So we intend to defer the maintenance until the next shutdown."

Her safest option, if she wants to CONNECT with her boss, is to simply ask what he wants the team to do. Sarah is playing a long game and is earning the right to be heard. Only once that has happened will she have the ability to influence decisions without threatening her boss.

Of course, there is no guarantee her boss will COMMIT to her recommendation, no matter how unthreateningly she couches it. If that happens, eventually Sarah needs to decide whether she wants to continue working at the power plant. Remember: chronic stress from working in a place where you do not feel fully appreciated will take a toll on your health.

JOB DESCRIPTIONS, HIRING, AND EVALUATIONS

Rosario works as the chief nursing officer at an urban hospital in California. The hospital is part of a large health care chain with centralized hiring and job postings. She has noticed that even some of her shift supervisors wait to be told what to do or to receive authorization for simple actions and are stuck in redwork. They do not view decision-making as part of their job description.

The standardized job posting used by the health care chain reads like a list of tasks to perform.

Take a look at the core activities of the job, focusing on the verbs. Here's a sampling of some of them.

1. Compile data . . .
2. Collaborate with Medical Director on . . .
3. Complete daily staff assignments . . .
4. Monitor daily reports and identify issues . . .
5. Resolve escalations . . .
    And so on . . . until . . .
14. Perform other duties as assigned.

The verbs in the responsibility list include compile, collaborate, complete, monitor, resolve, conduct, manage, direct, oversee, perform, create, administer, assist, provide, and supervise. These are predominantly Industrial Age verbs, where the view is that the supervisor does these things to the subordinate staff. There is a dearth of verbs about thinking, growth, and decision-making.

"Create" could be a blue verb because it implies the need to determine and initiate something. In this case, it is used to describe a leadership responsibility to create a culture of teamwork and ownership. This is positive, but there are no blue verbs about the job itself.

Since bluework both precedes redwork, in terms of decision-making, and follows redwork, in terms of reflection and learning, the description should contain verbs that describe bluework and redwork. Front-end bluework words about decision-making include decide, determine, propose, initiate, commit, recommend, and choose. Bluework verbs capturing the function of reflection and learning include reflect, learn, formulate hypothesis, test, experiment.

Rosario would also want to describe responsibilities in terms of outcomes, not as tasks. While the task might be to compile a report, the outcome is to provide transparency of data, measurement of performance, and trend data that ultimately would be used for incremental improvement.

The task to "administer performance and salary reviews" misses an opportunity to emphasize decision-making and team development. "Administer" seems deliberately chosen to ensure no thinking is involved. Blue verb alternatives would be determine, recommend, or consult on performance and salary reviews.

Another way in which the job description reveals our underlying structural bias for managing redwork in a command-and-control manner is a prevalence of verbs that are fundamentally reactive, passive, and coercive. These verbs include manage, direct, oversee, and supervise. Rosario could replace the standard passive last line of "perform other duties and special projects as assigned" to "perform other duties as they see the need for" to invite a higher level of proactivity, ownership, and engagement.

Verbs such as initiate, propose, intend, originate, launch, and start help here.

APPLICATION OF THE PLAYS

When thinking about applying the plays, try to read the situation and deliberately call the play you want. If you are in redwork, then to open up the possibility for collaboration will require you to CONTROL THE CLOCK.

If the team is in bluework mode, you may notice people who are still running the old plays: coerce, comply, continue, prove, and conform. In these cases, you will want to deliberately call the plays from the new playbook: COLLABORATE, COMMIT, COMPLETE, IMPROVE, and CONNECT.

Sometimes it is useful to think in terms of roles: the role of managing the redwork (this is the role that most of us have been programmed for), the role of managing the bluework, and the role of structuring the rhythmic oscillation between redwork and bluework.

CHAPTER 10

The Red-Blue
Operating System

I n 1972, a woman that the media referred to as Sandra Gillespie pulled
onto a Minneapolis highway in her new Ford Pinto. In the passenger seat rode thirteen-year-old "Robbie Carlton." As the car pulled
onto the highway, it stalled and the Pinto was rear-ended. The impact
speed was twenty-eight miles per hour.

The fuel tank in the Pinto ruptured and the car burst into flames.
Sandra was burned to death and Robbie survived with debilitating
burns over most of his body. Sadly, Sandra and Robbie were victims
not of unknown engineering variables but of a cost-benefit analysis
conducted by Ford.

Earlier we looked at how, in the 1960s, the American automakers
were challenged by the entry of the Volkswagen Beetle and Japanese
automakers into the US small-car market. At Ford, CEO Lee Iacocca
decided his company needed to respond with a small, fuel-efficient car
of its own. He set a goal of designing and bringing to market a car
under 2,000 pounds for under $2,000. He gave the design team
twenty-five months. They called it the Pinto.

Like some of you, the Ford Pinto was my first car. Mine was a blue
four-speed stick-shift. First gear stopped working and the right-hand

door handle fell off. Eventually, the Massachusetts practice of salting the roads during winter ate through the floor pan on the passenger side so the carpet served as the floor. Despite the mechanical issues, I fondly remember the newfound freedom that an automobile provided. Fortunately, I never had an accident in that car.

Ford's strategy to compete in the small-car market, as stated by the CEO, rested on the specific goal of a car under 2,000 pounds and under $2,000, but that was difficult to meet, and the engineers and designers made a series of compromise decisions early in the design process to achieve it. One of the trade-offs involved the fuel tank. In order to meet the space and weight requirements, the designers moved the fuel tank, typically located above the rear axle, to a position behind the rear axle. Now, rather than the rear axle providing protection for the fuel tank, it became the hot sharp metal object that the fuel tank got smashed into if the car were rear-ended.

As the Pinto went to market, engineers within Ford began to highlight the safety issues with the fuel tank. The company ran a cost-benefit analysis, estimating that the faulty fuel tanks would cost 180 deaths and 180 serious burn victims a year. The projected annual costs to Ford to settle the potential liability and death claims were estimated at $49.5 million annually.

On the other side of the equation, the estimate to improve the safety of the fuel tanks was $11 per car. Selling over 10 million cars and some light trucks with this design would cost the company $137 million annually. The cost to make the fuel tank safe was more than the financial cost to the company caused by the estimated deaths and injuries from the fuel tank. Decision: don't fix the fuel tank.

Ford's problem here was not unique. Strategy, which is then operationalized or stated as specific goals, is often viewed as the model by which to achieve a long-term vision. But what is the impact on goal setting within the organization when couched this way?

Specific goals at the strategic level set in motion a cascading mindset of prove-and-perform down the organization—locking people into redwork and raising barriers to bluework. They fulfill all our traditional Industrial Age plays—coercing people into complying and continuing with the work until the goal is met. Pausing, controlling the clock, taking time to collaborate, achieving a sense of completion, and celebration—these are seen as time wasters that get in the way. Learning is suppressed. Agility and adaptation are suppressed. Probability of long-term survival is reduced.

Creating a learning, adaptive organization requires implementing a redwork-bluework operating rhythm at the top—at a strategic level, then at the operational level, and finally at the tactical level.

THE PERILS OF GOAL SETTING

In a 2009 paper titled "Goals Gone Wild" published by the Harvard Business School, Lisa D. Ordóñez, Maurice Schweitzer, Adam Galinsky, and Max Bazerman explore the role of goals like Ford's "under 2,000 pounds, under $2,000" on organizational behavior and specifically the propensity toward unethical behavior.

Numerous studies have affirmed that setting specific, challenging goals boosts performance in the short term. Specific goals focus attention and reduce distraction. These are natural allies for redwork—a focusing of attention and adoption of a prove-and-perform mindset. But since bluework benefits from a wider perspective and embraces variability, goal setting can have unintended negative consequences.

Remember, one of the keys to delving into robust redwork is to take a thin slice and to provide the opportunity to control the clock. This control can come from leadership but it can also be signaled by the employees in the organization. Absent some sort of inoculation against that focus, the organization will crash forward in redwork despite signals they are off course.

Specific and challenging goals work by narrowing people's focus on a task, but this narrow focus results in an exclusion of what is perceived to be non-task-related information. It opens up wide blind spots where information could be present that calls into question the original direction of the strategy or goal, but that information is missed.

A fun way many leadership workshops demonstrate this is with the gorilla video. Participants are asked to watch a short video of people passing around a basketball and to count the number of basketball passes made by the team of white shirts or black shirts. The task is cognitively demanding and requires focus. In the middle of the video, a person in a gorilla suit crosses the court, in direct view of the camera. Many participants, when watching the video for the first time, completely fail to notice the gorilla.

Not only do goals cause a focus that can result in erroneous action, but the authors of "Goals Gone Wild" make the case that the presence of specific goals can actually induce unethical behavior.

When companies set specific strategic goals, the performance mindset becomes predominant and often the unhelpful variant of protect. Without specific mechanisms to allow employees to control the clock, employees feel incapable of controlling the outcome and are more likely to resort to unethical means to achieve the goal. This is why we end up with bad, even evil, behavior.

It is this combination of goals and top-down hierarchy that absolves people from owning their decisions, which is why we get VW engineers colluding on a diesel emission cheat, VA administrators creating shadow appointment lists, and Theranos forging blood-test results.

A single evil, unethical, or simply wrong person can derail an entire company only in top-down hierarchies, because it is the top-down nature of the hierarchy that relieves everyone else in the organization from responsibility for their decisions.

The Harvard Business School paper authors link goals with the propensity of unethical behavior within the ranks of an organization. Either people fudge the numbers or they fudge the process to reach the numbers. The authors think that "aggressive goal setting within an organization will foster an organizational climate ripe for unethical behavior."

There have been many cases of corporate dishonesty. Why do they keep occurring?

In 2014, the Veterans Administration suffered a series of scandals as a result of hospital administrators artificially showing shorter than actual wait times in order to receive bonuses. In 2011, the Veterans Health Administration shortened the desired wait time to fourteen days and attached financial bonuses to reaching this goal. This was partly in response to long wait times. Providing better care for veterans was collapsed into the goal of the fourteen-day wait time, and in 2012, the additional goal that operations would occur within seven days of the desired time. Since the VA process and resources remained largely the same, wait times did not change but they appeared to change. At the VA hospital in Phoenix, it was discovered that the fourteen-day objective was met by using a shadow waiting list. Veterans would be put on an unofficial list, sometimes as long as a year out. Then, when they came within two weeks of their appointments, they would be transferred to the official waiting list. The official records indicated high compliance with the fourteen-day waiting time goal, and cash bonuses were paid to executives. An investigation by CNN indicated that forty veterans had died waiting for appointments.

In 2015, the US Environmental Protection Agency issued a notice that Volkswagen had violated the Clean Air Act by intentionally pro-gramming its diesel engines to disable their emissions controls unless the car was being tested. The emissions level for nitrous oxide was forty times the limit during actual driving, but the vehicles would arti-ficially pass emissions testing.

In the decade after the financial crisis, Wells Fargo encouraged its employees to meet its goal of selling each client (the bank's existing customers) at least eight products. In response, employees began cre-ating fake accounts without clients' permission. At least 2 million fake accounts were created.

During the United States' invasion of Iraq, a strategic plan was drawn up with goals for units to achieve based upon certain assump-tions. One of the key assumptions was that the population would "welcome us with open arms." There was early evidence that this as-sumption was not valid. Yet, while frontline commanders knew this, the organization as a whole had taken a prove-and-perform mindset. The introduction of disproving or surprising information was struc-turally impeded from reaching the top. The result was an ineffective course of action that was allowed to persist for far too long.

In all these cases, the widespread violations make it implausible to blame a few corrupt individuals. There must be more symptomatic underlying causes.

STRICT GOALS + STEEP HIERARCHIES = UNETHICAL BEHAVIOR

In these cases and others, another pattern emerges that, combined with goal setting, provides a recipe for unethical behavior: cultures with steep power gradients and "tell me what to do" as the default interaction among employees. Reports from inside the Veterans Administration, Volkswagen, and Wells Fargo during the time of their scandals show high levels of a culture of compliance, fear, and pressure to meet targets.

Where does the idea come from that specific goals will improve performance? Studies on this have been, of necessity, short term and of generally few iterations. We don't ask people in a study to have a conversation with someone and repeat it a hundred times, seeing if the one hundredth conversation is better than the first. If the goal is picked well, then performance improves toward that goal, but this occurs to the exclusion of other goals.

In one study, two groups of people were asked to proofread a paper with grammar and content errors, but one group was asked only to find grammar errors. The second group was simply told to "do your best." The "do your best" group did better at finding both kinds of errors.

Remember, the redwork, prove-and-perform mindset is superior in the short run for achieving results, but the bluework, learn-and-grow mindset is more adaptive in the long run. Strategy, being a long-run endeavor, would benefit from more frequent bluework collaboration periods and the learning and growth mindset. Developing and executing company strategy should be couched as learning. In other words, not a "Here's our strategy" statement from the CEO but "Our hypothesis is that a strategy of abc will result in xyz," and put an expiration date on it.

The problem with goals, challenge goals, is that the strategies people use to achieve goals are often at odds with learning. That is, specific goals impede learning and adaptation.

Further, goals that are met give people permission to stop working. Goals serve as a cap on performance. A study of Uber drivers looked at the effect of surge pricing on driver availability. The logical behavior for an Uber driver is to work longer during high-demand, high-payout days, but it turns out the opposite occurs. Drivers seem to have an implicit daily goal. During high-demand days with surge pricing, they meet this goal faster. Once the goal is met, they are more likely to stop for the day. In other words, the goal might be something we stretch for, but it also sets a cap on performance.

Applying the redwork-bluework operating rhythm to strategy would mean viewing strategy as learning. Strategic direction would be set, and the organization would commit to it, but the commitment would be a thin slice of the whole—and it would not go out too far. While engaging in the strategy, operational goals would be set for learning objectives as well as performance objectives. The company would be focused on learning by being sensitive to indications that their strategy was on track or not.

The company would provide mechanisms for employees to control the clock by calling a pause. They would have the strategic equivalent of the Andon cord in the Toyota Production System, where workers can pull the cord, calling a pause, so that problems can be solved rather than managed.

Remember, the response of managers to workers pulling the Andon cord is to first say "thank you." In the same way, managers and leaders should react to unexpected and disproving information about their strategy with gratitude rather than digging in their heels, and listen instead of trying to paint a positive picture of things.

In addition, running the CONNECT play would underpin the culture of the organization with the benefit of a flatter power gradient. When disproving, uncomfortable, or undesirable information is noticed, companies that practice connection to flatten their hierarchies have a better chance to evaluate and react to it—they would get blindsided less. Think about the senior executives we've all heard about who were, or claimed to be, unaware of things happening in their companies.

First, employees would notice disproving information more because they would bring a wider perspective to work and not be locked into a prove-and-perform mindset. Second, when they notice the disproving information, the culture's flatter power gradient and pervasive connect mindset would make it easier for them to bring up the information. Finally, the mechanisms for controlling the clock, such as the strategic Andon cord, would make it easier for the organization to pause the redwork and shift to collaborate mode to fully evaluate what the new information meant in terms of their strategic decisions.

In a complex, fast-changing world, long-term survival is more about adaptation than achievement.

In our system, experiments are designed to have natural variations in order to discover the impact of various traits. The problem with goals is that they do exactly the opposite. They reduce variability. Reducing variability is the defining feature of redwork, and that is why goals work at improving the performance of redwork.

But at the same time, the reduction in variability squeezes out the natural variability that is needed to test whether there might not be better options and whether the current option is really going to be the best option in the future.

Kodak focused on film cameras. Its goal was to be better at selling film cameras.

Blockbuster focused on DVDs. Its goal was to be better at renting DVDs.

Setting a goal like Ford's 2,000-pound, $2,000 car should come from the doers. This separates the decision-maker from the decision-evaluator.

THE RED-BLUE ANNUAL CYCLE

At the operational level, many businesses conduct annual planning for the next year. The idea of these plans is rooted in the Industrial Age view that the future might be complicated, but it is knowable, and detailed enough planning will reveal the correct path. Then, a plan is created for what we will do next year. Often the plans lack learning goals entirely, or are sparse on detailing them.

What makes annual planning worse is that it often happens at a time when people tend to be most focused on redwork, without leadership meaningfully calling for a pause to transition into bluework. Further, these plans are "rolled out" to the team. This replicates the Industrial Age division between deciders and doers, between blueworkers and redworkers.

The CEO of a public organization in Scotland told me how the group's business planning cycle occurred during the last quarter of the calendar year, which was also its busiest time of the year. So not only was it difficult to take people out of execution during this time, but none of the redwork performed during that last quarter, which might amount to half the production work for the entire year, was utilized for learning because the plan for the next year was being formulated before the end of the period.

There are a couple options to fix this. One would be to delay planning to January, when the lessons of the fourth quarter could be incorporated. Another would be to shift the planning cycle a quarter or two, so that it did not coincide with the calendar quarter. Finally, it might be much better to treat each quarter as a business plan and then review and learn. Here the redwork-bluework cycle would be accelerated, as would learning.

JUST SELL ONE ENGINE

Here's a good example of a company that brought in a bluework expert to assist with managing the redwork-bluework operating rhythm.

Eric Ries, author of *The Lean Startup* and *The Startup Way*, was brought in by GE Aviation to assist with getting its next engine to market. GE was developing a new engine, eventually called the GEnx engine. The team was fixed on solving the technical problems—asking how to make the engine. This is a redwork perspective. The team was in the process of developing the engine with the idea that it would soon move to full-scale production. What the team members needed to know was not only whether they could design and manufacture the engine but whether they should. This would take them to bluework thinking.

Market analysis, interviews with customers, and feedback from trade shows would give them only so much help answering that question. What they needed to do was build the engine and see if anyone would buy it. At the time, the initial plan was to roll out the engine for five different use-cases, or markets, with the idea of selling engines. Ries explains what they did: refocus the initial rollout for one single use-case, with the idea of learning whether the engine had a future in that market and what changes should be made to adapt it to other markets.

The new plan was a success, and the GEnx engine has become GE's fastest-selling new engine, powering 747s and 787s with fuel efficiency up to 15 percent better than the engines it was replacing.

Although Ries does not call them redwork and bluework, notice the phases of the bluework-redwork-bluework cycle. First comes the CONTROL THE CLOCK play. This is the time-out the company called in order to develop a plan, and the commitment of time the executives spent in the brainstorming session collaborating rather than back at their desks working. As the COLLABORATE play was called, they had a hypothesis to test: that a new engine with certain design characteristics would have a demand signal in the market, and that they could manufacture it at a cost that would generate profits for GE Aviation.

The key was to determine the thinnest slice of product they could commit to, one that would give them initial feedback on their hypothesis. The answer was one engine.

I've seen technology companies actually test a product without making it. They create the images and descriptions, market it, then count the clicks as potential buyers show interest. If someone actually tries to buy the product, they are told that it is "sold out," or, more honestly, that there's "none available." In this way, the firms can reduce uncertainty in product development because they gauge the market before investing in the actual manufacture of the product.

Imagine the difference in the salesperson's interaction with the client between these two cases.

In case 1, GE Aviation executives set clear performance goals for selling the new engines. The factory has been retooled and workers are making engines. The unsold engines are piling up in a warehouse. The salesperson, when talking to the client, *really* wants to sell engines—and might be tempted to exaggerate benefits or minimize disadvantages. Likely feeling a sense of stress and narrowed perspective, she might also be tempted to resort to a shorter-term mindset, perhaps closing the deal to meet an immediate sales target, but on terms that pose a long-term disadvantage. Or the salesperson might be in an all-or-nothing position, where an acceptable counteroffer, still favorable to both parties, needs to be rejected because it does not meet the company's goal. Through all this, the client will perceive that he is being sold to.

Now in case 2, the actual case, GE Aviation commits to building only one engine. The salesperson who goes to sell it is charged with learning as much as possible about how the client perceives the engine. In the sales meeting, the salesperson will exude curiosity and have no benefit, no temptation, to describe the engine other than as accurately as possible. She will have a long-term perspective, willing to negotiate with a wider perspective on what an acceptable deal would be. She knows that the rest of the company is relying on her to return from the client meeting with as much information and as accurate a description of the client's reactions as possible.

The client will again perceive the salesperson's state of mind. He will notice her authentic curiosity and the calm and relaxed manner in describing the product, making no effort to sugarcoat things. The client will sense the salesperson's learning mindset rather than performance mindset, and not feel he is being sold to. It would feel more like two people working together to solve a problem.

REVISITING AGILE

A learning, adaptive, and agile approach to product development has been codified in a movement called "agile" software development. Agile software development started with small, cross-functional teams developing technology products. These teams had previously been run in a more traditional project management way, starting with detailed specifications requirements defined by the product owners. The problem was that these plans were too rigid and closed off options early in the development process, when uncertainty was greatest.

Agile development improves on this process by having teams work in short bursts called sprints. At the start of the sprint, the team reviews the backlog of work, and works with the product owner to select the work that will fit within the next increment. They self-organize around the work and commit to the work—this is the planning.

At the end of each sprint, the team has a working, testable product. The team members celebrate completion, invite feedback, and reflect on their product; this is called the retrospective. Then they commit to the next steps. In this way, they are starting development with the possibility of significant course adjustment early in the product development cycle, when change costs are lower.

As a product matures in development, change costs get higher financially and emotionally. Even if we could tolerate the financial and disruption costs, the psychological phenomenon of escalation of commitment weighs against decision-makers. Rigid adherence to legacy decisions can result in poorly performing products, abandonment, or overages in cost and schedule.

How long the sprints are and whether they are of fixed or variable duration is one of the decisions that teams working agilely need to make. Typical sprint cycles start at two to three weeks but can be as short as several hours.

Notice how the agile rhythm of planning-sprint-retrospective fits the redwork-bluework play cycle of collaborate-commit-complete-celebrate. This is what a redwork-bluework operating rhythm looks like when applied to product development.

The sprints include the redwork and are bookended by bluework. While in the production period of the sprint, the team designs and codes the product and is shielded from changes in direction. Leadership resists the urge to shower the team with new ideas and uses the discipline of the backlog to allow recording and to systematically decide upon new ideas and directions.

BLUEWORK AT THE TACTICAL LEVEL: DELIBERATE ACTION

On the submarine *Santa Fe*, one way we tried to practice the redwork-bluework operating system was with the habit of deliberate action. Deliberate action meant that we would pause, vocalize what we were about to do, and state our decision that it was the right thing to do just prior to doing it. We did this with specific actions like starting a pump or shutting a breaker, so that redwork-bluework was implemented at a micro level.

First, the pause meant we were controlling the clock.

Next, the vocalizing of intent invited collaboration. Team members nearby would have a chance to speak up. The code word we used was "hands off." This was our verbal Andon cord. If any of the other teammates were not convinced that what someone had just vocalized was the right thing to do, they could say "hands off." Notice, the test was not that they needed to be convinced it was wrong, only that they were not convinced it was right.

Then we would commit to the action and start the pump or shut the breaker.

Then we would reflect on whether the system was responding the way we thought it was going to. We would compare actual system response with the desired response.

When it comes to operating machinery or conducting an operational procedure, the habit of deliberate action will dramatically reduce errors and reduce error propagation.

We tried this in office environments with less success. In this case, deliberate action would mean a pause and final reflection before signing a piece of paper, approving a mortgage, submitting a bid, or sending an email. In most cases, deliberate action feels like overkill and seems unnecessary. This is because in business most of these actions have reversible actions—we can revise contracts and apologize for emails. Still, for important things that might have irreversible consequences or brand impacts, I believe the habit of deliberate action would be helpful.

SELF-REGULATION

One of the supporting personal traits needed for teams to embrace the redwork-bluework operating rhythm is a good degree of self-regulation. When we do not regulate ourselves, we are asking others to do it for us. Because many of the new plays require us to change the way we ask questions, talk, and interact, we need to make a commitment to ourselves to make these changes. Having a coach remind us is helpful, but only when we are open to being helped. Ultimately, we strive to internalize the changes in language that will reinforce and rewire our thought processes in a more adaptive, learning, growth-oriented way. It's up to us.

LIFELONG LEARNING

Beyond the strategic level, I believe that the idea of red-blue thinking will make our lives richer, more interesting, and more successful.

Cobblers in the fifteenth century did not have to worry much about a change in manufacturing processes occurring during their lifetime that would require relearning their craft. What they learned as teenage apprentices would be the same work process they would use as thirty-year-old cobblers, what they would teach their apprentices at forty years old, and what they would be using as fifty-year-old master cobblers.

Workers who hired on with Mr. Ford to build the Model T in 1908 could have worked on essentially the same assembly line for nineteen years, building the same model, using the same tools. They would not have had to worry about learning fundamentally new processes or being put out of work by a programmed robot.

Our life rhythms adapted to this structure: (1) get educated, (2) apply your education, (3) retire and hope to live a few more years. Schooling lasted from age five to twenty-one and then we went off to work. So our life pattern was to start with bluework (cognitive, reflective, learning, improving), then shift to redwork (physical, active, doing, proving). The rhythm was not so much a back-and-forth between bluework and redwork but a one-time learn followed by a continuous do, do, do, then die. This worked because it was likely that the conditions forty years on into our working life would be the same as the conditions that existed back when we were educated.

We also saw in the education system a desire to create humans who would conform to the six plays of the Industrial Age. Education was about obeying the clock, complying, and proving. This legacy continues to weigh heavily on the current classroom.

But the situation has, of course, changed. It would be unlikely that someone graduating from high school or college today could apply his or her specific skills or trade in two or three decades without significant modification and relearning.

Therefore, in the modern world, to maintain relevance we need to apply the rhythm of blue-red-blue to our lives. No longer is "learn once, then do till retirement" going to work. What is needed now is a restructuring of this approach—one in line with the bluework-redwork rhythm laid out here. We should think of our careers in chunks, maybe ten or twenty years of doing, followed by a period of learning.

During our time of doing, the overall emphasis is on redwork. While there are smaller periods of bluework inside that redwork—Bill Gates took a week off once or twice a year to sequester himself in a cabin without distractions and with lots of reading—the emphasis is on the doing. We earn money, we practice our skills, we prove our worth. Although not dominant all the time, our "be good" self plays a big role here.

Then we pause; we shift to bluework. We reflect on how our lives are going. We give our brains time to rest. We look dispassionately at our careers and seek to embrace an improve mindset. At this point our "get better" self is dominant. We take classes, we enroll in school again, we develop new skills or a new line of work altogether. To be most effective we would engage others in these periods of reflection.

At least two things make this hard. First, the education system is not designed for this approach. Online courses and university programs designed for older people returning to school certainly exist, but the fundamental structure remains learn, graduate, and now do!

The second thing that makes this hard is that our brains seem to be designed for the "(1) learn, (2) do" model. They are more elastic when younger and it is easier to develop the new connections in our brains that are associated with new ideas and learning. James Watt invented the working steam engine when he was in his late thirties, Edison invented the lightbulb in his thirties, the Wright Brothers were in their thirties when they flew their airplane. There are some outliers. Marconi invented the radio in his twenties and Einstein developed the special theory of relativity when he was twenty-six. On the other hand, Gutenberg was in his fifties when he developed the printing press.

It seems that the inventions occur early in life but not too early. It takes time to apply learning by interacting in the real world, testing and tinkering. Inventions don't happen the day we graduate from school because all that most of us have at that point is bluework. Invention and innovation require both—bluework and redwork.

But rare is the invention that occurs late in life. Why is that? Do we stop learning? Do our brains just get tired? After all, it would seem that as we accumulate more and more knowledge about the world, and experience more interactions with it, we should become more and more prolific innovators. That is not the case (yet).

Brain development slows markedly in our twenties, and the volume of our prefrontal cortex starts shrinking in our forties. Turns out forty was the life expectancy of humans basically forever—up till now. But the key is that brain development slows, it does not stop. So don't despair, our brains have the ability to learn new things for decades.

My life mostly followed the learn-do model. I went to the Naval Academy and had two years of nuclear power schooling and then was launched into the fleet to perform. I did earn two master's degrees after that—one online and one in person. In retrospect, neither seemed to be much of a pause-and-reflect period. Maybe it was because I viewed them strictly in the context of helping me be a better naval officer. Maybe it was because I was immature and did not take sufficient advantage of the opportunities.

After twenty-eight years I left the navy, wrote a book, and became a global keynote speaker. These are markedly different careers and require markedly different skills. Even the two more recent activities differ—being onstage in front of a crowd and delivering something interesting, compelling, useful, and fun as opposed to the work of writing. So I feel that I have had a blue-red-blue cycle in my life.

Now I am wondering if it's not time for another period of bluework for my life. Not imposed or happenstance but deliberate, planned, life changing. That will require me to control the clock of my life (*gasp*). No more excuses, no more "too busy," no more the cotton candy of busyness.

I claimed this book was about learning and that the correct rhythm of blue-red-blue would help apply learning in your job but also in your life. It won't happen just churning away in redwork. You will need to invoke these plays, starting with controlling the clock. Start small, work on yourself. Run experiments at work, and in your life.

I am interested in your stories—how you inject bluework in life and work—do you learn a new language, do you move to a different country, do you go back to school and get a degree? Share that with me at david@turntheshiparound.com or on our LinkedIn page for Intent-Based Leadership.

I wish you well on your journey.

THE REDWORK-BLUEWORK OPERATING SYSTEM

There are two modes of human activity: thinking and doing.

We call thinking bluework. It is cognitive, complex, creative, and uncertain. Variability is an ally to bluework. During bluework, we collaborate, invoke the "get better" self, seek to improve, make decisions, and develop hypotheses.

We call doing redwork. It is often physical, skill based, focused, and deliberate. Variability is an enemy to redwork. During redwork, we work, invoke the "be good" self, seek to prove, and perform our jobs.

Implementing a redwork-bluework operating system means deliberately practicing the rhythm of redwork followed by bluework.

Leaders have three domains in which to influence the system. The first domain is determining the overall balance between red and blue—with more frequent bluework at the beginning of a project when there is more uncertainty and the focus should be on learning. Then they extend the length of the redwork periods, spacing out the bluework later in the project as the focus shifts toward production and most major decisions have been made.

The second domain is within the bluework periods—getting everyone involved in bluework rather than leadership only, and managing the bluework periods with a goal of embracing variability.

The third domain is within the redwork periods—setting goals and a focus for the team. This is the domain leaders will be most familiar with and which received the least attention among these plays. I often see ways of doing the redwork better. There are many tools available, such as Lean, to assist leaders in this domain.

The rhythmic oscillation between redwork and bluework can be applied at the strategic, operational, and tactical levels. It applies to teams and individuals. It can be applied in our lives.

The outcome of the redwork-bluework rhythm is learning—learning at work, at home, and at life.

Saving *El Faro*

El *Faro* and her crew met a tragic fate and lives were lost. With their demise, they left us with a tremendously valuable learning tool: the transcript of their conversations on board. By studying these conversations, and considering how they might have played out differently, I am not looking to place blame or attribute bad intentions to anyone. Every person on board surely believed they were doing what was in the best interests of their mission and their team. However, it was their ingrained patterns of language, drawing on an outdated playbook, that turned their best intentions into a disastrous situation.

Every one of us makes the same mistakes. The stakes may not be as high when we go in to work every day, but the effect of our words on our coworkers' behavior is no different.

My hope for this book is that we can learn from the tragedy of *El Faro* and take steps so that tragedies like this never occur again. I imagine a world in which organizations are more conscious of how language affects our behavior, in which leaders are equipped to run a new playbook that makes us all safer and more effective at work.

In this chapter, I reimagine the story of *El Faro* with the same team, same equipment, same deadlines, same professional training, and same weather conditions. The only difference is that they view their work in the rhythmic cycle from blue to red to blue, enabled by the power of connection. This difference manifests in the simplest of ways: how they talk to each other.

MONDAY

In port, Jacksonville, Florida
Over 1,000 miles from storm center

Before *El Faro* starts its journey to San Juan, the play is to CONNECT, not conform. The officers establish rapport with the crew, and the captain with the officers.

The captain serves as a filter. He works hard not to transmit any stress he may be feeling to the crew. His mental state is "care, don't care." He cares deeply and passionately about the people and cargo entrusted to his care, and not about the bureaucratic consequences of any choices made on board. The CONNECT play allows him to feel part of a team and mitigates his fear.

In the CONNECT play, the captain does two important things before getting under way. First, he works to lower the power gradient. The power gradient is felt by the subordinates, but must be lowered by the senior person. In this case, the captain is fifty-three years old, the chief mate is fifty-four years old, and the third mate is forty-six. Age establishes a natural power gradient, so these men already have a lower power gradient between them. The second mate—the navigator, and one of two women on board—is thirty-four. Almost twenty years younger and a minority by gender, she stands to be most affected by the power gradient, and she is also most likely to offer intellectual variability which will aid any bluework the team might encounter. This makes it even more important to create an environment where she feels safe speaking up.

The captain has a one-on-one meeting with her. He says, "I am glad you are on our team—your difference in age and gender means you're likely to have a different perspective. You may see things the rest of us miss, and you know things the rest of us don't. You may have ideas or concerns that won't be echoed by others, but that doesn't mean you are wrong. You may be the only one who is right. I encourage you to speak up. On my side, I commit to listening to what you tell us. This doesn't mean we will always do what you want, but I am committing to listening with curiosity and interest. Here is a yellow card—if you don't think I'm listening, then I invite you to flash the yellow card at me, like a referee. Or you should feel free to come tell me separately, if that's what you prefer—remember, you might be the only one thinking right."

To the team, he might say, "Some of you have operated with different captains with different styles. Here's my commitment on how I operate. I am responsible for navigating this ship safely to Puerto Rico, and I believe that we will all be better off if each one of us knows what we all know and sees what we all see. My intention is that, as officers, we will all discuss the key decisions involved in this journey. If the group is split and I need to make a decision, it will be after we've heard everything. I made a decision a couple months ago to take the Old Bahama Channel. That cost us six hours on the schedule. It may or may not have been necessary, we'll never know, and I had to go to headquarters to explain it. That's on me. I will take care of headquarters."

The second important thing the captain does is set up the CONTROL THE CLOCK play. This includes giving the pause a name.

As the captain briefs the team, he says, "I want to remind everyone that we are in hurricane season. It's possible, even likely, that you will receive weather updates that should cause us to take a planning pause and determine what route we should take. I want to call these pauses, for whatever reason you feel you need one, a 'mariners' minute.' Just say, 'I'm calling a mariners' minute.' The following will happen. All officers will muster on the bridge and we'll talk about what to do. I'd like each of you to do that once during your first underway watch for practice so that we get the language and response down and see it's easy. We'll all practice coming to the bridge for collaboration."

WEDNESDAY

6:00 A.M., SEPTEMBER 30, 2015
APPROACHING THE TOP OF THE BAHAMAS,
600 MILES FROM STORM CENTER

Normally, the ship would take the exposed Atlantic route without much thought. It could hardly be considered a decision point, but this time, a weather update indicates Tropical Storm Joaquin is now Hurricane Joaquin. This trigger event sparks the need to get out of the automatic redwork (driving the Atlantic route to Puerto Rico) and into bluework (making a decision about the route).

The plays needed next are CONTROL THE CLOCK, COLLABORATE, and COMMIT.

6:05 A.M., SEPTEMBER 30, 2015
The officer on watch runs the CONTROL THE CLOCK play. In the most effective organizations, the first person to learn of the need to control the clock does so. Knowing that an email alert might get lost, he sends a physical note to all officers that a meeting will be held at 6:30 a.m. to discuss the ship's route to Puerto Rico.

A less optimal response would have been for the captain to notice the need for bluework and call the meeting, but the captain should only be a backup to the watch officer. Still, this is preferred to no one calling the play and the team marching on in redwork.

. . .

6:10 A.M., SEPTEMBER 30, 2015

The captain receives the message along with the other officers.

6:15 A.M., SEPTEMBER 30, 2015

The second mate, the ship's navigator, arrives on the bridge and has a discussion with the watch officer about who will run the meeting. They decide the second mate will run the meeting because the topic will be how to approach the transit to Puerto Rico with an oncoming storm. Neither one expects the captain to run the meeting.

They know that during the COLLABORATE and COMMIT parts of the cycle, the team's decision will be more resilient if they act as decision-makers and allow the captain to be a detached decision-evaluator. They know that the more the captain gets involved, the more the crew will be under the influence of escalation of commitment, and the more likely they will be to stick with the predetermined course of action.

6:29 A.M., SEPTEMBER 30, 2015

Everyone arrives on the bridge. The officers gather around the chart table while the captain stands just a little behind and off to the side.

6:30 A.M., SEPTEMBER 30, 2015, MEETING START

The second mate starts the meeting without waiting for the captain to nod or say anything. She does not even look to the captain for approval. She speaks to and looks at the other officers. "As you know, we have a decision to make. We are approaching a decision point, which we will call decision point 1. The decision is whether to turn right and take the Old Bahama Channel or stick to the standard Atlantic route to Puerto Rico. The reason we need to collaborate on this decision is that Tropical Storm Joaquin has been upgraded to a hurricane."

The second mate asks for a vote using fist-to-five: "How strongly do you feel about either option? A vote strongly urging the Old Bahama Channel is a zero vote, while a vote strongly urging the standard route is a five vote." The second mate is using *vote first, then discuss*, and the *fist-to-five* tool. Since the group is small and psychological safety is high, fist-to-five is a quick and effective tool.

The greatest variability occurs prior to group discussion. If the second mate is worried that people won't be honest, she might ask for anonymous votes, possibly using probability cards.

The second mate has asked the question starting with "how," avoiding the binary question "Should we take the Old Bahama Channel or the Atlantic route?" Her job at this point is to anchor the endpoints and ask the question in a probabilistic way that invites subtle variations of enthusiasm and maximum variability.

"One-two-three, vote!"

The chief mate, second mate, third mate, and chief engineer all raise their hands. The votes are 5, 3, 1, 0, respectively. The chief mate has voted strongly for the efficient Atlantic route, and the engineer has voted strongly for the protected Old Bahama Channel. The captain does not vote because he does not want to influence the discussion that will follow and would rather observe the team dynamics. He has the authority to veto the final vote, so he does not need to talk now.

The second mate embraces variability and is being curious, not compelling.

In a neutral tone, she asks the chief engineer, "Chief, you showed a zero. Tell us about that." Even her choice of words—"you showed a zero," as opposed to "you voted a zero"—is deliberate. This helps separate the position from the person and invites dissent. The second mate also avoids asking, "Why did you vote that way?" as this may indicate disapproval and put the voter on the defensive.

The chief engineer explains, "We have a forty-year-old ship powered by a steam plant. As the ship enters higher seas, maintaining propulsion will be necessary to keep the ship on track, and the production of electrical power will be vital to running any bilge pumps. The rocking and rolling is likely to cause disruption to the lube oil systems, which may result in automatic shutdowns to our equipment. If it does shut down, it will be difficult to restart."

The chief mate, who voted most strongly to take the standard route, seeks first to understand: "How many degrees of roll do you think it will take to disrupt lube oil systems?" He does not try to convince the chief engineer that the ship "can take it," but responds instead with curiosity.

The chief engineer: "The ship was originally designed to take thirty-degree rolls, but with the wear and tear on the gear and the fact that we are operating at the low end of our lube oil reserves, I'd guess more like twenty- to twenty-five-degree rolls would start triggering shutdowns. I'd be only 60 percent confident that we could maintain propulsion with twenty-five-degree rolls."

Though the chief engineer cannot know for sure, he gives his best estimate using a probabilistic response. He also includes the potentially embarrassing fact that they are low on lube oil—not so low that a refill was mandated, but at the low end of the normal operating band. This could be viewed as a mistake in operational planning, but the captain remains quiet.

The second mate then invites the chief mate, who voted 5, to explain his thinking. The chief mate notes the efficiency of the shorter Atlantic route and the benefit to the ship's customers and the company. The captain notes that the third mate, the most junior in the group, has been quiet. "Third Mate, you've been quiet, and you showed one finger. What's on your mind?" The leader's job in the bluework play of COLLABORATE is not to drive consensus but to invite discussion, especially from the quieter outliers.

The third mate tells a short story: "Well, I lived in the Bahamas for ten years and, I don't know, but this storm scares me. We really got hammered by Andrew back in 1992. Badly hammered. I'm worried that we won't have an escape route once we make this decision. How much of a commitment are we making?"

The third mate feels it is safe to express his anxiety about sailing into a hurricane based on a past experience, and he asks an important question: Once this decision is made, what are the chances to revisit? Can they make a small commitment with a preplanned CONTROL THE CLOCK pause?

The second mate speaks up: "I think we have one additional decision point, down near Rum Cay. Let's call that decision point 2. There's a channel there that cuts through the Bahamas. At that point, if we have taken the Atlantic route, we will be able to deviate south and join the Old Bahama Channel just north of Cuba. At our planned speed of twenty knots, we will reach that decision point around midnight tonight. That's about eighteen hours. But between now and Rum Cay, we will have the Bahamas on our right with little chance to tuck in behind them."

The captain chimes in: "I just want to say something here. A couple months ago, I elected to take the Old Bahama Channel when a storm threatened. I ended up going to corporate to discuss the decision, and I'm still here—so I don't want people's votes to be swayed by protecting my reputation. We should do what is right, for us and for the company." The captain wants people to vote based on the weather and the condition of the ship, not bureaucratic consequences. He wants the right decision for the right reasons.

The chief mate has information to add as well: "You know, at the end of the season, we are going to head up to Alaska, and we are likely to hit a lot of bad weather. I would really like to see how the ship does in some big water so we'll know if there are material or procedural changes we need to make before the Alaska operations begin." I like the emphasis on learning here. The mindset during bluework should be biased toward growth, mastery, and learning. The choice of path should be influenced by not only the best path for short-term production value, but also what we could learn. Also, the statement is made first of fact, and then of the chief mate's feelings. It is not a statement trying to compel or convince others to vote for one route or another. This is a good statement.

The second mate senses it is time to move toward COMMITMENT: "OK, let's vote again."

The chief engineer asks, "Are we voting for the entire track to San Juan, or just from here to the Rum Cay cutoff?"

The second mate says, "This vote is only to the Rum Cay cutoff. Let's think about this as two legs and two decision points. I want to decouple those." She knows it will be easier to commit to a small segment than the entire route.

The votes are 5, 5, 3, 2. The team has shifted toward taking the Atlantic route. Knowing that there is an escape plan halfway down the Bahamas at Rum Cay makes it safer to make the shorter decision, even with the warning from the chief engineer. Shorter commitments allow more learning and more risk-embracing behavior.

The second mate: "OK, here's what I propose: we take the Atlantic route now. My hypothesis is that we will be able to monitor the weather before it gets too bad. We monitor the weather reports as well as our onboard measurements of winds and waves. At midnight, we will have another meeting to decide between taking the cutoff to the Old Bahama Channel and continuing along the Atlantic route."

The second mate is taking them to COMMIT, but committing to as thin a slice as possible. She is presenting the period of redwork (driving to the Rum Cay cutoff) and the next bluework decision point (midnight). Because she has told everyone that there will be a subsequent decision, and because they know that their votes will matter, she has activated a learning and growth mindset. They will be observant of the conditions and have a wider perspective in order to shape their next vote.

The second mate could have said she intended to follow this plan, which would have been a more assertive statement. Instead, she chooses the word "propose" to give any member of the group an opportunity to voice dissent.

The second mate is the best person to propose the plan to the group because it fits within her role as the navigator. Further, she is the youngest and the social pressure to agree will be slightest.

The captain approves the plan. "All right, that's our plan. Let's see how it goes. I am particularly interested in the ship's rolls and how the engineering plant is holding up. We are heading into heavy weather, so everyone review your procedures for that. Let's have another meeting at eight to present preparations for heavy weather."

A decision has been made. Additionally, since the ship will be operating in heavy weather, additional measures (such as locking topside doors, lashing down the cargo, and monitoring water levels in the bilge) ought to be implemented. This is part of the redwork that supports the decision to take the Atlantic track. Since the ship will likely not be entering heavy weather for several hours, there is time for each officer to review his or her own procedures rather than having the captain tell everyone what to do. This allows them to take ownership and initiative.

The chief mate has an idea. "I also think we ought to let operational headquarters know what we are doing. I will prepare a message." He is anticipating that operational headquarters will direct their routing or question it. Rather than passively waiting for either, he is proposing that *El Faro* preemptively notify headquarters of the plan. We would refer to this as "feeding the beast." He is also being proactive by taking the initiative to prepare (but not send) the message.

During the next few watches, throughout the day and toward midnight, the officers note changes in winds, waves, and weather. They have been motivated to do this because they know they will participate in the decision meeting and that their input will matter. They know they will have control over their destiny.

MIDNIGHT, SEPTEMBER 30, 2015, MEETING START

At the midnight meeting, the officers run through the fist-to-five voting again. This time, because the storm has increased to over 100 mph winds, the ship is already rolling hard, and there are no other options for safety, they propose taking the cutoff to the safer channel. The captain knows this will delay the ship six hours and what the costs will be. He also knows that there's a chance they could take the Atlantic route and that things will work out. Still, he approves the decision, and they notify operational headquarters.

FRIDAY

9:00 A.M., OCTOBER 2, 2015

El Faro arrives in San Juan. There is damage topside to some instruments, and some of the cargo has broken loose and gotten damaged. The ship arrives six hours late, but they do arrive, and all thirty-three crew members survive.

Taking the Old Bahama Channel has saved the ship.

SAVING *EL FARO* USING THE NEW PLAYBOOK

With the CONNECT play, saving *El Faro* starts before the ship gets under way. The captain establishes psychological safety now, knowing that when it comes to future bluework, an atmosphere of psychological safety will invite greater diversity of discussion, more creativity, and more resilient problem-solving.

He also establishes the expected norm that the person who sees a need to CONTROL THE CLOCK has the authority to do so. The team is thinking two and three steps ahead so that when the next decision point comes, they are ready.

Even in a demanding operational environment, the crew applies a learning and growth mindset, thus invoking the IMPROVE play. Members work to tame their "be good" selves and elevate their "get better" selves.

They have confidence that they will be listened to and that they have control over their lives. In the absence of that, they would not participate.

A junior person runs the decision meetings, allowing the captain to remain in the role of decision-evaluator. This inoculates the team against the temptation toward escalation of commitment.

During meetings, they practice voting first, then discussing, and being curious instead of compelling. Confident that they will be heard, they do not need to clamor for attention.

ACKNOWLEDGMENTS

I've often said that none of *my* good ideas were my good ideas and this is one of those cases.

There were several streams of intellectual thought that fed into these ideas. First, there was the idea that language mattered—from the earliest recorded "great speech" in the words Thucydides attributes to Pericles through the powerful words of Winston Churchill and Martin Luther King Jr. A brilliant but unexpected book on this subject is *How to Talk So Kids Will Listen & Listen So Kids Will Talk* by Adele Faber and Elaine Mazlish. Next, there was the framework of action and rest, doing and thinking, focus and reflection which became redwork/bluework and the overall framing of our lives as a journey of learning—primed for me by the work of Viktor Frankl.

I need to acknowledge all the leaders who have tried the ideas in *Turn the Ship Around!*, striving to make the world of work better and providing invaluable feedback on what works and what doesn't, as well as inspirational stories of transformation.

The team at Portfolio/Penguin was superb in pushing me when needed and supporting me when needed. In particular, I'd like to thank my editor, Kaushik Viswanath.

I would like to acknowledge my team at Turn the Ship Around who served as sparring partners, sounding boards, and truth tellers, including Chuck Dunphy, Cathy Kostelansky, Jayme Welch, Jeff Leap, Peter

Russian, Andy Worshek, and Dr. Mike Gillespie. They all served to advance the manuscript in various ways, listened to my frustrations and gripes, and kept the company humming while I was immersed in this project.

Special appreciation goes to Jayme, who analyzed the *El Faro* transcript in detail. The analysis was critical work yielding insight into how teams actually communicate. None of this could have been done if it were not for the voice recordings of the crews of ships and aircraft made public in the investigation transcripts by the National Transportation Safety Board.

A great big shout-out goes to my writing partner, the "bookitect," Dave Moldawer. Dave provided structure, word engineering, and a sounding board during a critical period when I felt like I had reached a dead end.

I would like to acknowledge my wife, Jane, who suffered book-writing holidays, my gripes of frustrations and, during writing periods, getting up at 5:00 a.m. to get in a couple hours of writing before the work day started.

FURTHER READING

The Progress Principle by Teresa Amabile and Steven Kramer

The Art of Action by Stephen Bungay

Descartes' Error by Antonio Damasio

Bringing Out the Best in People by Aubrey C. Daniels

Mindset by Carol S. Dweck

The Fearless Organization by Amy C. Edmondson

How to Talk So Kids Will Listen and Listen So Kids Will Talk by
  Adele Faber and Elaine Mazlish

No Hard Feelings by Liz Fosslien and Mollie West Duffy

Behemoth by Joshua B. Freeman

Only the Paranoid Survive by Andrew S. Grove

How Could This Happen? edited by Jan U. Hagen

Thinking, Fast and Slow by Daniel Kahneman

The One Best Way by Robert Kanigel

Punished by Rewards by Alfie Kohn

Fire on the Horizon by John Konrad and Tom Shroder

Superminds by Thomas W. Malone

Nonviolent Communication by Marshall B. Rosenberg

Accounting for Slavery by Caitlin Rosenthal

Humble Leadership by Edgar H. Schein and Peter Schein

Leaders Eat Last by Simon Sinek

Clean Language by Wendy Sullivan and Judy Rees

The Wisdom of Crowds by James Surowiecki

Black Box Thinking by Matthew Syed

Misbehaving by Richard H. Thaler

Multipliers by Liz Wiseman

GLOSSARY

ANDON CORD   *Andon* is the Japanese word for lantern. The Andon cord was a system installed in Toyota factories that allowed the workers to signal they had a problem on the line and needed to shift out of redwork and into bluework.

"BE GOOD" SELF   The part of the self that wants to project (and protect) an image of competence in the world, deserving of praise and recognition. The "be good" self needs to be tamed in order to execute the IMPROVE play.

BLUEWORK   Thinking, cognitive, creative, deciding work. Bluework benefits from embracing variability.

BLUEWORKERS   The class of people assigned to do the bluework in Industrial Age organizational design. They were called white-collar, nonunion, salaried thinkers and leaders.

COERCE   The Industrial Age play where we goad, manipulate, order, motivate, inspire, or threaten people to do what we want them to do.

COLLABORATE   The play where we learn from others, thereby making our product, ideas, and lives better.

COMMIT   The play where we decide what we intend to do and dedicate ourselves to action.

COMPLETE   The play at the end of redwork where we pause to reflect on what we have accomplished, celebrate that, and invite others to tell their stories.

COMPLY   The Industrial Age play of doing what we're told.

CONFORM   The Industrial Age play where people hide behind their positions and deny connection with other people.

CONNECT   The enabling play that makes all the other plays more effective. Connect is caring for others and leveling the power gradient. Connect means viewing yourself as doing *with*, not *to* or *for*.

CONTINUE   The Industrial Age play of continuing redwork, or if pausing, proceeding directly on to the next project.

CONTROL THE CLOCK   The new play where we are able to call a pause or time-out in order to exit the pressures of redwork and shift to the thinking of bluework.

CREW RESOURCE MANAGEMENT (CRM)   A system of speaking among pilots and copilots that reduces the power gradient by giving the copilot the words to say to express concern and priming pilots to pay attention to words of concern.

CURIOSITY   The desire to learn more about how another sees, what another thinks, or what they propose as a course of action.

ESCALATION OF COMMITMENT   The psychological phenomenon where humans tend to stick with a previous smaller commitment. "Throw bad money after good" captures the effect of this bias.

FIXED MINDSET   A term used by Carol Dweck in her book *Mindset* to describe the belief that we are fixed in our abilities.

"GET BETTER" SELF   The part of the self that wants to grow and get better; it yearns for learning and is seeking and curious. The "get better" self needs to be active for the IMPROVE play.

GROWTH MINDSET   A term used by Carol Dweck in her book *Mindset* to describe the belief that we can continue to grow and improve.

IMPROVE   The play at the end of redwork where we pause to reflect on what we have learned. Improve comes from reflection on the past and modification of current plans, processes, or designs in order to do or make something better in the future. Improve is the domain of the "get better" self.

INDUSTRIAL AGE   The period when humans developed large complex organizations based on machines. Factories, assembly lines, plantations, and railroads were dominant during the Industrial Age. The Industrial Age organizational design was optimized to use humans to reduce variability and comply with their masters' instructions. This fundamental structure shapes our organizational design and language today.

INTENT-BASED LEADERSHIP (IBL)   A system of leadership that pushes authority to those with the information. The goal of IBL is to create organizations where people are healthier and happier because they have more control over their lives. The origin story of IBL is told in my book *Turn the Ship Around!*.

OBEY THE CLOCK   The Industrial Age play where we feel the stress of having to get so much done within a certain period of time.

OVERCLAIMING   The psychological phenomenon where humans tend to claim more credit for a shared task than they actually deserve. The reason for over-claiming is availability bias. When making decisions and answering questions, the brain puts more weight on information that is more easily available. We are naturally more familiar with our own actions than those of others.

PATIENT ELLIOT   The name assigned to a patient whom Dr. Antonio Damasio operated on for a brain tumor. Patient Elliot lost all emotions and the ability to make decisions. Patient Elliot demonstrates the intimate link between emotions and decision-making.

POWER GRADIENT   The amount of hierarchical social distance from one person to another. A proxy for power gradient could be pay scale, office size, equity, age, longevity, skill level, attractiveness, or carpet thickness. Information flows inversely to the steepness of the power gradient. Steep power gradients inhibit communications, variability of ideas, and creativity. In psychology, this is close to the term "social gradient."

PROTECT MINDSET   A mindset motivated to avoid the exposure of one's own incompetence.

PROVE   The Industrial Age play where demonstration of competency or avoiding exposure of incompetency is paramount. Prove is the domain of the "be good" self.

PROVE MINDSET   A mindset motivated to achieve something, prove competence, show the ability to get something done. A prove mindset is positively correlated with performance in redwork tasks.

PSYCHOLOGICAL SAFETY   A term coined by Amy Edmondson to describe how comfortable it is for people in a group or organization to share information that may make them vulnerable.

REDWORK   Doing, action, process, production work. Redwork benefits from reducing variability.

REDWORK-BLUEWORK OPERATING SYSTEM (RBOS)   RBOS (pronounced "our-boss") is a system that deliberately structures the rhythmic dance between doing and deciding, between redwork and bluework. RBOS can be applied at the strategic, operational, or tactical level.

REDWORKERS   The class of people assigned to do the redwork in Industrial Age organizational design. These are called blue-collar, union, hourly workers, doers, and followers. In effective organizations there are no redworkers; there are people who sometimes operate in redwork and sometimes operate in bluework.

REPTILE BRAIN   The oldest part of the brain that regulates breathing, heartbeat, and base impulses. This system is motivated for self-preservation. Stress pushes humans back into their reptile brains.

SABBATICAL   A break from one's career. Traditionally sabbaticals were only found in academic careers, but today anyone can take one. An application of redwork-bluework at the lifelong level.

SELF-DETERMINATION THEORY   A psychological theory formulated by Edward Deci and Richard Ryan to explain intrinsic motivation. The theory posits that competence, relatedness, and autonomy are at the core of human intrinsic motivation.

SHARE OF VOICE   Share of voice is the proportion of words attributed to each person in a conversation and is an excellent indicator of the power gradient within an organization.

TEAM LANGUAGE COEFFICIENT (TLC)   A mathematical calculation that measures the deviation from a perfectly balanced share of voice. A perfectly balanced share of voice results in a Team Language Coefficient of 0.0. A situation where one person says all the words and everyone else is silent is perfectly unbalanced and results in a Team Language Coefficient of 1.0. In a three-person team where two people say half the words each and the third person is silent, the score is 0.5.

TRUST   The feeling that we are aligned in our goals and that you say what you mean. Trust does not include the idea of competence. We would not say, "I trust you to make that decision," because that includes the competence to make the decision in addition to desire to make the right decision. This pollutes the concept of trust. Trust is transparency over time.

VARIABILITY   The spread in a characteristic. Variability can be across time and across different members of a population. Variability can be thought of as diversity. The purpose of diversity programs is to increase the chance of greater variability in cognitive creativity. Variability is an enemy to redwork and an ally to bluework.

NOTES

CHAPTER 1: LOSING *EL FARO*

17 *El Faro* **set sail:** United States Coast Guard (2017). Steam Ship El Faro (O.N. 561732) Sinking and Loss of the Vessel with 33 Persons Missing and Presumed Deceased Northeast of Acklins and Crooked Island, Bahamas, on October 1, 2015. Retrieved from media.defense.gov/2017/Oct/01/2001820187/-1/-1/0/FINAL%20PDF%20ROI%2024%20SEP%2017.pdf.

21 Looking at the transcript: This reference and all quotes from the voyage and the data on share of voice come from the NTSB's investigation transcript of *El Faro*'s black box. National Transportation Safety Board (2017). Group Chairman's Factual Report of Investigation. Attachment 1 to Addendum, Voyage Data Recorder—Audio Transcript. Revised: August 8, 2017. Retrieved from dms.ntsb.gov/public/58000-58499/58116/606566.pdf.

33 In his book *Superminds*: T. W. Malone (2018). *Superminds: The Surprising Power of People and Computers Thinking Together.* New York: Little, Brown and Company.

CHAPTER 2: THE NEW PLAYBOOK

38 the correct answer is 130 percent: M. Ross and F. Sicoly (1979). Egocentric biases in availability and attribution. *Journal of Personality and Social Psychology* 37(3), 322–36. Retrieved from dx.doi.org/10.1037/0022-3514.37.3.322.

39 in his enlightening book: J. Surowieki (2004). *The Wisdom of Crowds: Why the Many Are Smarter Than the Few and How Collective Wisdom Shapes Business, Economies, Societies, and Nations.* New York: Doubleday.

43 color of calm and creativity: QSX Software Group (2015). Color Wheel Pro—See Color Theory in Action. Color Meaning. Retrieved from color-wheel-pro.com/color-meaning.html.

47 *The Principles of Scientific Management*: F. W. Taylor (1911). *The Principles of Scientific Management.* New York: Harper & Brothers.

48 "we have other men for thinking": R. Kanigel (1997). *The One Best Way: Frederick Winslow Taylor and the Enigma of Efficiency.* New York: Viking.

50 526 workers died in industrial accidents: Centers for Disease Control and Prevention (1999). Achievements in Public Health, 1900–1999: Improvements in Workplace Safety—United States, 1900–1999. *MMWR Morbidity and Mortality Weekly Report* 48(22), 461–69. Retrieved from cdc.gov/mmwr/preview/mmwrhtml/mm4822a1.htm.

50 **work environment affects workers' values:** M. Obschonka (2018). Research: The Industrial Revolution left psychological scars that can still be seen today. *Harvard Business Review* (March 26). Retrieved from hbr.org/2018/03/research-the-industrial-revolution-left-psychological-scars-that-can-still-be-seen-today.

53 **Japan produced more cars:** C. Lin (1994). The Japanese Automotive Industry: Recent Developments and Future Competitive Outlook. Office for the Study of Automotive Transportation. Report: UMTRI-94-13. Retrieved from deepblue.lib.umich.edu/bitstream/handle/2027.42/1064/87139.0001.001.pdf?sequence=2.

64 **relationship between stress and learning:** R. M. Yerkes and J. D. Dodson (1908). The relation of strength of stimulus to rapidity of habit-formation. *Journal of Comparative Neurology and Psychology* 18(5), 459–82.

69 **The agile approach:** Manifesto for Agile Software Development. Retrieved from agilemanifesto.org.

CHAPTER 3: EXITING REDWORK: CONTROL THE CLOCK

75 **integrity of the voting process:** ABC News (2017). Oscars 2017: Warren Beatty not to blame for Moonlight–La La Land envelope stuff-up. Retrieved from abc.net.au/news/2017-02-28/oscars-stuff-up-dont-blame-warren-beatty/8309160.

77 **disagreed about who would read the card:** I. Mohr (2017). Warren Beatty and Faye Dunaway couldn't stop fighting before Oscars. Retrieved from pagesix.com/2017/02/28/warren-beatty-and-faye-dunaway-couldnt-stop-fighting-before-oscars/.

84 **"when do you want me to launch":** *Los Angeles Times* staff (1986). Challenger disaster: The 24 hours of pre-launch debate that could have prevented a tragedy. Retrieved from latimes.com/science/la-sci-challenger-24-hours-pre-launch-debate-20160128-htmlstory.html.

89 **ceremony attended by fifteen thousand people:** Boeing (2007). Boeing Celebrates the Premiere of the 787 Dreamliner. News release. Retrieved from boeing.mediaroom.com/2007-07-08-Boeing-Celebrates-the-Premiere-of-the-787-Dreamliner.

89 **"most successful launch in commercial airplane history":** Boeing (2006). Charting the Course. Annual report. Retrieved from annualreports.com/HostedData/AnnualReportArchive/b/NYSE_BA_2006.pdf.

90 **off by a factor of twenty:** Boeing (n.d.). Boeing 787 Commercial Transport Historical Snapshot. Retrieved from boeing.com/history/products/787.page.

93 **Andon cord should be pulled:** C. Duhigg (2017). *Smarter Faster Better: The Transformative Power of Real Productivity.* New York: Random House.

93 **Idle and bored, he cried "wolf":** T. Simondi (n.d.). Fables of Aesop: A Complete Collection. The Boy Who Cried Wolf. Retrieved from fablesofaesop.com/the-boy-who-cried-wolf.html.

95 **use CRM to force a pause and collaborate:** NASA (1979). Resource Management on the Flight Deck. Proceedings of a NASA/Industry Workshop Held at San Francisco, CA. Retrieved from ntrs.nasa.gov/search.jsp?R=19800013796.

CHAPTER 4: INTO THE BLUEWORK: COLLABORATE

121 *Clean Language: Revealing Metaphors and Opening Minds:* W. Sullivan and J. Rees (2008). *Clean Language: Revealing Metaphors and Opening Minds.* Bancyfelin, Wales: Crown House.

CHAPTER 5: LEAVING BLUEWORK BEHIND: COMMIT

140 66 percent of workers were not engaged: J. Harter (2018). Employee Engagement on the Rise in the U.S. Retrieved from news.gallup.com/poll/241649/employee-engagement-rise.aspx.

144 "Space: the final frontier": D. C. Fontana and G. Roddenberry (1966). Charlie X. Television series episode. *Star Trek*. Culver City, CA. Desilu Studios.

152 "Once we suffer large casualties": G. Ball (1965). A Compromise Solution for South Viet-Nam. Foreign Relations of the United States, 1964–1968, III, Document 40. Retrieved from history.state.gov/historicaldocuments/frus1964-68v03/d40.

153 When Professor Staw published: B. M. Staw (1976). Knee-deep in the Big Muddy: A study of escalating commitment to a chosen course of action. *Organizational Behavior and Human Performance* 16(1), 27–44.

155 separate the decision-maker: A. Grant (2013). How to Escape from Bad Decisions: Four Key Steps to Avoid Throwing Good Money After Bad. Retrieved from psychologytoday.com /us/blog/give-and-take/201307/how-escape-bad-decisions.

CHAPTER 6: THE END OF REDWORK: COMPLETE

178 Of the group praised: Dweck, Carol. *Mindset*. London: Robinson, 2017.

181 Sadly, most of them: Erin Fothergill, Juen Guo, Lilian Howard, Jennifer C. Kerns, Nicolas D. Knuth, Robert Brychta, Kong Y. Chen, Monica C. Skarulis, Mary Walter, Peter J. Walter, and Kevin D. Hall. "Persistent Metabolic Adaptation 6 Years after "The Biggest Loser" Competition - Fothergill - 2016 - Obesity - Wiley Online Library." *Obesity*. May 2, 2016. onlinelibrary.wiley.com/doi/full/10.1002/oby.21538.

182 In a study conducted at the Stanford: S. C. Huang and J. Aaker (2019). It's the Journey, Not the Destination: How Metaphor Drives Growth After Goal Attainment. *Journal of Personality and Social Psychology*, 14.

183 In another study: S. C. Huang and J. Aaker (2019). It's the Journey, Not the Destination: How Metaphor Drives Growth After Goal Attainment. *Journal of Personality and Social Psychology*, 11.

CHAPTER 7: COMPLETING THE CYCLE: IMPROVE

188 "Instead of focusing on": C. Duhigg (2017). *Smarter Faster Better: The Transformative Power of Real Productivity*. New York: Random House.

196 "To take action in": A. Edmondson (2003). Managing the risk of learning: Psychological safety in work teams. In M. A. West, D. Tjosvild, and K. G. Smith, eds., *International Handbook of Organizational Teamwork and Co-operative Working*. West Sussex, England: John Wiley & Sons.

197 two modes working in concert: A. Edmondson, R. M. J. Bohmer, and G. Pisano (2001). Disrupted routines. *Administrative Science Quarterly* 46(4), 685–716.

197 period of learning rather than a period of achieving: C. S. Dweck and E. L. Leggett (1988). A social-cognitive approach to motivation and personality. *Psychological Review* 95(2), 256–73.

199 three fundamental components of intrinsic motivation: R. M. Ryan and E. L. Deci (2000). Self-determination theory and the facilitation of intrinsic motivation, social development, and well-being. *American Psychologist* 55(1), 68–78. DOI: 10.1037//0003-066X.55.1.68.

203 **depression that comes with learned helplessness:** L. Y. Abramson, M. E. Seligman, and J. D. Teasdale (1978). Learned helplessness in humans: Critique and reformulation. *Journal of Abnormal Psychology* 87(1), 49–74. Retrieved from dx.doi.org/10.1037/0021-843X.87.1.49.

208 **cases when the crowd gets it wrong:** J. Surowieki (2004). *The Wisdom of Crowds: Why the Many Are Smarter Than the Few and How Collective Wisdom Shapes Business, Economies, Societies, and Nations.* New York: Doubleday.

209 **1,751 airline cockpit and crew members:** J. U. Hagen, ed. (2018). *How Could This Happen? Managing Errors in Organizations,* 48. Cham, Switzerland: Palgrave Macmillan; see also Bienefeld, N., and G. Grote (2012). Silence that may kill: When aircrew members don't speak up and why. *Aviation Psychology and Applied Human Factors* 2, 1–10.

CHAPTER 8: THE ENABLING PLAY: CONNECT

229 **"I support the division of Jerusalem":** O. Idan, E. Halperin, B. Hameiri, and R. Tagar (2018). A rose by any other name? A subtle linguistic cue impacts anger and corresponding policy support in intractable conflict. *Psychological Science* 29(6). Retrieved from researchgate.net /publication/322150387_A_Rose_by_Any_Other_Name_A_Subtle_Linguistic_Cue_Im pacts_Anger_and_Corresponding_Policy_Support_in_Intractable_Conflict.

234 **Fast bowler Mark Wood:** Mark Wood. "Mark Wood on Cricket World Cup, Liam Plunkett & Northumberland's Beaches - BBC Sport." *BBC News.* July 2, 2019. Retrieved from bbc.com /sport/cricket/48847826.

236 **the relationship between emotions and decision-making:** A. R. Damasio (1994). *Descartes' Error: Emotion, Reason, and the Human Brain.* New York: Putnam's Sons.

237 **participants are each given a pot of money:** A. Bechara, H. Damasio, D. Tranel, and A. R. Damasio (2005). The Iowa Gambling Task and the somatic marker hypothesis: Some questions and answers. *Trends in Cognitive Sciences* 9(4), 159–62. DOI: 10.1016/j.tics .2005.02.002.

241 **accidents occurred with the pilot:** National Transportation Safety Board, Safety Recommenda- tions (1994). A Review of Flightcrew-Involved, Major Accidents of U.S. Air Carriers, 1978 through 1990, Safety Study. Retrieved from ntsb.gov/safety/safety-recs/recletters/A94_1_5.pdf.

241 **power gradient follows the order:** J. Tunga, L. B. Barreiroa, Z. P. Johnson, et al. (2012). So- cial environment is associated with gene regulatory variation in the rhesus macaque immune system. *PNAS* 109(17). Retrieved from pnas.org/cgi/doi/10.1073/pnas.1202734109.

244 **This led to a more successful implementation:** A. Edmondson (2003). Managing the risk of learning: Psychological safety in work teams. In M. A. West, D. Tjosvild, and K. G. Smith, eds., *International Handbook of Organizational Teamwork and Co-operative Working.* West Sussex, England: John Wiley & Sons.

CHAPTER 9: APPLYING THE REDWORK-BLUEWORK
PRINCIPLES IN WORKPLACE SITUATIONS

275 **reads like a list of tasks to perform:** Utilization Review (UM) Nurse Supervisor (n.d.). LinkedIn, Cognizant, Job Description. Retrieved from linkedin.com/jobs/view/963470952.

CHAPTER 10: THE RED-BLUE OPERATING SYSTEM

279 **fuel tank in the Pinto ruptured:** M. Dowie (1977). Pinto madness. *Mother Jones* (September/ October). Retrieved from motherjones.com/politics/1977/09/pinto-madness.

280 **don't fix the fuel tank:** B. Wojdyla (2011). The top automotive engineering failures: The Ford Pinto fuel tanks. *Popular Mechanics* (May 20). Retrieved from popularmechanics.com/cars /a6700/top-automotive-engineering-failures-ford-pinto-fuel-tanks.

281 **propensity toward unethical behavior:** L. D. Ordóñez, M. Schweitzer, A. Galinsky, and M. Bazerman (2009). Goals gone wild: The systematic side effects of over-prescribing goal setting. *Harvard Business Review*. Retrieved from hbswk.hbs.edu/item/goals-gone wild-the -systematic-side-effects-of-over-prescribing goal-setting.

285 **The second group was simply:** B. M. Staw and R. D. Boettger (1990). Task revision: A neglected form of work performance. *Academy of Management Journal* 33(3), 534–59.

289 **GE was developing a new engine:** E. Reis (2017). Teaching GE to think like a startup. *Fortune* (October 17). Retrieved from fortune.com/2017/10/17/teaching-ge-the-startup-way-excerpt.

INDEX

Aaker, Jennifer, 182–83
Academy Awards (2017), 76, *163*
  Beatty at, 75–81, 90–91, 98, 105, 141
  being wrong and, 79–80
  bluework and, 79, 81
  coerce and, 105
  Dunaway at, 75–81, 105
  obey the clock and, 81
  prove or protect mindset and, 90–91
  redwork and, 78–79, 81
action
  commit and, 138, 144–45, 158
  deliberate, 293
action bias, 138–39, 157
Agile management, 69
  change management scenario and, 263
  improve play and, 211–12
  Prime Directive and, 211
  sprint cycle and, 100–101
The Agile Manifesto, 69
agile software development, 291–92
Amabile, Teresa, 183, 201
anchoring bias
  overclaiming and, 61
  reduce-variability and, 61, 63
Andon cord, 92–93, 286, 317
annual cycle, 287–88
anonymous blind electronic
  polling, 108–9
applying principles of redwork-
  bluework, 277

Assist and, 247–49
assistant plant manager scenario and,
  259–60
change initiative scenario and, 254–57
control the clock and, 266–67
global engine repair company scenario
  and, 257–58
job description and evaluation
  scenario, 274–76
maintenance crew scenario and,
  272–74
overcommitment scenario and,
  269–71
product owner at bank scenario and,
  261–62
scientist trial scenario and exiting
  redwork, 252–54
United Airlines and, 268–69
when to pivot in redwork-bluework,
  249–52
Asch, Solomon, 125–26
Asda, 201–2
Assist, 247–49
assistant plant manager scenario, 259–60

Ball, George, 152
Barings Bank, 97–98
Bazerman, Max, 281, 282–83
Beatty, Warren, 75–81, 90–91, 98,
  105, 141
Bechara, Antoine, 237

"be good" self, 220, 299, 317
    defensive mode and, 195
    improve play and, 194–98, 205–6
    prove and, 319
being wrong. *See* wrong, being
bias, 168
    action, 138–39, 157
    anchoring, 61, 63
    bad behavior and, 198
    clean question and, 121
    collaboration and, 107
    interference and, 191
    Kahneman on, 60–61
    overconfidence, 62
The Biggest Loser (television show),
    181–82
blue-collar workers, 46
bluework, 73, *139*, 149, 162, 180, 317.
    See also applying principles of
    redwork-bluework; rhythm of
    redwork-bluework; Sue (technology
    executive)
    Academy Awards (2017) and, 79, 81
    Andon cord and, 93
    bias and, 62
    brain size and, 60
    celebrate and, 173–74
    collaborate and, 135, 136
    commit and, 147–48, 158
    connect play and, 217–18
    control the clock and, 193
    Deming on redworkers and, 52–53
    errors and, 57–59
    El Faro and, 57
    "get better" self and, 194–98, 204,
        205–6, 299, 318
    hypothesis and, 132–33
    improve mindset and, 66–67
    improve play and, 189, 193, 212
    Japan and, 53
    language and, 45, 275–76
    leadership plays for, 249–50
    life rhythms and, 295, 296–98
    Santa Fe and, 43
    sprint cycle and, 101
    stress and, 65, 72
    timeline, 206–7

TLC and, 46
    trapped in, 250–51
    variability and, 299
    vote first and, 209
blueworkers, 105, 288, 317
    coerce and, 136
    improve and, 193–94
    Industrial Age and, 46–49
    Taylor and, 48–49, 51, 53
Boeing 787 Dreamliner, 89–90
boy who cried wolf, 93–94
brain
    bluework and, 60
    decision-making and, 59
    development, 297
    reptile brain, 64, 65, 79, 80, 320
Brexit, 153
Bringing Out the Best in People
    (Daniels), 174–75

can-do culture, 4
can-think culture, 4
celebrate
    behavior and, 174–76
    bluework, redwork and, 173–74
    complete and, 168, 171–78, 184
    descriptive statements and, 177–78
    failing to, 171–72
    Industrial Age and, 173
    observe and celebrate leadership, 183
    power gradient and, 226
    Santa Fe and, 175–76
    small wins, 183
    with, not for, 176–78
change initiative scenario, 254, 257
    collaborate and, 256
    commit and, 255, 256
    control the clock and, 255
change management scenario, 262
    Agile management and, 263
    commit and, 264–66
chunk it small but do it all, 146–47, 158
Clean Language, 120–21
coerce, 10, 130, 270, 317
    Academy Awards (2017) and, 105
    blueworkers and, 136
    collaborate and, 105–6

comply and, 135
El Faro and, 22, 40, 106
NASA and, 106
collaborate, 10, 71, 212, 289, 317
  bias and, 107
  bluework and, 135, 136
  change initiative scenario and, 256
  coerce and, 105–6
  commit and, 158
  curiosity and, 116–25, 318
  dissent and, 125–29, 136
  hypothesis and, 132–35
  information and, 130–32
  play, 107–8, 148, 162
  redwork and, 135
  saving *El Faro* and, 305, 308
  TLC and, 136
  vote first as, 108–16, 209, 319
Columbia space shuttle, 222
commit, 10, 71, 317
  action and, 138, 144–45, 158
  bluework and, 147–48, 158
  change initiative scenario and, 255, 256
  change management scenario and, 264–66
  chunk it small but do it all, 146–47, 158
  collaborate and, 158
  could, would, should and, 149–50
  decision-evaluator, decision-maker and, 155–58
  Ella's Kitchen and, 145
  escalation of commitment, 21, 147, 150–55, 166, 168, 318
  intent and, 157
  language and, 137–38
  to learn, 142–44, 158
  overcommitment scenario, 269–71
  play, 141–47, 158, 162
  redwork and, 142, 147–48, 158
  saving *El Faro* and, 305, 309–10
  seeking system and, 143
  self-talk and, 137
  statements to, 147–49
  Sue and, 143
competence, 320
complete, 11, 71, 317
  behavior focus and, 178–79, 184

celebration and, 168, 171–78, 184
chunk work for frequent completes
  early, few completes late, 169–76, 170, 184
continue or, 163–64, 165, 166–68
control the clock and, 165
failure to, 164–65
El Faro and, 163, 164
Ford and, 159–61
Frozen and, 187–88
how to, 168
journey focus and, 179–84
play, 168–69, 185
in practice, 162–63
redwork and, 158, 162, 168, 184, 185, 191
comply, 10, 158, 317
  coerce and, 135
  consequences of, 139–41
  engaged workers and, 139–40
  El Faro and, 28, 40, 141
  responsibility and, 140
  Santa Fe and, 140–41
conform, 11, 32, 218, 220, 317
  El Faro and, 23, 28
connect, 11, 71, 245, 317. See also power gradient
  admit you don't know and, 231–32
  bluework and, 217–18
  Deepwater Horizon and, 213–16
  emotions and, 236–37
  fear and, 217
  hierarchy first and, 216–19
  Industrial Age and, 218–19
  Iowa Gambling Task and, 237–41
  Patient Elliot and, 236–37, 319
  play, 219–20, 244
  red-blue operating system and, 286–87
  saving *El Faro* and, 302–3
  trust and, 234–36
  vulnerability and, 233–34
consensus, 41–42, 125
continue, 11, 59, 318
  complete or, 163–64, 165, 166–68
  El Faro and, 21, 28, 165

control the clock, 10, 71, 102, 270,
    289, 318
  applying principles of redwork-
    bluework and, 266–67
  bluework and, 193
  calling pause and, 95–99
  change initiative scenario and, 255
  complete and, 165
  Frozen and, 187–88
  life and, 197–98
  maintenance crew scenario and, 273
  make pause possible and, 82–90
  naming the pause and, 91–95
  play for, 82, 162
  preplanning next pause to, 100–101
  redwork exit and, 100–101, 103,
    281–82
  saving *El Faro* and, 303–4
  speaking up and, 81–82
Covey, Stephen R., 116
Crew Resource Management
    (CRM), 318
  naming pause and, 95
  as red-blue approach, 54–55
Csikszentmihalyi, Mihaly, 96–97
culture
  calling pause and, 97–98
  can-do, can-think, 4
  language and, 6
curiosity, 318
  better questions and, 125
  Covey on, 116
  Iraq invasion and, 117–18
  leaders speak last and, 116
  sins of questioning and, 119–24

Damasio, Antonio, 236–37, 319
Daniels, Aubrey, 174–75
Dao, David, 268
Deci, Edward, 199, 320
decision-evaluator, 155–58
decision-maker, 155–58
decision-making
  brain size and, 59
  emotions and, 32, 236, 238–39, 319
  errors in, 58
  factors of poor, 34

El Faro and, 20–21, 23, 25, 26–27,
    32, 34, 38, 57, 62, 146–47
  system 1 and 2, 62
  validation and, 106
  wisdom of the crowd and, 38–39
  wisdom of the loud and, 38
Deepwater Horizon, 213–16
deep-water oil rig, 87–89
Deming, W. Edwards
  on bluework for redworkers, 52–53
  TQL and, 51–53, 54, 190, 194
depression, 203
dissent, 136
  Asch and, 125–26
  cards for, 126–27
  curious questions and, 128–29
  disharmony and, 128
diversity, 320
Dodson, John, 64
doing and thinking, 14
  embrace-variability and, 41
  El Faro and, 40–41
  Fred, Sue and, 12, 40
  learning and, 13
dot voting, 111
Dunaway, Faye, 75–81, 105
Dweck, Carol
  growth mindset and, 318
  praise and, 178

"early out" meetings and, 253–54
Edmondson, Amy, 196–97,
    244, 319
education system, 295–96
Ella's Kitchen, 145
embrace-variability, 41, 63
emotions, 2
  decision-making and, 32, 236,
    238–39, 319
  intuition and, 238–39
  Patient Elliot and, 236–37, 319
errors
  bluework and, 57–59
  in redwork, 57–58
escalation of commitment, 147, 168, 318
  Brexit and, 153
  digital cameras and, 154

ego threat and, 155
El Faro and, 21, 150–51, 154, 166
redwork and, 153–54, 155
Staw on, 151–53
Vietnam War and, 151–52, 153
ETH Zürich study, 209–11, 220

failure
to celebrate, 171–72
to complete, 164–65
"early out" meetings and, 253–54
El Faro, 15–16, 19, 49, 98, 163, 209
bluework on, 57
coerce and, 22, 40, 106
complete and, 163, 164
comply and, 28, 40, 141
conform and, 23, 28
continue and, 21, 28, 165
decision-evaluator, decision-maker
and, 156–57
decision-making and, 20–21, 23, 25,
26–27, 32, 34, 38, 57, 62, 146–47
doing and thinking on, 40–41
escalation of commitment and, 21,
150–51, 154, 166
hierarchy and, 217
hurricane Joaquin and, 17–18, 20,
23–24, 26–29
hypothesis and, 133–34
language and, 19, 21–22, 24–25,
26–29, 30–32
obey the clock and, 21, 40
pause and, 83
permission-based environment and,
22–23
playbook and, 35–36, 39–40
prove and, 40
redwork and, 57, 64, 68
rhythm of redwork-bluework for,
165–66
self-affirming questions and, 123
share of voice and, 32–36, 33, 34
sinking of, 29–30
size of, 17
technical competence and, 20
timeline for, 206–8
TLC and, 34, 34–35

turning points for, 18, 20, 23, 26,
40, 57, 134
vulnerability and, 233–34
El Faro, saving, 301, 312
collaborate and, 305, 308
commit and, 305, 309–10
connect and, 302–3
control the clock and, 303–4
feeding the beast and, 311
fist-to-five voting and, 306–8, 311
power gradient and, 302–3
fist-to-five voting, 111–14
saving El Faro and,
306–8, 311
fixed mindset, 318
flow, 96–97
Ford, Henry
complete and, 159–61
Model T and, 159–61, 294
plays of, 161
Taylor and, 48, 159
Ford Pinto, 287
goal setting and, 279, 280–81
Fred (manufacturing executive),
11, 14, 251
can-do attitude of, 31
doing and thinking for, 12, 40
plays of, 161–62
redwork and, 43
redworkers and, 218–19
Frozen (film)
complete, control the clock and,
187–88
"get better" selves and, 196
improve play and, 187–89, 196, 201,
205, 206

Galinsky, Adam, 281, 282–83
Galton, Francis, 108
GE Aviation, 288–91
General Motors Corporation, 160–61
"get better" self
Frozen and, 196
improve play and, 194–98, 204,
205–6, 318
global engine repair company scenario,
257–58

goal setting
Ford Pinto and, 279, 280–81
performance and, 285–86
prove-and-perform mindset and, 281
red-blue operating system and,
281–84
unethical behavior and, 282–87
"Goals Gone Wild" (Ordóñez,
Schweitzer, Galinsky,
Bazerman), 281
unethical behavior and, 282–83
Grant, Adam, 155
Grove, Andy, 155–56
Grove, David, 121
growth mindset, 318
Gruden, Jon, 9

hierarchy, 2
first, 216–19
Huang, Szu-Chi, 182–83
hypothesis, 149
bluework and, 132–33
El Faro and, 133–34
redwork and, 133

IBL. See intent-based leadership
If Japan Can, Why Can't We?
(documentary), 53
improve-and-grow mindset, 170
improve mindset, 66–67
improve play, 11, 71, 142–43, 165, 185
achieve excellence and, 205–6
Agile management and, 211–12
Asda and, 201–2
"be good" self and, 194–98, 205–6
bluework and, 189, 193, 212
blueworkers and, 193–94
discontinuous improvement and,
192–93
ETH Zürich study and, 209–11, 220
executing, 203, 212
forward focus and, 204
freedom, innovation and, 200–201
Frozen and, 187–89, 196, 201,
205, 206
"get better" self and, 194–98, 204,
205–6, 318

interference and, 191
learned helplessness and, 202–3
motivation and, 198–99
outward focus and, 204–5
process focus and, 205
redwork and, 191–92, 212
Self-Determination Theory and,
199, 320
thinking as team and, 208–9
timeline for, 206–8
when to, 190
income inequality, 32–33
Industrial Age, 55, 72, 171, 251–52,
295, 318. See also coerce; conform;
continue
blueworkers, redworkers and, 46–49
celebrate and, 173
connect and, 218–19
division of labor in, 81
doers in, 14–15
job description and, 275
language in, 14–15
Munoz and, 268–69
obey the clock and, 15, 21
playbooks and, 10, 38
reduce-variability and, 70–71, 190
redwork and, 46, 47, 163
stress and, 65
trust and, 234–35
vulnerability and, 232
information
censorship and power gradient, 221
meeting time, 130–31
parking and, 131–32
intent-based leadership (IBL), 8,
55, 318
intuition, 238–39
Iowa Gambling Task, 237–41
Iraq invasion, 117–18, 284

Japan, 53, 54
Jerusalem, 228
job description and evaluation scenario,
274–76
journey, 183, 184
The Biggest Loser and, 181–82
goal and, 181–82

observation and, 179–80
story questions and, 180–81
judgment, 228–29, 230–31

Kahneman, Daniel
on modes of thinking, 62
Thinking, Fast and Slow by, 60–61
Kramer, Steven, 183

language
Assist and, 248–49
bluework and, 45, 275–76
commit and, 137–38
culture and, 6
El Faro and, 19, 21–22, 24–25,
26–29, 30–32
in Industrial Age, 14–15
leadership and, 5–7
power gradient and,
229–30, 242–43
redwork and, 44–45, 67–68
Santa Fe and, 4–5, 6–7, 8
self-awareness and, 8–9
learned helplessness, 202–3
learning, 197, 291
commitment and, 142–44, 158
doing, thinking and, 13
inventions and, 296
red-blue operating system and lifelong,
294–98
rhythm of redwork-bluework and,
169, 300
life rhythms, 295–98

Mac, Shane, 247–49
Maier, Steven, 202–3
maintenance crew scenario, 272–74
Malone, Thomas, 34
Marquet, L. David, 7
May, Theresa, 153
McNerney, James, 90
metacognition, 100
Model T, 159–61, 294
Moore, Gordon, 155–56
morale
performance and, 7
Santa Fe and, 3, 5, 7

motivation
extrinsic, 198–99
intrinsic, 199, 320
Munoz, Oscar, 268–69
NASA, 164
Challenger space shuttle and,
83–84, 106
coerce and, 106
Naval Academy, 1
Navy, 69–70

Oakland Raiders, 9–10
obey the clock, 10, 105, 161, 318
Academy Awards (2017) and, 81
Challenger space shuttle and,
83–84
El Faro and, 21, 40
Industrial Age and, 15, 21
Navy and, 69–70
as stressor, 21
Obschonka, Martin, 50
observe and celebrate leadership, 183
Ordóñez, Lisa D., 281, 282–83
outliers, 145
idea swap and, 117
vote first and, 110, 111, 115–16
overclaiming, 37, 61, 319
overcommitment scenario, 269–71
overconfidence bias, 62

Patient Elliot, 236–37, 319
pause, calling
culture and, 97–98
signals and, 98–99
stress and, 95–96
pause, make possible
Boeing 787 Dreamliner and, 89–90
Challenger space shuttle and, 83–84
construction site and, 84–86
deep-water oil rig and, 87–89
El Faro and, 83
preempting and, 83–84
pause, naming
Andon cord and, 92–93
being wrong and, 93–94
boy who cried wolf and, 93–94
CRM and, 95

pause, naming *(Cont.)*
  practice and, 91–92
  Santa Fe and, 91
pause, preplanning next, 100–101
permission-based environment, 22–23
playbooks. *See also specific topics*
  El Faro and, 35–36, 39–40
  Industrial Age and, 10, 38
  Oakland Raiders, 9–10
positive psychology, 203
power gradient, 220
  celebration and, 226
  communication patterns and, 222
  enforcing, 224–25
  flat, 223
  flattening, 225–26, 227, 228, 244
  information censorship and, 221
  judgment and, 228–29, 230–31
  language and, 229–30, 242–43
  measuring, 221
  new and established group members
    and, 241–42
  pilots and, 240–41
  RBS and, 223–24
  saving *El Faro* and, 302–3
  share of voice and, 224
  trust and, 239–40, 245
  unethical behavior and, 284
Prime Directive, 211
The Principles of Scientific Management
  (Taylor), 47
probability cards, 109–11, *111*, *114*
product owner at bank scenario, 261–62
protect mindset, 65–66, 319
prove, 11, 142
  "be good" self and, 319
  El Faro and, 40
prove-and-perform mindset, 65, 162,
    170, 267, 319
  global engine repair company scenario
    and, 257
  goal setting and, 281
  redwork and, 66, 67, 72, 285
  Santa Fe and, 3–4
prove or protect mindset, 90–91
psychological safety, 207, 217, 219
  vote first and, 108, 110, 111–12, 319

RBOS. *See* redwork-bluework operating
  system
RBS. *See* Royal Bank of Scotland
red-blue approaches, 68
  Agile approach, 69
  CRM as, 54–55
  TQL as, 54
red-blue operating system, 299–300
  agile software development and,
    291–92
  annual cycle and, 287–88
  connect and, 286–87
  Ford Pinto and, 279–81
  GE Aviation and, 288–91
  goal setting and, 281–84
  lifelong learning and, 294–98
  product development and, 292
  Santa Fe and, 292–93
  self-regulation and, 294
  strategy and, 286
  unethical behavior and, 282–87
reduce-variability, 41–43
  anchoring bias and, 61, 63
  Industrial Age and, 70–71, 190
  Taylor and, 47–49
redwork, 73, *139*, 149, 319. *See also*
    applying principles of redwork-
    bluework; rhythm of redwork-
    bluework
  Academy Awards (2017) and,
    78–79, 81
  "be good" self and, 194–98, *195*,
    205–6, 220, 299, 317, 319
  blue-collar workers and, 46
  celebrate and, 173–74
  collaborate and, 135
  commit and, 142, 147–48, 158
  complete and, 158, 162, 168, 184,
    185, 191
  control the clock and exiting,
    100–101, 103, 281–82
  errors in, 57–58
  escalation of commitment and,
    153–54, 155
  experiments and, 133
  El Faro and, 57, 64, 68
  flow and, 96–97

Fred and, 43
hypothesis and, 133
improve play and, 191–92, 212
industrial accidents and, 50
Industrial Age and, 46–47, 163
Japan and, 53
language and, 44–45, 67–68
leadership plays for, 219
Navy and, 69–70
prove-and-perform mindset and, 66,
   67, 72, 285
prove or protect mindset and, 90–91
Santa Fe and, 43–44
stress and, 64–65, 70, 96
timeline, 206
TLC and, 45–46
redwork-bluework operating system
   (RBOS), 319
redworkers, 51, 105, 138, 194, 288, 319
Deming on bluework and, 52–53
Fred and, 218–19
industrial accidents and, 50
Industrial Age and, 46–49
Taylor and, 48–49, 53
work environment and, 50
relatedness, 210
reptile brain, 64, 65, 320
being wrong and, 80
stress and, 79
rhythm of redwork-bluework, 55–59,
   170, *170*, 297. *See also* red-blue
   operating system
bad behavior and, 198
cycle length and, 147
for *El Faro*, 165–66
learning and, 169, 300
planning and, 184, 299
when to pivot and, 249–52
Ries, Eric, 288–91
Royal Bank of Scotland (RBS), 223–24
Ryan, Richard, 199, 320

sabbatical, 320
Santa Fe, USS
bluework and, 43
celebration and, 175–76
comply and, 140–41

IBL and, 55
language and, 4–5, 6–7, 8
morale and, 3, 5, 7
naming pause on, 91
organizations and lessons of, 8
prove-and-perform leadership
   and, 3–4
red-blue operating system and,
   292–93
redwork and, 43–44
Schweitzer, Maurice, 281,
   282–83
scientist trial scenario and exiting
   redwork, 252
"early out" meetings and, 253–54
seeking system, 143
Self-Determination Theory,
   199, 320
self-preservation, 21, 65, 79
self-regulation, 294
self-talk, 137
Seligman, Martin, 202–3
*The Seven Habits of Highly Effective
   People* (Covey), 116
share of voice
divergent thinkers and, 46
El Faro and, 32–36, *33, 34*
power gradient and, 224
TLC and, 33, *33,* 45–46, 320
sins of questioning, seven
aggressive questioning, 124
binary questions, 121–22
dirty questions, 120–21
leading questions, 119–20
question stacking, 119
self-affirming questions, 123–24
"why" questions, 120
Slack, 256
Sloan, Alfred, 160–61
SSDD (same stuff different day), 168
Star Trek (television series), 143–44
Staw, Barry, 151–53
stress
bluework and, 65, 72
calling pause and, 95–96
Industrial Age and, 65
obey the clock and, 21

stress *(Cont.)*
  redwork and, 64–65, 70, 96
  reptile brain and, 79
Sue (technology executive), 14, 43, 150,
    189, 250
  commit and, 143
  doing and thinking for, 12, 40
Sullenberger, Chesley "Sully," 54, 124
superiority, 1–2
Superminds (Malone), 34
Surowiecki, James, 39, 108, 208
system 1 and 2 thinking, 62–63

Taylor, Frederick Winslow, 223
  blueworkers and, 48–49, 51, 53
  Ford and, 48, 159
  *The Principles of Scientific
    Management* by, 47
  problems with work approach of,
    49–50
  reducing-variability and, 47–49
  redworkers and, 48–49, 53
Team Language Coefficient (TLC)
  binary questions and, 122
  bluework and, 46
  collaborate and, 136
  El Faro and, 34, 34–35
  redwork and, 45–46
  share of voice and, 33, 33, 45–46, 320
Thinking, Fast and Slow (Kahneman),
    60–61
TLC. *See* team language coefficient
Total Quality Leadership (TQL), 51–52,
    53, 54, 190, 194
Toyoda, Sakichi, 92
Toyota Production System, 53, 54
  Andon cord and, 92–93, 286, 317
TQL. *See* Total Quality Leadership
trust
  competence and, 320
  connect and, 234–36
  Industrial Age and, 234–35
  power gradient and, 239–40, 245
Turn the Ship Around! (Marquet), 7

Uber, 285–86
unethical behavior
  goal setting and, 282–87
  power gradient and, 284
United Airlines, 268–69

variability, 287
  bluework and, 299
  consensus and, 41–42
  diversity and, 41, 320
  embrace-variability, 41, 63
  manufacturing and, 53
  reduce-variability, 41–43, 47–49, 61,
    63, 70–71, 190
Veterans Administration,
    283, 284–85
Vietnam War, 151–52, 153
Volkswagen, 283–85
vote first
  anonymous blind electronic
    polling, 108–9
  bluework and, 209
  dot voting, 111
  fist-to-five voting, 111–14
  outliers and, 110, 111, 115–16
  probability cards and, 109–11,
    111, 114
  psychological safety and, 108, 110,
    111–12, 319
vulnerability
  avoiding, 2
  El Faro and, 233–34
  Industrial Age and, 232

Wells Fargo, 284–85
The Wisdom of Crowds (Surowiecki),
    39, 108, 208
wrong, being
  Academy Awards and, 79–80
  boy who cried wolf and, 93–94
  naming pause and, 93–94
  reptile brain and, 80

Yerkes, Robert, 64

If you enjoyed *Leadership Is Language*, pick up David Marquet's *Turn the Ship Around!* and *The Turn the Ship Around! Workbook.*

"This is the best how-to manual anywhere for managers on delegating, training, and driving flawless execution." *–Fortune*

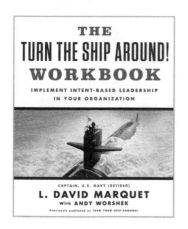

Extensive questions and lessons on how to delegate and inspire others.

Get Marquet's acclaimed books wherever books are sold.

For more tools and resources, visit intentbasedleadership.com.